Primary teacher
YEARBOOKS

TEACHING YEAR FOUR

Edited by Lucy Hall

Published by Scholastic Ltd.
Villiers House
Clarendon Avenue
Leamington Spa
Warwickshire CV32 5PR
Text © 1999 Nick Phillips; David Waugh; Peter Clarke; Terry Jennings; Paul Noble;
Margaret Mackintosh; Dorothy Tipton; Gillian Robinson; Pauline Boorman; Richard Ager;
Lynn Newton; Douglas Newton; Geoffrey Teece
© 1999 Scholastic Ltd.
1234567890   9012345678

Authors

Nick Phillips, David Waugh, Peter Clarke, Terry Jennings, Paul Noble,
Margaret Mackintosh, Dorothy Tipton, Gillian Robinson, Pauline Boorman, Richard Ager,
Lynn Newton, Douglas Newton, Geoffrey Teece

Series Editor
Lucy Hall

Editor
Helen Skelton

Series Designer
Lynne Joesbury

Designer
Claire Belcher

Illustrations
B L Kearley Ltd

Cover photograph
Fiona Pragoff

Designed using Adobe Pagemaker

British Library Cataloguing-in-Publication Data
A catalogue record for this book is available from the British Library

ISBN 0 590 53822 5

Contents

Preface

Primary school teachers don't say, as secondary teachers would, 'I teach history'. They say 'I teach year 4s' or 'I teach a reception class'. Why, then, have all the books for primary teachers been wholly subject-orientated? It seems that primary teachers are supposed to buy about 13 different books and read through them all to extract the relevant bits.

It was about 20 years ago that the thought occurred to me that it would make teachers' lives much easier if all the information about teaching their year group was provided in *one* book. Since then I have been waiting for someone to do it. But no-one did. So, finally, fourteen different authors, Scholastic and I have put together the seven *Primary Teacher Yearbooks.*

I should like to thank all the authors. They faced a difficult task in tailoring their writing to a common format and structuring their guidance, about what to teach and what to expect from children, so that it correlated with the seven different stages of the primary school. They have all been extremely patient.

Particular thanks are due to Paul Noble, who not only wrote 13 chapters in the series, but was also deeply involved in the development of the project from the very beginning. His practical, knowledgeable advice and cheerful imperturbability kept the whole project stuck together.

We all hope that you will find your Yearbook useful and that it meets your needs – whichever class you teach.

Lucy Hall, Series Editor

Your Class

Planning your classroom

Your classroom should be planned and organized to enable you to teach effectively and for the children to learn efficiently. While there is no easy or simple formula to follow, your organization should reflect your philosophy, together with the school's policy for teaching and learning.

Find out what the school expects from you. If this is not written down, talk to the headteacher or a colleague. Consider the space available. Keep a record of ideas and list the main items of furniture and equipment in the room. Next, draw an outline plan of the classroom. On the plan mark:

- radiators and power points;
- sink;
- where wall displays are fixed;
- white board;
- any immovable items of furniture.

Make copies of the plan and experiment with your ideas until you think you have the best possible design. Remember to include:

- any 'gathering area' for the class;
- an area for the class library;
- where your desk will be, if you intend to have one.

Your main teaching area will need to reflect:

- the number of groups you have decided to have;
- the size of the groups;
- how the groups will be arranged in the room;
- provision for collaborative as well as independent learning;
- how you wish the children to move around the room.

Examine the available resources, decide which ones you will need and banish anything else to a cupboard or into storage. If there are any obvious gaps, see the headteacher and make urgent requests to have them filled. Arrange the resources you will be using so that they are easily accessible and maintained in designated areas. Label your cupboards, racks, shelves, trays and areas. If you organize your room in this way it will help to encourage independence and responsibility among the children. You will be building on past practices and preparing for the future.

Display

What part will displays and centres of interest play in your room? For your displays, try using the backs of movable furniture as well as the mounted wall boards. A table pushed against a unit not only looks effective but it helps to break up the room into separate workshop areas.

Year 4 children still enjoy and learn from handling artefacts and items of interest. Using captions and information sheets that make children want to find out more is sound practice. Children of this age enjoy the opportunity of being responsible for displays themselves. This can be particularly effective when it is a group response to a topic.

The key pointers for display are:
- written work should be on unlined paper;
- work should rarely be displayed unmounted;
- choose backing materials carefully;
- children's work should be named and displays titled;
- there is no point in displaying work copied from secondary sources;
- draw attention to your displays and remember, what goes up must come down;
- displays should work for children, not children for displays.

The children

Year 4 children will normally feel quite confident about their position in the school, whether it is an all-through primary or a junior school. Your authority will need to be established from day one. Establish the ground rules and make sure the children are aware of class routines and practices. In the early days you will need to remind some children of these quite frequently.

Try not to present the class with a set of regulations. After talking to them about what you expect, encourage them to develop a list of positive points that could form the class charter. For example, rather than focusing on the negative such as 'do not tease or bully anyone else,' something about showing respect towards each other is much more positive. You may also want to establish a reward and punishment system with the class in this way.

Your children will need to know not only what you expect from them but what they can expect from you. Explain:
- why the room is organized as it is;
- why they are sitting where they are;
- where the resources are stored;
- how resources and equipment should be used and maintained;
- what to do when they first enter the classroom in the morning;
- how they attract your attention when they are need help;
- where they should put finished work.

A carefully planned classroom with well-organized resources, together with a class that appreciates what is expected of them and feels valued and respected, should enable you all to enjoy a rewarding year together.

Social and emotional development
General behaviour

Some individuals will inevitably try and take advantage of their new-found confidence, especially if you are unfamiliar with the school. Find out what you can about the 'characters' in the class from the Year 3 teacher but do keep an open mind. Children respond differently to different teachers, just as teachers find it easier to a form relationship with one child than another. As the professional, however, you have to work even harder at the more challenging situations – which can often prove to be the most rewarding

Take care how you organize the groups and insist on working arrangements which are effective. Be aware of conflict between children (or even families). Watch to see which children work well together and which do not. Be prepared to change groupings for different activities or if learning is being disrupted.

Give the children independence and responsibilities and ensure that they appreciate what the boundaries are. A positive behaviour policy agreed and established in the class will help provide a sound reference. It must, though, be owned by the class as a community. That way, any misdemeanours will be as much a case for peer group pressure in a positive way as for you to respond to.

Concentration and motivation

Levels of concentration and self-motivation will inevitably vary. Most Year 4 children should be able to work independently on a task for a complete session. Naturally, this will depend upon the activity, but you will need to encourage self-discipline and structure opportunities for the children to practise. Try to stand back from the class and observe the children from time to time. Note how long individuals or groups are focused and concentrate on a task. Identify children who may need intervention and support. Build in specific times for these children in your planning, and gradually increase your expectations. If individuals are having difficulties, talk it through with them. Try to establish the reasons for their poor concentration. It may be a simple matter that you can easily address, or you may have to agree targets with the child for focused working times. Use any reward system that you have to encourage the child. Compare levels of concentration between the sessions you have observed so that you have a clear idea of the situation in your class. If practical, carry out a monitoring session, focusing on groups or individuals, when another teacher is available to take responsibility for the rest of the class.

You are the most important motivating factor for the children. However, there may be children who, for a variety of reasons, are not readily stimulated. This is where your skills as a teacher will be tested. Use appropriate strategies for different children such as your particular relationship with the child on a one-to-one exchange; promote an aspect of the child's work or contribution to the class or school; and find out what does stimulate the child as this can help you find a way through. Think in terms of setting achievable targets over a short term. It may be a question of showing children what they can achieve and that their contribution is valued. If necessary, seek advice from colleagues.

Friendships

The relationships that exist and develop between the children will have a significant influence on the ethos and attitude of the class. Avoid organizing children into single-sex groupings. Find out which friendships are positive for learning and which are best avoided. Teachers who have had the class before you will be in a good position to offer constructive advice. Ensuring that you have children together who will motivate and encourage each other and are not antagonistic or a negative influence is a balancing act. It is probable that the only sensible approach is to introduce a system of flexible groupings for different activities. Inevitably you will learn from your mistakes!

Changes at home

The birth of a new brother or sister, while being an exciting family event, can have an effect on the behaviour, attitude and performance of children. Changes at home may result in less attention and a feeling of isolation and insecurity. You will need to be aware. Give the child opportunities to talk to you about how they feel and help them to understand that they will remain just as important once all the initial euphoria has subsided.

Other changes in circumstances, such as parents' separation or divorce, a parent in prison or the death of a relative, will have a dramatic effect. A change in character will be the first symptom, for instance, the outgoing, confident child who becomes withdrawn, the friendly, popular pupil who is suddenly falling out with friends or the happy child who is moody and difficult in class.

Your relationship with the child is crucial. If you do notice a change in behaviour or attitude, seek the child out at an appropriate time. Gently encourage the child to talk to you. Explain what you have noticed and give reassurance that you are concerned and want to help. At the same time, ask around. Check whether a letter has come in to the school office. Talk to the headteacher and, if you do have an opportunity to see the parents on the playground, let them know that you are concerned. After discussing the matter with the headteacher, you may decide that you need to make a more formal contact with the parents by telephone or by writing to them, inviting them to come and see you.

The important point is to appreciate what the problem is so that you can guide and support the child and modify your response accordingly.

Children with special needs

Disruptive children

A child may be disruptive for a number of reasons. Try not to be caught out. Gather as much information about the children as possible before you start. This should include reading reports and records and talking to colleagues who have been involved with the class but, again, do give the children the opportunity for a fresh start. The special educational needs co-ordinator (SENCO) will have a wealth of information to share with you about any children with statements or any that he/she has been involved with. Use this to your advantage and be prepared.

Having established ground rules with the class, make sure you stick to them. Strategies for responding to inappropriate behaviour need to be sensitive and fair. These might include a warning system that progresses to a range of known punishments that eventually involve senior staff and the child's parents or carers.

All children should be treated equally but some will be more demanding. When challenged, follow the systems that are in place and never be afraid to seek advice.

Able children

Particularly able children should be seen as a challenge rather than a problem. Such children will have a potential to excel in one or more areas of learning and their needs should be met. It is your responsibility as their teacher to develop an appropriate learning programme for them. This should be established in consultation with the SENCO, parents and possibly a local authority officer.

It is not uncommon for especially able children to experience difficulties socially and emotionally. An academically gifted Year 4 child may well find it hard relating to other members of the class and will not always be accepted. Able children may even try to hide their talent and be disruptive or apathetic in class.

Do your homework. Make sure you have the background information you need by checking back through records and reports. Develop a relationship of trust with able children by being open with them about their needs, and involving them in aspects of planning their learning. Guide them in their learning, keep them in touch with the class as a whole and, most importantly, plan challenging activities that match their ability and learning potential.

Mobile children

Children of travelling or other mobile families have the same entitlement at school as do children of the settled population. Schools have a responsibility to provide for mobile children, however short their stay may be.

Roadside travellers are usually highly mobile and, as a result, often educationally disadvantaged. The whole process of their introduction to the class needs to be handled with great sensitivity. The headteacher will have made contact with the proper authorities and support will be available to you and to the children. If you are to have travellers' children in your class:

● make sure you have as much basic information about them as possible, such as their names, how old they are, where they are staying, if there is any friction between their family and the family of any other child in your class;
● be prepared for them: have their place ready, name their tray and books;
● talk to the class before the new child/children arrives, just as you would about any new pupil(s);
● liaise closely with the support agencies and ask for as much help, advice and guidance as you feel you need.

For children of families in the forces, the same principles apply. The school may have a long-standing relationship with any one of the services. If this is the case, it is likely that a number of service children will already be in the school and supportive, effective networks will be established. If so, use them. Decide what the child's needs are and organize the learning to best meet these. Always look at the positive and build on the strengths, as you would with any child. Make the time in your class, however short, a happy and worthwhile period in their education.

Children with learning difficulties

All information and records about any children in your class with learning difficulties should be made available to you before you meet the class. Study the information thoroughly and make notes of the key points and any questions you may have for the special needs teacher. You will need to be aware of:

● which children have learning difficulties and what is specific to each;
● the level each is working at;
● what their planned learning programme is;
● what their targets are;
● the support available within school;
● the extent of involvement of all external agencies.

Whatever a child's difficulty, plan carefully for his/her learning. Agree targets that are achievable and review these with the child and the parents. Liaise closely with the support staff at the school and maintain clear, helpful and regularly updated records.

Ensure that the child is, and feels, integrated in the class group. Recognize successes and achievements and focus on strengths where you can. Be especially sensitive at stressful times when there are class assessments or tests.

Physically disabled children and children with health problems

Children in your Year 4 class with any physical disabilities or significant health problems may have spent some time at your school. This previous experience will be helpful to you. Practices will be established and the family, school and child should feel confident with each other.

Your first task is to find out as much background information as you can about the child. Seek out the parents before they come looking for you. It is better to take the initiative so that the parents feel you understand and care. A change in teacher for any child and his/her parents can be unsettling. Parents of children with a disability will naturally be more anxious and need reassurance.

By Year 4, children with disabilities or health problems will have developed coping strategies. Spend time talking openly and honestly to each child. Establish what their strategies are, what they see as their needs and how they would like you to help. Maintain close links with the child's parents. Seek advice regularly. Monitor the involvement of external agencies and take particular care to remember the children's needs when arranging visits or special events.

'Looked after' children

A child who is 'looked after' by a local authority will be in their care if he/she has been placed there by a court order. The local authority will be responsible for acting as 'corporate parents' and the child may be placed in a residential or foster home. The effect of such a placement, together with the traumas resulting from the court order, will be devastating for the child. Their reaction may be extreme and they will need sensitive, guided support from you.

School can have a strong and beneficial influence on children in care. It is often the one environment that is stable and where the 'looked after' children's experiences are the same as their peers. Guard against lowering your expectations. Determine what their educational needs are. Set up a plan which is challenging and has achievable targets. Remember to share this with the child and his/her carers. It is possible that the child may move suddenly from your school so always ensure that records and assessments are maintained and easily transferable.

As a school, you will be able to draw on the information maintained by social workers and others involved with the child. If possible, you or the headteacher should attend the meetings about the child which are held regularly with the carers and social workers. Keep up to date with developments and be especially aware of any changes in behaviour. Avoid potentially damaging situations over school lunches, games kit and contributions for trips. Also, be vigilant about bullying. Year 4 children will not fully appreciate the consequences and, if provoked, may resort to taunting.

If things go wrong inform the head. Contact the casework officer and the carers. Early intervention and identification of the problems are crucial for the well-being of the child.

Health education

Substance abuse

In Year 4, you should be aware of the signs of substance abuse. Helpful literature will normally be available in school or through the health authority. Take time to look through the information, check to see where the topic fits into the school's PSE scheme of work and plan accordingly.

Sharing information with the class will be important. They need to know the facts, the reality of the situation and that you are aware. Reassure them that you have the knowledge and understanding to advise and support them should they experience difficulties or be tempted. If you detect a change in character or behaviour that may be linked to substance abuse, take your concerns to a senior member of staff immediately.

Sex education

Sex education is the responsibility of the school's governors. They will decide whether it is to form part of the school's curriculum. Find out what your governors' policy says. If you do not feel comfortable with any elements allocated to the Year 4 curriculum, discuss the matter with the headteacher. You are able to 'opt out' if you so wish.

Before you embark on any sex education teaching, inform the parents. You may find it helpful to organize a special meeting with parents where you can outline what will be included and share any material, such as videos you will be using with the children.

Parents will need to know when the lessons will be taking place, whether any other members of staff or the school nurse will be involved and how they can support their children's learning.

This is not an easy subject and many children will find it embarrassing. It can affect their behaviour during the lessons so do maintain a professional and factual manner at all times.

Citizenship and moral development

Racial prejudice/multicultural issues

'Effective learning could take place only when pupils had a feeling of self confidence, well being and security, flourishing in conditions conducive to equality of opportunity, mutual respect and co-operation.' (HMI Report: *Racial Bullying in Schools*) (*date of report?*)

Somewhere in one of your school's policies will be a statement about guaranteeing equal opportunities to all children. It is your responsibility to ensure that this is not just a fine statement but what happens in your classroom. Racial harassment can take many different forms, including:
- name calling;
- ridiculing children because of the colour of their skin or their language;
- the threat of physical violence;
- racist abuse, insults, jokes, verbal threats;
- refusal to co-operate with children or adults in school because of the colour of their skin, race, religion or language.

Any kind of harassment demands an immediate and effective response from you. This will involve reporting any incident to the headteacher and dealing with the children concerned. Make sure you have completely established the facts of any such incident. Demonstrate to the child concerned that you have taken the matter seriously by recording the abuse. Discuss the allegations, your concerns and disappointment with the perpetrator before administering any appropriate punishment. It is also essential that the victim receives a genuine apology and reassurance that there will be no further incidents. However, you will need to remind the child how he/she should respond if there is any repetition of racial abuse. Finally, do not forget that parents will need to be informed and reports sent to the local authority.

Encourage the children in your class to talk to you about any racist behaviour. As part of the curriculum, children need opportunities to learn and develop informed attitudes. Encourage tolerance but do not be tolerant of any racist behaviour. Be proud of a classroom where equality of opportunity, mutual respect and co-operation allow all your children to flourish.

Bullying

This is an emotive topic. Your school will have well-rehearsed procedures and practices that both staff and children should be aware of. Familiarize yourself with the policy so that you know the steps to take.

Do not wait for a problem before discussing the subject with the children. Establish with the class from an early stage what is understood by the term 'bullying', that it can involve more than physical intimidation, what is unacceptable and how they should respond if they are a victim or an observer. Impress upon the children how important it is to be a 'telling' class and that this is responsible behaviour which protects the well-being of all.

When you witness or are told about an incident:
- talk to both parties independently to establish their perception (reassure victims that any threats of reprisal against them will not be tolerated and remind them of the school's supervision arrangements so they know who to approach and when);
- talk to other children who may have witnessed what happened;

● discuss the case with the headteacher or a colleague who knows the children;

● keep a log of your 'interviews' so that you have a comprehensive record;

● if appropriate, bring both parties together to discuss the situation;

● you or the headteacher should then inform the parents of the children concerned of the incident and of the action you will be taking.

You may need to meet with the parents and explain again what has happened. Both sets of parents will be angry for different reasons and probably defensive. Unfortunately the school may be equally 'blamed', so do keep comprehensive notes and have another member of staff with you at any potentially difficult interview.

Gender

Your conduct and attitude will influence how the children regard and value each other. Gender is not an organizing principle or a classroom management strategy that you should consider. Do not use sex segregation to motivate or control children. Your role is to promote equality by changing stereotypical ideas about boys and girls that children often come to school with.

To achieve this, take great care with your planning, as well as the classroom management and organization to ensure that both boys and girls receive a broad-based education with opportunities to follow up specific interests and activities that may not conform with tradition. A programme of personal and social education should deal with gender issues and help to make the children more generally aware.

Addressing this issue needs to be part of a whole-school policy and should include a considered approach not only to the curriculum but to assemblies, planning, classroom practices and even playtimes. However, efforts being made in your classroom or in the school toward equal opportunities will be limited by powerful influences from outside. This makes your role even more important.

Respect for property

This is not so much a class matter as a whole-school issue. Respect for others and other people's property will form part of the ethos of any good school. This should percolate down to the way children regard their belongings and the school's resources. It is essential that children develop a sense of ownership and responsibility for school and class equipment. This is their school, their classroom and their resources. All are provided to help them.

Respect for property should be included as a heading in any statement that is agreed with the class. Year 4 children will be aware of the cost and value of their own and school resources. Draw the children's attention to anything that is new. Introduce strict practices for checking and maintaining class equipment. Regularly go through cloakroom areas with the class and take seriously any accusation of theft.

Stranger danger

It is probable that the majority of children will be making their own way to and from school without an adult to accompany them. This can leave them vulnerable to possible abduction or even assault. As part of your PSE programme, remind the class of the 'stranger danger' message. Invite the police liaison officer to talk to the children during the year. Warn the class of any reported sightings that may be a potential threat to them but at the same time avoid overstating the case. Being aware and conscientious is an important part of the children's development and growing independence.

Reports

Report writing is not the most enjoyable part of a teacher's duties but it is a duty, and you should ensure that your reports are helpful and worthwhile for parents, children and colleagues. Whatever the arrangements are at your school for compiling children's reports, make sure you are well prepared in advance. Collect the information you will need over a period of time and follow these steps:

Step 1 Check when the hand-in date for the report is and work backwards, blocking in time so that you have a schedule, for example, three reports a night for four nights a week over a three-week period.

Step 2 Give yourself a date by which all your assessments have to be completed.

Step 3 Check to see who else will need to write on your children's reports and agree a time scale with them.

Step 4 Gather all the information you will need to base your reports on.

Step 5 If possible, persuade a literate friend to check through your reports once you have written them. Otherwise, check all spelling and punctuation very carefully.

Reports should provide a summary of significant achievements, not total coverage. Include some details of areas where the child has experienced difficulties, together with an indication of what they should focus on in the future. Comments about children's behaviour or attitude should not come as a surprise to parents. Avoid bland statements. Be specific to ensure that what you say is of value. Remember, other teachers who have the children after you, have to live by what you say. Be as accurate as you can with the statements you make.

The parents
Communication with parents

Parents will always be especially interested in any newly appointed member of staff and even if you are long established at the school, they will probably know more of your reputation than of you!

If the opportunity arises, meet with the parents before the new year or at an early stage in your first term. Most parents will want to know:

- how you manage the class in terms of the groups and activities;
- what the topics will be for the year;
- whether there will be homework and what your expectations of the children are;
- about any visits that you may have arranged or will be organizing;
- details and dates of any set testing;
- how they can help;
- what they should do if there is ever a problem and how they make contact with you.

For any meeting you have with parents, keep a record of who attends and then send a copy of the important points from your notes to parents who did not come to the meeting. Be as visible and available as you can at regular times. Give parents the opportunity to talk to you on the playground before or after school. You will often prevent a minor problem developing into something more significant if you deal with it at an early stage.

Person-to-person communication with parents of children in Year 4 can be difficult to organize and will not occur as naturally or as frequently as it does with parents of younger children. Children may be making their own way to and from school so the opportunities for informal chats with parents are fewer.

The school will have established procedures for class teachers to meet with parents, such as the traditional open evening or end-of-year report discussions, but written communication between home and school will be as important as the way you manage the more formal occasions. If you have not had an opportunity to meet with parents before you take over the class, write to them and introduce yourself. Parents will be interested to know something of your background and special interests, as well as the learning their children will be involved in during the year. Your aim is to reassure parents that you know what you are doing and that you value their contributions and support. Give them an outline of the year's work.

As the year unfolds, send out simple reminder slips about special events such as class assemblies and whole-school happenings. Newsletters and circulars from the school office do not always reach home, even in the hands of Year 4 children!

After-school meetings

When there are evening or after-school meetings with parents, ensure that the parents:
● have been given a reasonable amount of notice;
● are clear about the focus of the meeting: is it to discuss their child's progress or a teaching and learning matter?
● are aware of the appointment time and the period available.

Be prepared and check carefully that you have all relevant information with you. Parents can rightly be insulted by teachers who spend part of the limited time rummaging through papers, looking for the right child's tray, or talking about the hard day they have had. If it is a consultation, think carefully about:
● where you will talk with the parents;
● where parents will wait;
● how you are going to maintain confidentiality and prevent parents from overhearing other parents' consultation or looking through other children's trays.
● whether children's work will be accessible for parents to look at before their appointment;
● whether you will make this an opportunity to share the class achievements with parents through displays.

Whatever stage of the day or evening you meet with parents, imagine that each appointment is your first. Be bright, cheerful and professional. Know what the main points are that you need to make but give the parents an opportunity to talk. Keep the conversation crisp and relevant. At the end of the consultation, sum up the main points and note down anything that you have agreed. Always offer a follow-up meeting if appropriate to the discussion.

Parents in the classroom

Help from parents can be invaluable and make a real difference to the quality of classroom life. However, before you make any arrangements, check to see what the school's policy is. There will probably be police enquiry forms to complete and the school may have a prepared information sheet for volunteers.

You will need to establish whether parents of children in your class can work in the same classroom as their children. Decide upon the optimum times when you would like help, the particular skills you are looking for and how you are going to 'advertise' this.

Draw up a brief guidance sheet for parents that includes some details of how they can help and what you are looking for. Parents who work in your room will need to be aware of school procedures: for example, the evacuation of the premises, access to the staffroom and school office.

Talk to the parents about confidentiality and what they should do if they ever have any concerns or are approached by another parent. Make them feel welcome and valued and thank them at the end of the session. It can be helpful for both you and the parents to keep a book between you where you list the tasks and arrangements for the session. That way, they will know what to do without interrupting you when they arrive. Always remember that parents will form an opinion about you and your teaching. This can be to your advantage but there are potentially damaging repercussions if things go wrong. To avoid this, you will need to have established a positive working relationship with parents. Be aware of their strengths and weaknesses and value their contributions to class life. A small gift at Christmas or the end of the year and invitations to help with class visits are usually much appreciated.

Dealing with problems

Not all parents will agree with, or even want to understand, school policies or practices. While major disputes will be directed at the headteacher or senior staff, you may be the first 'representative' parents focus their attention on. Should this be the case, outwardly remain calm and always be polite. Never raise your voice, even if the parent is shouting and screaming! Try and manoeuvre the parent away from children or other 'interested' parties, and make sure you call on an appropriate colleague for assistance. Listen to what the parent has to say. Take down notes. This can have a calming effect and will be helpful later. Assure the parent that you are interested and taking what they have to say seriously. Explain your position or the school's policy but avoid an argument. Advise the parent of correct procedures for any complaints and ask for it to be put in writing.

When faced with aggressive parents, you may not be able to calm them. Seek help immediately; again try to lead the parent away from children and, if necessary, call the police for assistance. Individuals can be totally unreasonable. Often the grievance will not be directly school related but you can be seen as a soft target. Whatever the situation you find yourself in, the safety of the children and your own safety is your first responsibility. Be cautious and always seek support.

The Year 4 year

In many respects, Year 4 is a year of consolidation. Important groundwork needs to be covered both in terms of the curriculum and children's development. Potentially it can be a lost year, when individuals are allowed to drift and progress is not maintained. This is a conclusion drawn by OFSTED and something you should be very aware of.

Monitor attainment carefully and be vigilant about any changes in attitude or working practice. A successful Year 4 year will consolidate what has happened before and prepare the children for the future.

Curriculum and Classroom Planning

Materials and resources

Getting organized in advance

It is well worth investing time in your classroom before the new term. Make an audit of the resources and start to keep a 'needs list'. Once you are clear about priorities, see if your headteacher can help to provide any missing items – you may not get everything you want immediately but at least your needs will be on record.

Organize resources so that they are accessible and in designated areas. Year 4 children should be independent and able to help themselves to consumables and equipment as and when they need to.

Dispose of tatty, inappropriate or dated books that you know the children will not look at. Mend any books that are worth keeping but which are damaged. Check that tools work, that brushes have enough bristles and that your computer is operational. Your aim is to present your class with good quality equipment and well-cared-for resources. It is more likely that they will then present you with good work.

Library resources

If you are new to the school, you will need to find out what the school's policy is for the library. Is there a set time for your class or is it always open for anyone who needs to use the resources? Browse through the shelves. Familiarize yourself with the stock and look out for books which will

back up your year's plans. Arrange to withdraw books you will need for topic work or as part of a display before term begins. Read a selection of the fiction suitable for your class so you can recommend books. Get to know the system, the different methods for retrieving information and borrowing arrangements. At the earliest opportunity, talk to your class about library skills and practise them. A library 'treasure hunt' can be helpful: small groups of children have to locate particular books, articles or other reference material and information. You can even make it into a competition between the groups. This helps children to be familiar and aware of their library as well as developing important skills.

Check the books in the class library so you know exactly what you've got, sort them into appropriate categories and display them as attractively as possible. Arrange well in advance to borrow collections of books from the school library service or local children's library to complement the work you are planning through the year.

Audio visual resources

School televisions and video recorders tend to possess a range of special peculiarities. Never assume that they will be straightforward. Practise beforehand and make sure you have the tape at the appropriate place. Check the audio tapes you want to use to make sure that they aren't worn or damaged.

Information technology

It is possible that a number of the children in your class may be used to more sophisticated computer systems at home than the ones available to you at school. Other children will have little out-of-school practice. (It is these children in particular who need time on the computer.) Set up a system to record computer use so that you can be sure that everyone is spending an appropriate amount of time on this. Get to know the programs available to you so that you can match these with the children's needs. Put away any disks that aren't relevant and make sure the rest are clearly labelled and conveniently stored. When planning, decide how and where computers will support learning and make sure that the children use the word processing package as a natural part of their work.

People

As part of your forward planning, don't forget to show how you will make use of other people: a classroom assistant, perhaps, support staff, parents, governors or contacts from outside the immediate school environment, such as the school nurse or police liaison officer.

If you are lucky enough to have a class assistant, use his/her time carefully. You may decide that, while the majority of his/her hours should be spent supporting the children, there will be administrative tasks such as photocopying, filing and covering boards, which the classroom assistant can do to free valuable time for you.

If you have a large number of volunteer parents, make sure that you don't take on more help than you can cope with. Remember that you will have to train them and plan for them. Organize a book with tasks clearly identified for anyone who is helping in the classroom on a regular basis. People like to know what is expected of them. Preparation will save time for you in the end.

Visits

Always plan your visits in advance. You should have a clear idea of what you intend to organize, and why, at the beginning of the school year. Ensure that you include a range and, with voluntary contributions rather than charging in mind, be conscious of the costs involved.

Your school and local authority will have a policy that you should follow. It is important that you check the details carefully before embarking on any school journey or day excursion. For each visit, find out if you will need a first-aider. Always have a first-aid kit with you. A mobile phone is now an essential item and you should aim for an adult–child ratio of at least 1–15, preferably 1–10.

Inform parents of visits well in advance and make sure that consent slips are signed and returned. Never take a child without a parent's or carer's permission.

Display

Having read through the school's policy for display, check to see if you have the material and other resources you will need. If you have a budget to order your own items, plan and place orders well in advance. Alternatively, you may have to make 'requests' to the colleague who guards the stock cupboard!

If you are purchasing from a class budget, carefully work out your requirements and keep a record of items that you have and will need. Slightly more expensive backing paper will last longer and will not fade as quickly. Invest in border strips to go round the edges of your display but be careful about the colour contrasts you choose. Limit yourself to a select range of colours. Collect a variety of pieces of fabric for drapes – local shops may be persuaded to part with end cuts, markets can offer fabric at reasonable prices and parents will often make donations.

Plan your displays for the room. Have a range showing different aspects of the curriculum. Year 4 children will enjoy having some responsibility for organizing and contributing to displays so involve them in your planning.

Requirements of the curriculum

Your school will be used to adapting to change and adopting new practices. Seek advice and support from senior staff if you have any doubts or difficulties with planning. Share your draft timetable and termly plans with a colleague. This can be a reciprocal arrangement.

School-generated as well as national documentation will guide and instruct you. The recent literacy and numeracy initiatives clearly outline what you will be expected to cover. Use these frameworks and support materials to ensure that your planning is both appropriate and in accordance with policy.

Check on the school statement for the teaching of religious education. This is another sensitive area. Make sure you know about any children, such as Jehovah's Witnesses, who will not be included and who may have other restrictions (such as not being photographed) applying to them.

Time
Official recommendations

The DfEE's recommended minimum time for Key Stage 2 children is $23\frac{1}{2}$ hours. This does not include breaks, lunch time or assembly and probably underestimates the time spent, inevitably, on non-teaching activities. When deciding on the percentage allocations for curriculum subjects, you will need to take account of the QCA document, the Literacy and Numeracy Hours, the National Curriculum, the school's curriculum and any established special priorities. For a typical Year 4 class the breakdown might look like this:

	Engl.	Maths	Sci.	IT	D&T	Hist.	Geog.	Art	Music	PE	RE	PSE
Hrs/pw	6.5	5	2	1.5	1	1	1	1.75	1	1.75	0.75	0.75
%	27	21	8	6	4	4	4	7	4	7	3	3

Do not attempt to cover all subject areas each week. Think in terms of blocks of time over a longer period so that you can do justice to a topic or activity.

Timetable

Your timetable will need to be flexible but carefully balanced to ensure that opportunities exist to cover a broad curriculum. Make sure the allocations during the day are of a reasonable length and that you arrange to do the most demanding activities when the children's concentration level is at its highest.

On your timetable, first include the 'immovable feasts' such as assemblies, acts of worship or set times when another teacher takes your class. Then plot on your Literacy and Numeracy Hours. Work in your PE, hall, games and any drama times (but, obviously, not all on the same day). Include other curriculum areas around these so that you have sensible periods of time and a good range of disciplines on each day.

Long-/medium-/short-term planning

There is no single approach to planning or any common understanding of what each stage should include. Your school will have developed a system that works for them and meets their needs.

Long-term planning

Long-term planning may be included in a school's curriculum framework and in schemes of work for individual subjects. These will be quite specific and should form the core from which you take your plans.

You may be fortunate enough to be a member of a team for planning. This can provide you with opportunities to share reflections on past practices and activities as well as to plan together for the future. You can use each others' strengths, support each other and help with resource issues. Being a member of a team for planning will be particularly helpful for newly qualified teachers.

Medium-term planning

Your medium-term planning might include an overview sheet for the half term that shows what you will be covering, subject by subject. This can be helpful for anyone looking at intended coverage and can be shared with parents.

You will then need to break this planning down and add some more details. A half-termly grid is a helpful tool.

If you use the grid, highlight what you have covered at the end of each week. This then gives you an immediate record, is visually reassuring, informative and very useful to any supply teacher who takes over your class.

Short-term planning

Short-term planning may be for a fortnight or just for the week. A sheet like this allows you to include as much information as you need to deliver the curriculum. You can show the assessments you intend to make and any evaluations that will help you to inform what you need to do in the future.

Fortnightly plan

Week beginning _____   Group/Year group _____

Subj. Ref.	Learning intentions	Activities	Resources	Groupings	Evaluation

Your daily plans will be drawn from the fortnightly or weekly sheets. Normally it will be left to you to devise a format, but it will mainly be concerned with how you intend to organize the class or groups. In many respects daily plans are a memory jogger.

The teaching

Class, group and individual teaching must all form part of your repertoire. 'Fitness for purpose' should be your maxim. You should be clear about what your learning intentions are and how you can best offer children the most appropriate learning experiences.

Class teaching

Teaching the class as a whole should prove to be particularly enjoyable and rewarding for you as a teacher. It involves a combination of thoughtful planning and natural flair. Make your instructions clear, pace the lessons so that children's attention does not wander and provide opportunities for them to contribute. Correct and assess their responses so that they can progress and, at the end of the lesson, draw the class back together to review and reinforce the main teaching points. It is, of course, this style of teaching that you will mostly be using in the Literacy and Numeracy Hours.

The ability range in a typical Year 4 class is significant but this should not make you shy away from class teaching. Consider where children are positioned in the class; those you need to maintain regular eye contact with; those children who need to be encouraged. The follow up or group activity can then be differentiated allowing children of all abilities to respond.

Group teaching

Teaching children in groups is an equally important strategy. Not only does it allow resources to be shared but it provides planned opportunities for children to interact together and with you. Focusing on teaching particular groups while other groups work with a class assistant or on independent tasks is an effective approach. Year 4 children should be responsible enough to work in this way, because they have developed the skills they need to learn independently. However, group activities can be counter-productive if there are too many groups, too many different activities at the same time or if the criteria for grouping the children has not been carefully considered.

Decide if there will be times when it is best to group the children by ability. If you do decide to do this, then plan accordingly. Organize the children sensitively and flexibly. Be open with the children but do not label the groups. Often grouping by ability will be an effective strategy to use with teaching aspects of mathematics. By Year 4, some schools may have introduced ability setting for maths.

Individual teaching

To teach every child in the class individually would be extremely difficult, if not impossible. Interaction with the child can be superficial and the real amount of teaching time the child experiences will be minimal. However, there will be times when it is appropriate to focus on and support an individual pupil. Children of all abilities, but particularly those with special educational needs, will benefit from one-to-one teaching. It is up to you to decide if, while being best for the child, it is manageable. Can the other children in the class work independently and usefully without your immediate attention?

Differentiation by task/outcome

Knowing what individual children are capable of, and what their needs are, is a challenge. By Year 4 a significant amount of information will have been gathered and you will need to make good use of this when planning. However, your own professional judgement will be just as important as far as evaluations and assessments are concerned.

When you are planning, think in terms of three broad groups of children which will include children of above average, average and below average abilities. (Children with particular needs such as statemented or gifted pupils, should have individual programmes adjusted for them). Decide how you might differentiate an activity for three groups and match the children by need and ability. For example, your teaching point may be to encourage the children to develop an understanding of 'time' related to a history-based topic. Following the initial introductions, appropriately designed activity cards with varying degrees of information, guidance and questions at different levels could be given to the three groups.

For some activities, it may be a question of what is commonly called 'differentiation by outcome', where the children should take the activity to the extent of their individual ability. An example of this would be in responding to a piece of creative writing.

Know exactly what it is that you intend the children should learn. Make sure that your class know what the learning intention is and why it is important. For example, tell them that they are going to learn about speech marks and why they need to know about this form of punctuation. Plan in advance how you can best provide a differentiated approach that is manageable and that achieves your objectives.

Teaching points

Whatever your method of organization, strategy or style of delivery, 'fitness for purpose' is your guiding consideration. For example discuss written work and how it should be laid out on the page. Where should the date and title be? What about margins and how should paragraphs be set out? What should you do if you make a mistake and need to correct a word? With maths work, is it best to record in pencil? Where should workings be shown? How should work be referenced to text books you are using?

● Teach your class using a variety of methods, including to the whole class, in smaller groups of various compositions, and individually.

● Remember that it is never appropriate to use one method exclusively.

● Ensure that you have a manageable number of groups and learning activities provided at any one time.

● Use your time effectively to instruct, question, explain, listen and assess.

Recording and presentation

By Year 4 children will normally enjoy taking a pride in the way they record and present their work. Basic skills will have been mastered and this is a time to build on their new-found confidence.

Your school may well have agreed practices for how children should record and present their work. Do not assume that the class will have remembered or even appreciated what these are. Go over them again with the children and reinforce what you regard as the main points.

If no such policy exists, draw one up with the class. You will need to have ideas of your own as a guide, before you embark on discussions. This will set the standards for the year. Keep the policy on display and, when necessary, remind the children to look at it. (What did we decide about underlining?)

While the processes that the children work through are important, the presentation of the final product will say as much about their level of attainment as it will about you as their teacher. Use it to motivate and build a firm foundation in terms of attitude and responsibility that will support the children in the future.

Homework

All schools are now expected to have a policy outlining the amount and range of homework that children should aim to do. For Year 4 children, the recognized amount is 40 minutes each day. This should include an emphasis on reading, with perhaps regular spellings and multiplication tables to learn. Follow-up work, related to class or individual topics is also appropriate, and your school may have provision for basic number reinforcement exercises to be done at home. Make sure that parents and children are aware of the expectations. A homework diary can be a helpful form of communication between home and school. Be consistent and reasonable with your expectations as well as fair on yourself as far as the demands of marking are concerned. Include regular reading practice, spellings and tables to learn, areas related to class or individual topics to follow up. You might also decide to have homework diaries so that children can record what they have to do and parents are aware of the expectations.

SATs and assessment

It is possible that you will be expected to administer the interim year for SATs during the summer term. This will provide future teachers with important information for planning and the school with an indication of how far individuals have progressed since the Key Stage 1 SATs.

For all other assessments, follow the school's set procedures. Keep formative assessment information in a file for each child. Use the sheets to include all significant achievements under general subject headings. Also include other relevant details in a personal and social development section.

Keep your records up to date. This avoids a desperate search for the information you need just before a meeting with parents or summer report writing. At appropriate stages in a topic, include planned opportunities for assessment for particular children. If you organize this on a regular basis, then it will be manageable. Your records will not only provide you with valuable information, but they will also be your evidence if you are challenged by a parent, colleague or inspector!

English
including Literacy Hour

By the time children reach Year 4, there will be an increasing gap between the abilities of the most and least able. Those at the upper end of the ability range may now be keen, independent readers and some may write for pleasure outside the classroom. Some will be confident orally and will be eager to contribute to class and group discussions. Children at the lower end of the ability range may still be struggling with basic skills in reading and writing and some may be reluctant participants in oral work. They may have problems with text books and worksheets in subjects such as mathematics and, because they cannot read instructions accurately, they may be very dependent upon you.

By the end of Year 4, children should have reached at least Level 3 in the core subjects of the National Curriculum, and the attainment targets provide useful yardsticks against which to measure their progress. Many children may have progressed further and will have a good understanding of the purpose and value of literacy in their everyday lives. Others will lack this comprehension and it is important that, at this stage in particular, time is devoted to literacy activities which children can see as useful to them both in school and outside school.

What should they be able to do?

By the end of Year 4, children should be developing an awareness of standard English and beginning to be able to vary the way in which they speak according to context. They should be able to show that they have listened carefully by making relevant comments during oral lessons, and they should be increasingly able to explore and communicate their ideas.

In reading, they will be able to draw upon different strategies to gain meaning from a range of texts. There should be a growing independence in their literary work with an increasing emphasis on their ability to use information skills to select books and find information.

Writing, for most children, should be developing in accuracy, with sentences being punctuated; spelling of regular words generally correct; and handwriting fluent, legible and joined. There will be a broadening of the range of vocabulary used and writing may be adapted according to readership.

Key areas

The key areas in English are speaking and listening, reading and writing. Year 4 will, for many children, represent a time when they begin to demonstrate consistently that they are able to modify and present the production elements of speaking and writing according to the needs of their listeners and readers. During Year 4, you should ensure that children are given lots of opportunities to speak and write for a range of different real audiences. The provision of real audiences should act as a spur to children to show greater accuracy in their presentation and to make the content of what they say and write more interesting. Those children who have not yet learned to appreciate the needs of their audiences may sometimes benefit from working alongside those whose language skills are more sophisticated.

It is important to match activities carefully to children's needs and stages of development. Take particular care to avoid those activities which neither challenge children nor reinforce what they have already learned. At this stage, for example, many children will be given exercises such as comprehension work, Cloze work or grammatical work. There is nothing wrong with this and the activities can be useful in allowing you to check that children have grasped certain concepts and are able to apply them. However, before you give any exercises to children, examine them carefully and eliminate those which are lengthy, unsupervised, and which involve repetitive work.

Identify clear learning objectives for each lesson along the lines of *By the end of the lesson the children will be able to …* Exercises may offer an opportunity for children to show that they have understood something, but you should not see them as having a significant role in teaching concepts. As the teacher, you have an important role to play in the direct teaching of concepts through lessons such as the Literacy Hour. Exercises should act as reinforcements of those concepts and should enable you to assess the effectiveness of your teaching and the extent to which the children have learned.

Key area: Speaking

During Year 4, children should be developing their abilities to talk to an audience and be aware of that audience's needs. Make use of story time to show the children how a skilled reader can bring the text to life by using a range of expressions and even accents, and how the pace of reading can be changed to add excitement or to demonstrate the feelings of the characters. For example, a scene which involves a chase may be read more quickly than one in which the character is expressing sadness or boredom. Discuss the techniques by referring to your own reading aloud. However, the children could talk about the ways in which readers of taped stories perform or those they hear on schools' radio or television.

You could make opportunities for children to work together to plan and discuss topics and presentations. Extend this into drama work, with scripts being produced. By the time they reach Year 4, most children are capable of being assigned different roles for talking activities and they should be made to feel that their contributions are both valuable and important. Look for opportunities for them to discuss each other's performances and to analyse the qualities which make for effective communication.

Key area: Listening

At Year 4, children should be given lots of opportunities to listen to stories and presentations and to comment on them. Many will be able to make notes on what they have heard and you should discuss ways of making succinct notes which are easy to record and to understand.

Many teachers find that children are less able to listen carefully since the advent of regular television watching, which has the added stimulus of the visual image. This makes it all the more important that you should encourage children to develop listening skills at school.

Key area: Reading

At this stage, children should begin to explore the texts they read and hear in greater detail, and be encouraged to express opinions about what they have read. Try to develop discussions about the ways in which authors use varied and interesting vocabulary to enhance descriptions. Make use of character grids which list the characters in stories and poems. Ask children to draw upon their own vocabularies, as well as word banks which you provide and discuss, to list the attributes of the people about whom they read. It is through discussion about the ways in which authors write that children's own writing will become more thoughtful and varied.

Many children will have previously enjoyed nursery rhymes and poems written for young children. At Year 4, they are ready to experience a much greater range of poetry and you should provide them with a variety of material. This could include humorous work by authors such as McGough, Rosen, Ahlberg, Dahl and Milligan, but it should also include more serious and thought-provoking poems. Have a collection of anthologies available in the classroom so that selections can be read to and by the children regularly. The role of rhyming poetry in developing phonic awareness is well established by research, and children should be encouraged to discuss the rhyming schemes which poets employ.

They should also be exposed to non-rhyming poetry and be encouraged to write such poems themselves, since this genre allows them to express their ideas concisely, but without worrying about finding rhyming words which may be included in their writing for their rhyming qualities rather than their literary appropriateness.

The range of literature available to children should be growing and they should be encouraged to explore a variety of children's stories and poems as well as texts which were not necessarily written for children. These might include newspaper articles, magazine features, sports results, television listings, and various reference books including catalogues, dictionaries, thesauruses, encyclopaedias and telephone directories. At Year 4, children will need to develop their understanding of literacy as a vital life skill and you should take every opportunity to present them with accessible materials which enable them to behave as real readers.

Year 4 children should be increasingly able to discuss what they have read by referring to evidence acquired from the text. They might, for example, be asked to look at a novel with a historical setting and then talk about differences between the period in which the story is set and the present day. They should be encouraged to draw upon their reading to support their views.

You can also ask them to talk about language which has been deliberately adapted by the author to add historical authenticity or to indicate dialect. Such discussion will help children to think about the language we use now and may lead to a debate about standard and non-standard English.

You will still need to reinforce word attack skills and phonic knowledge; do not assume that children who read quite fluently will not benefit from occasional reminders about ways in which to approach unfamiliar words. At this stage, it is worth talking with children about making use of context to determine the meaning of a new word. Suggest that they read ahead and then return to the word and try to decide what the word might mean. They should be encouraged to look first at the initial letter sound of the word and then use this clue, in conjunction with the context, to try to work out how to say the word and to discern what the word means. Praise intelligent guesses and encourage children to make use of dictionaries to look up new words which they meet.

Tri-words

tricycle
tripod
triple
triangle

Spend time talking about words and their structure and encouraging children to apply what they learn about some words to others. For example, they may look at prefixes such as un- and tri- in words like 'unusual', 'unlikely', 'tricycle' and 'triangle' and then be asked to draw conclusions about other words with similar prefixes. It is this development of an ability to make inferences from what they learn about words which will help them to become more independent readers, capable of making informed attempts at deciphering new words. The once much-maligned spelling list has a role here, provided that words are discussed at length and children are shown how other words have similar features and similar meanings. If used intelligently, the weekly spelling list can be a useful device for encouraging children to take an interest in words and to begin to extrapolate from the words listed, so that they can apply their knowledge to new words with similar structures. For example, in discussing a word like *submarine*, you can take the opportunity to talk about other words which begin with the prefix *sub-* and other words which include *marine*.

There should be plenty of opportunities to talk about words with the same phonemes and different spellings (for example, 'shoot' and 'sugar'), as well as those with similar spelling patterns and different pronunciation (for example, 'cough' and 'though'). The use of a phonic programme such as THRASS, which provides a range of graphemes to represent phonemes, is particularly useful here. (*Teaching, Handwriting, Reading and Spelling Skills*, A Davies and D Ritchie.)

Key area: Writing

By the time they reach Year 4, many children will be capable of writing at some length, but may lack the ability to vary vocabulary and sentence structure. A growing awareness of the devices which authors deploy to make their writing more interesting will help children to reflect upon their own work. Equally, if they are asked to plan their work before writing at length, they may find it easier to consider their audience and ways in which their writing might be improved.

There should be a wide range of different writing genres available to the children through their reading and you should show them many examples in order to stimulate their writing. There should be opportunities for persuasive writing and factual accounts, as well as letter-writing and creative writing such as stories and poems. Encourage them to discuss ways in which they might improve their writing and use terms such as 'adjective' and 'adverb' in these discussions. At Year 4, most children are ready to consider ways in which they might edit their work to make it more concise and accessible to the reader. Focus attention on particular aspects of writing when they do this so that they look for opportunities to, for example, vary verbs and adjectives.

Year 4 children should be making use of writing aids such as dictionaries and thesauruses and word banks, and you should praise them for attempting to use more complex and interesting vocabulary even when a word is used incorrectly or spelled wrongly. After all, if they feel reluctant to be adventurous in their choice of words because they fear criticism, you will not be able to find opportunities to teach them new spellings and to introduce a broader span of vocabulary and spelling to the whole class. See the writing lesson as providing you with the chance to extend everyone's knowledge and skills through careful and positive intervention at strategic moments.

Revise and reinforce their knowledge of punctuation (commas, full stops, question marks, speech marks) and, since much of their writing can involve listing, you can show them how to use colons to precede lists. During Year 4, the National Literacy Strategy suggests you focus on the apostrophe, too. The important thing to remember is that there is no need to try and do everything at once.

Continue to provide regular handwriting practice and make children aware that different styles are required on different occasions. For example, they may need to print in block capitals when labelling a diagram; they may be more concerned with getting ideas down quickly than with presentation when making notes or drafting work; and they will need to take great care over presentation when writing for others.

Practical ideas

Literacy Hour

The teaching framework devised by the National Literacy Project is, of course, the foundation for the Literacy Hour. You must dedicate one hour a day to the teaching of reading and writing in a rhythmic transition from whole-class teaching to small-group work and back again. During this hour, children should be engaged in work at:
- whole text level, involving comprehension and composition;
- sentence level involving grammar and punctuation;
- word level involving vocabulary and spelling.

Those of the following activities which are particularly suitable for use in the Literacy Hour are marked thus ✅.

Speaking and listening

Speaking and listening develop best when children are given real purposes for their discussions and when they are aware that there is an audience for what they have to say. At Year 4, part of the speaking and listening programme might involve children in preparing presentations, perhaps in a group and with notes being made as *aides-mémoire*.

Drama

● Drama has an important role in Year 4, because it provides a medium through which children can explore language and can accustom themselves to the needs of an audience. It also allows children whose oral skills may be less well developed to have an opportunity to work with others in presentations. Those for whom English is a second language may, for example, be involved in dramatic activities which rely on actions to a greater extent than dialogue, but which enable them to participate within a language-based context.

● Oral work should be an integral feature of activities across the curriculum and children should be encouraged to talk confidently about their work and the topics which they are studying. You could, for example, ask them to work with others to identify key points from a religious story and dramatize and perform the story for the rest of the class. Their version of events might be compared with those of other groups and lead to a class discussion.

Using tape recorders

Cassette recorders which enable group discussions and productions to be recorded are invaluable, as they allow children to consider their use of language and provide you with material which may be used as part of ongoing assessment and recording. You might also make use of tape recordings occasionally as an alternative or addition to chalk and talk when introducing a topic to the children.

Try recording a mock interview with an historical character or a reading from a story or eye-witness account, and then asking the children to listen carefully and pick out the main points. This could lead to class discussion and then repeated listening as children seek support for their views.

In Year 4, children are increasingly able to reflect upon their own performance as speakers and listeners and, if this is encouraged within a supportive classroom environment, they will develop both their skills and their confidence.

Reading

At this stage, children will need to continue to develop their reading skills, and you should continue to introduce them to attractive and interesting literature so that they see a real need to develop those skills to enable them to enjoy the literature to the full. Where possible, teach skills through the use of literature so that children see the context in which words, phrases and grammatical structures are used. It is also important that children at Year 4 develop an interest in, and ability to use, non-fiction texts both as reference sources and as everyday reading matter.

Reading skills
Letter strings

As children's vocabularies increase, they will encounter more and more words which have letter groupings in common with other words. If they are to develop as readers and spellers, they will need to develop a sound knowledge of the phonic correspondence to a wide range of letter strings.

● Try giving the children specially prepared passages, or simply old newspapers and asking them to use highlighter pens to colour groups of letters which occur in several different words. They might, for example, look for words which include 'ough'. Having found a number of such words, they could go on to use a dictionary to find the words' meanings. They could then use a different colour and look for words which included, say, 'tion'. This activity could be followed up at home with children making collections of words with common graphemes.

● You could put up a sheet headed *At-ten-tion!* and ask children to fill it with 'tion' words. If it fits your teaching style, you could, for a short while, ask the children to come to attention when they hear the grapheme being used. When a grapheme is reliably consistent like this one, intensive concentration on it can mean that nearly all of the class will learn to deal with it confidently in their reading and writing.

Reading practice

● Try to ensure that children have lots of opportunities to practise their reading together and with experienced readers. Hearing them read can be a valuable activity, but only if you are able to devote your undivided attention to the reader. When a child is expected to read at one side of you while you mark work or help other children with problems at the other side, the reader is unlikely to benefit from the experience. In fact, since it demonstrates that the teacher is not really listening to the reader, it projects a poor image of the value of reading aloud.

● Where possible, hear individuals at times when you will not be distracted by others and make use of group reading sessions to hear children taking turns to read from multiple copies of the same story, poem, play or other text. Group reading will enable you to make teaching points and should also provide children with a real reason to read with expression, as well as developing their listening skills as they follow the text when it is not their own turn to read aloud. Group reading is advocated by many authorities on reading, not least OFSTED, whose 1996 report, *The Teaching of Reading in 45 Inner London Primary Schools*, strongly favoured this

approach and described hearing individuals as being in many cases, 'an unproductive exercise of such short duration that very little actual teaching took place'. The National Literacy Strategy focuses on guided group reading during the Literacy Hour and regards it as 'a fundamental part of each school's literacy programme'.

● A more productive way to approach individual reading might be to make use of reading conferences at which the child discusses with you the kind of reading he or she enjoys, and you use the opportunity to assess his or her progress, making use of miscue analysis and running records to keep an account of ways in which the child approaches text. This will enable you to identify the child's strengths and address them in future planning.

Fiction

Children's discussions of the story books they read can enable them to gain a greater insight into the ways in which texts are constructed and may allow them to develop their abilities to read critically and to write more adventurously. The National Curriculum for English and the National Literacy Strategy require teachers to provide opportunities for children to examine literature in some depth at Key Stage 2.

'Pupils should be taught to consider in detail the quality and depth of what they read. They should be encouraged to respond imaginatively to the plot, characters, ideas, vocabulary and organization of language in literature. They should be taught to use inference and deduction. Pupils should be taught to evaluate the texts they read, and to refer to relevant passages or episodes to support their opinions.' (Programme of Study for Reading at KS2)

The ideas for work in the classroom which are included in this section are intended to allow children to gain greater insight into the works of fiction which they read. At this stage, children may already have well-developed tastes for some kinds of fiction and may have decided that other types have little appeal for them. It is important to wean them away from such a restricted literary diet, and you should give them plenty of opportunities to discover different authors and different types of novel. Many will be ready to read, or may already have read, full-scale children's novels, while others will only experience these when more experienced readers read aloud to them. By providing a wide variety of literature, reading extracts from it aloud and discussing it imaginatively, you should find that children's interest is aroused and many will, at Year 4, begin to acquire the reading habit.

Considering characters and plots

There are many activities which you can introduce to encourage children to think carefully about the characters in the stories they hear and read.

● Children can write short pieces describing a day in the life of a leading character say 30 years after the events in the story (see *Curriculum Bank: Writing KS2*, D Waugh and N McGuinn, Scholastic, pp 30-31 and 117 for a lesson plan and examples). They could be asked to think about the traits which a character displays in the story and decide how the person might turn out if he or she continued to behave in the same way as in the story.

● Before they read a story, ask the children to examine the publisher's blurb on the back of the book, then they can return to it afterwards and rewrite it in their own way. They could design an alternative book cover and could consider ways of making the book attractive and enticing to potential readers – perhaps writing an advertisement for it.

● Another activity could include retelling the story in a concise way, perhaps in a mini-saga with a strict word limit, perhaps 100 words. This encourages the children to think carefully about the key events and use words economically to tell the story. They might then go on to discuss the merits of writing at greater length in order to make the story more interesting for the reader.

● Ask the children to produce alternative endings for a story and compare these with the original. Discussions could centre around their interpretations of the fates which they felt each character deserved. You could also ask them to put themselves into the positions of the characters in a story and consider how they would have reacted to circumstances. Ted Hughes' *The Iron Man* is an ideal book for encouraging children to do this. Their initial feelings about the Iron Man might be that he is an evil force but, as the story unfolds, this is clearly not the case. Children could consider how the other central character, Hogarth, reacted initially and how they would react if they encountered a monster. They could also consider the feelings of the Iron Man and could compare his image with those of other giants in stories which they know.

Poetry

Many people were put off poetry at school because they were made to learn inappropriate poems in order to recite them to the class. Equally, some people found that the poetry they were introduced to was dull or virtually incomprehensible. There are many interesting, moving and humorous poems available which can, when used well, stimulate children's interest in this important medium.

● Try selections from each of the following types:

▶ 'nonsense' poems;

▶ free verse without rhyme;

▶ haiku and other forms of poetry from different cultures;

▶ humorous poetry, including limericks;

▶ nursery rhymes and jingles;

▶ poems written by children in your class and by other children of the same age which have been published;

▶ psalms, prayers, hymn lyrics, and so on;

▶ classic and modern poetry.

You can simply invite children to listen to poems being read to them, but poetry also provides starting points for discussion which, if exploited, can give children a greater insight into language use and the scope for expressing emotions in a concise way. Children can be swept along and excited by poetry with a strong metre ('The Charge of the Light Brigade') even when they don't understand all of it.

● The children can discuss, in pairs or groups, ways of presenting a poem to others; perhaps as a whole-class choral version with sound effects. They can also make use of movement and actions to accompany reading or reciting. Anthologies of favourite poems can be created (perhaps on the computer) and illustrated and children can make posters with captions from poems illustrating a part of a poem.

● In selecting poems and stories for children, look for examples which are set in a wide range of social and cultural contexts. Your class should have access to a wide range of genres and should be encouraged to discuss the different ways in which authors make use of style and vocabulary.

● Analysis of texts may appear potentially dull, and some may argue that such an activity could detract from children's enjoyment of stories and poems. However, their pleasure may be enhanced if the activities are made interesting and exciting and if they afford children opportunities to gain a greater insight into their reading.

Non-fiction

◉ Many children in Year 4 will have well-developed interests and hobbies which may include cars, pets, sport, pop music, riding, computers and making collections. These interests can provide useful starting points for developing their reference skills, if books for the classroom are chosen carefully. Unwilling readers are often more prepared to tackle information books than fiction. Try to include accessible books for your Year 4s which contain the features of standard text books, such as contents pages, indexes, glossaries, maps, charts, illustrations and diagrams. Show children how to use these to find out more about the subjects in which they are interested. You might ask them to prepare a talk for the class by finding information from books at school, at home or in the local library or, if they have access to one, from a CD-ROM.

Time should be spent on dictionary work and you can encourage children to keep a dictionary of their own. This should develop into something more useful than a word book and should be referred to and updated regularly. The dictionary can act as a reference point for spellings and, provided it is looked at regularly, should prevent you from being followed around the classroom by children seeking spellings. Use the Literacy Hour to work on spellings and definitions and ask the children to update their dictionaries at such times.

Give a pair of children two telephone directories (collect old ones), a stop watch and a list of names and addresses for which they have to find the telephone numbers. *Who can complete the list most quickly?* Children who are not very interested in dictionaries can see the advantages of being familiar with alphabetical order in a practical context like this.

Developing information skills

Ensure that there is a reference area in the classroom and show children how to use it.

Spend time discussing reference books with the children and demonstrate that you make use of them. Discuss the different styles, layouts and purposes of the text and ensure that you provide a range of elementary reference books which are suitable for the children's varying reading abilities.

Introduce simple databases and show groups of children how they can record and recover information. If the resources are available, you could introduce them to the Internet and to CD-Rom to show the range of data and information which we can gain access to.

Writing

During their time in Year 4, children should develop a growing awareness of the ways in which they can make use of devices such as punctuation, varied sentence structures, vocabulary choice and phrasing to enhance their writing and make it more interesting for their readers. Their discussion about stories and poems could be extended into written work in which they, for example, write another verse for a well-known poem or song or further dialogue for a conversation between two characters from a story. They might try to emulate the style used by an author to produce stories and poems of their own.

Drafting

You should encourage children to plan and draft their work where this is appropriate and they should always be aware that they are writing for someone else, unless their writing takes the form of notes or a personal diary or log. This will mean talking with them about the importance of secretarial skills and the need to present writing so that it may be read easily.

To develop an appreciation of the drafting process, introduce a writing activity which is highly structured and which involves note-making followed by revising and editing. Inviting children to write about an item of food which you provide can be particularly successful. Ask them to make notes about the food's appearance, followed by its feel, its smell and then its taste. When they have done this, they can begin to edit their notes so that they produce a piece of descriptive writing based upon the notes but refined and honed until it can be presented to others. Encourage them to use a thesaurus to find varied words for their descriptions.

When talking about drafting, suggest that the children consider abbreviations which allow them to develop a form of shorthand. They might begin by learning the common symbols or abbreviations for *because* (•.•), *and* (&) *therefore* (.•.) and *approximately* (approx.). You could go on to explore abbreviations in Literacy Hour work, perhaps looking at acronyms (for example, SAT, RoSPA, quango, ERIC) and at dictionary listings of abbreviations.

English

Grammatical agreement

A common problem for many children at Year 4 is the concept of grammatical agreement. They may say 'I aren't' or 'we was' or 'you was' because that is the way in which those with whom they live and play speak. They will need to understand that this is not standard English and that it is not acceptable in writing.

✅ Oral work in the Literacy Hour might be based upon personal pronouns and verbs followed up by written work. You might begin by reading a passage from a book or one which you have written specially. For a second reading, miss out the personal pronouns and ask the children to suggest what they might be. Next, read the passage without the verbs which accompany the personal pronouns and again ask the children for their ideas. Finally, show the children the passage, if possible on an overhead projection, and let them see if they were correct. Emphasize to them that sometimes more than one answer may be possible (for example, 'I was', 'she was', 'it was'), but that some things are always incorrect (for example, 'we was', 'they was', 'you was'). The children could go on to complete sentences or passages which have been specially prepared and then to copy pieces from their books, missing words out, before asking their friends to attempt to complete them.

Comparatives

✅ In their mathematical work at this stage, children should be becoming increasingly familiar with terms such as 'tall', 'taller' and 'tallest' and 'heavy', 'heavier' and 'heaviest'. However, they frequently misuse these comparatives and may, for example, claim to be the oldest of two children or say that the best team won a football match. They will learn the appropriate endings most easily if they are given practical examples and are asked to select the correct words.

✅ Ask two children to come to the front of the class and ask the other children who is the taller, heavier, smaller, and so on. (Be careful to choose children who won't mind comparisons of this kind.) Next, introduce a third child and ask who is the tallest, heaviest, smallest and so on. This can be developed into a written reinforcement exercise and you might ask children to use highlighters to find examples of comparatives and superlatives in newspapers and other texts. You could also ask them to be language detectives and deduce information from text about the numbers of people involved in certain incidents. For example, a sentence like, 'Sarah was Mr Jones' eldest daughter' should tell the reader that there were more than two daughters.

Vocabulary extension

✅ An important element in the drafting process is the development of interesting use of words so that repetition is avoided and the reader can really appreciate the topic which he or she is reading about. Children often rely heavily on adjectives such as *nice* and *good*. As a Literacy Hour activity read and show to the children a passage in which these adjectives are over-used. Ask them to suggest alternatives which you can substitute on an overhead projection or on the board. This could be followed by group, paired or individual work in which the children make use of simple thesauruses to develop and improve another passage.

Language study

As they develop as readers and writers, children will need to explore in greater detail the reasons why authors make choices about the ways in which they organize their work.

✅ Discuss with them the ways in which stories have a beginning, a middle and an ending and help them to identify some of the devices which are commonly used to signal each section. For example, authors may indicate the ending of a story by using 'finally', 'at last' or 'in the end'. At the beginning, they might use 'One day', 'A long time ago', 'There was once', 'Once upon a time' or a statement about a character which arouses the reader's interest. This should then translate into their own writing and might include activities such as writing a beginning for a story for which someone else writes the middle and a third person writes the ending. This could be a whole-class activity with everyone writing a beginning then passing it on, and everyone writing a middle before passing it on and so on. The authors of each section would then have a real incentive to read other people's work in order to find out what happened to their original stories.

○ As part of Literacy Hour work, you could give children a set of jumbled sentences which, when put together in the right order, form a coherent story. Encourage them to discuss the reasons for their choices and to talk about the vocabulary in the sentences.

○ Talk to them about using pronouns to replace repeated names, or about varying conjunctions and breaking lengthy passages into sentences and paragraphs. Show them how authors invert sentences and use different forms of verbs. Rather than writing 'We went to the castle and then we went to the sea', they might write 'After going to the castle, we went to the sea'.

○ Show them how the position of a word can change the meaning of a sentence. *In how many places can you put the word 'only' into this sentence?* 'I will help you tomorrow'. *Does the sentence mean the same each time?*

Letters

● Children are often most aware of their audience when they are asked to write a letter and this can be especially true when they enter into correspondence with someone who makes a real effort with presentation too. They could write to children in another school here or abroad, or to younger or older children within their own school. They might write to their parents to tell them of a forthcoming school event or they could write to curators at museums, or public relations officers at businesses which they might visit.

● Another letter-writing activity which you can use at the beginning of the year involves you in writing to the children telling them about some of the things which they will be doing in your class during the year. This could also be a good opportunity to pass on information about class rules, days on which they will need PE clothes, aprons or dinner money. It also offers an opportunity for you to give the children some feeling of ownership of the classroom by

asking them to look at the layout and think about ways of improving it. You could invite them to share any worries they have about the coming year and to let you know who their friends are and whom they enjoy working with. The letters could be a private correspondence between you and each child and you should assure them that what they write will only be seen by you.

Educational visits

Educational visits can provide a rich source of writing activities. Children could write:

◗ Letters to the place they will be visiting to ask questions both before and after the visit.

◗ Thank you letters after the visit.

◗ A report on the journey (factual or humorous).

◗ Forms other than prose to describe the visit. For example, if they visit a factory or an industrial museum they could record the production process in list, diagram or chart form. A visit to a supermarket could be recorded by making a map and labelling the places where different activities took place.

◗ A quiz for other class members to test their memories of the visit.

◗ An evaluation of the visit with comments on the organization, enjoyability, educational value and so on of the occasion. Suggestions for improvement. (This could be a group effort.)

Persuasive writing

In Year 4, children should be encouraged to regard writing as a powerful tool for persuasion.

● Ask the children to make collections of advertisements from newspapers and magazines and then display these and discuss them. Look at the ways in which varied fonts, particular words and striking illustrations are used to attract the reader's

attention. *Which advertisements do you think are most effective? Why?* They could follow this up by making their own advertisement for a school event such as a bazaar, party, play or assembly. Their work should be planned in rough initially to ensure accurate spelling and careful positioning of words. Take the opportunity to talk with them about the size and style of print and the impression which this makes upon the reader.

● Have children compare reports from different newspapers on the same event and then produce their own reports, either written or presented as TV or radio news items. This could lead into the production of a class newspaper in which the children make use of headlines and other features of newspaper layout. A DTP program on the computer is a valuable tool for this activity.

◉ Look out for local issues that children can have a view about – the siting of a car park, the closing of a branch library, the building of a hypermarket, the need for a zebra crossing or school crossing patrol, vandalism. Ask them to write briefly, but convincingly, about what they feel about the issue – perhaps as a letter to the editor of the local newspaper. Then ask them to try and write equally persuasively on the other side.

● Other persuasive writing could include taking an event from a story which the children consider demonstrates an example of injustice, and asking them to write from their own point of view, or that of one of the characters, putting the case for doing things differently. A poem such as Allan Ahlberg's 'It's Not Fair', from *Please Mrs Butler* (Puffin), could

be used as a starting point for children to identify those things which they consider to be unfair, and to write persuasively offering their solutions.

Writing based upon literature

Literature can provide a powerful stimulus for children's writing. They can follow hearing or reading a story by producing 'character grids' so that they can consider traits of different characters. (Are they kind, happy, popular and so on.) You can provide a selection of words (generous, considerate, clever, devious…) but children may prefer to choose their own. They could then compare their views of the characters with those of their classmates and you might ask them to follow individual work by paired or group work in which each member's ideas become part of a collective description.

Spelling

◉ The children can collect and display families of words with similar spellings to reinforce the idea that they can apply what they learn about one word to others. They might also make collections of plural nouns, so that they can begin to appreciate that there are irregularities which need to be learned, as well as regular patterns which can be widely applied.

Homophones

Discuss with the class those often troublesome words which sound the same but are spelled differently. Tell them about problems you have, or have had, with these words and of strategies you employ. For example, *Many people get mixed up between 'stationery' writing paper and 'stationary' standing still* (put them on the board) *but you can remember which is which because envelope has 'e' in it and so does the writing paper word.* (Point it out.)) Encourage the children to volunteer their difficulties with homophones. Write them on the board. *Has anyone got any ways of remembering which word is which? Can we think of one for this pair?* Strategies may seem far-fetched but usually work. One child, plagued by 'which' and 'witch' sorted it out by thinking 'All those black clothes would be very itchy'.

Some mnemonics come easily – beach/beech not only has a double *ee* for tree in one word but an *a* for sand in the other. Here/hear can be sorted out because the listening one has an *ear* in it. Others require greater ingenuity.

When you have had your brainstorming session on strategies, you could display the words and strategies under a *Homophone Help Line* heading and ask children to add more problem words as they come across them. Show definitions pictorially, if possible.

Chanting

For real problem words you could try the old-fashioned method of chanting. One secondary school maths teacher ensured whole generations of children could spell 'parallel' for ever because he regularly made them chant 'p-a-r-a-double-l-e-l'. If you find one or two words are consistently mis-spelled you could give them this treatment but it would be boring, time-consuming and ineffective to apply to all mis-spellings.

Spell-checker

Make sure that all the children are aware of the spell-check facility in the word-processing package, know how to use it – and do so. Then tell the children that they have their own spell-checker in their head and should use it for work not done on the computer. Remind them of the *Look–cover–write–check* strategy. There are lots and lots of words they have often seen in writing and the right spelling is probably there in their heads, if they look really hard at what they have written and switch on their mental spell-checker. Sometimes you can suggest that children spell-check each other's work. It is much more fun to look for other people's mistakes than your own!

Spelling rules

◉ Tell the children some of these (*q* is always followed by *u*; words do not end with *v* and rarely end with *i* or *u*) but let them work out others for themselves. Offer groups of words which follow a spelling rule and ask the children to identify the rule and add some exceptions (of which there are usually plenty). For example, *hop, drop, slip, pat, slam, hopped, dropped, slipped, patted, slammed* show a clear pattern and the children should be able to identify the rule. Encourage them to state it clearly using the correct terms ('consonant', 'past tense') teaching them these, if necessary. How many of them know the correct past tense of the many exceptions like sit, run, cut, sleep, hit? *Isn't it strange that sit, hit, and fit all do different things in the past tense?* If you are enthusiastic, knowledgeable and entertained by the extraordinary way our language works, then the children will enjoy it, too.

Punctuation

◉ During Year 4, children should be increasingly aware of the ways in which English writing is punctuated. Group reading and class and group discussion might be focused upon punctuation, and a range of activities can be used to highlight its importance. For example, you can use an overhead projector for a passage in which all the punctuation

marks are covered by Blu-tack. (Or write it on the board and cover the punctuation with sticky labels.) Show the passage to the children and ask them to read it and then suggest what the hidden punctuation marks might be. Such discussions enable children to think carefully about the reasons for punctuation and the different roles which different marks have.

◉ Write on the board an example of writing where the meaning can be totally changed by the position of the punctuation: *the boy sat down on the television there was a herd of elephants in his bedroom his father was tidying up.* Tell the children that this needs punctuation and quickly add full stops and capitals: *The boy sat down on the television. There was a herd of elephants in his bedroom. His father was tidying up.*

Do they think this is what the author meant? *Could we punctuate it differently? How?* Together you can find a more likely version: *The boy sat down. On the television there was a herd of elephants. In his bedroom, his father was tidying up.*

Discuss with them how punctuation has a very real purpose in making clear exactly what the author means. Can they write something which means different things with different punctuation? You can probably show them examples of ambiguity in their own writing caused by poor punctuation.

> They all had skins ● When they saw Torto without a skin ● they were horrified ●
> ● But he has no skin ● cried Porcupine ● ● It ● s disgusting ● ● cried Yak ● ● It ● s indecent ● ●
> ● He's not normal ● leave him to himself ● ● said Sloth ●

Commas

● Use lists to show the function of commas in separating items and encourage children to create their own sentences which make use of commas in this way. Children could list things they have to do, favourite celebrities, favourite songs and so on. The lists could be discussed and explanations for choices made. The activity could, therefore, incorporate an element of oral work as well as helping children with the use of punctuation.

Question and exclamation marks

● Similarly, the use of question and exclamation marks can be reinforced by asking children to write their own examples. Various games may be played to reinforce the use of question marks and some may lead from oral to written work. For example, in one game the children work in pairs asking each other questions. Every sentence has to be a question, so the conversation might go:

How old are you?
Why do you want to know?
Don't you know?
You don't, do you?

This could then be followed by a written conversation with emphasis being placed upon using question marks only when appropriate.

● Exclamation marks might be discussed through the use of a drama script or a passage of dialogue from an exciting story. Children could be encouraged to look for exclamation marks when reading aloud in groups and to use them to guide their expression and tone. If the stories are recorded using a tape recorder, the children will appreciate even more the importance of using punctuation to guide expression, since they will no longer be able to rely upon gesture and facial expression. Such oral work can be followed by writing which encourages children to be expressive and to add dramatic touches through the use of punctuation. It is worth pointing out that exclamation marks lose their power if they are over-used.

Apostrophes

● The National Literacy Strategy requires Year 4 children to learn to use the apostrophe.

Begin with the possessive apostrophe because this will become increasingly familiar to Year 4s. (*Gary's football went over the fence. Helen's lunch box has disappeared!*) Enlist a helper to go round the class picking up items and holding them up while everyone announces ownership and you write 'Simon's pencil', 'teacher's board rubber' on the board, saying 'apostrophe' as you write it. Then ask children to come

out and point to the apostrophes – discuss how they show 'belongs to'. Give them an exercise to do converting 'the book belonging to Polly', 'the dog belonging to the man', 'the button of the shirt' and so on. When everyone is quite comfortable with this, go on, another time, to plurals.

This is where confusion can creep in. Emphasize from the start that Polly can have dozens of books, the man can have a billion dogs, the shirt can be covered with buttons but, because there is only one owner, the apostrophe stays before the *s* always. Now go on to say that, if there is more than one owner, we show it by putting the apostrophe after the *s*. 'The cars' horns ... the cats' dinner ... the elephants' footprints. Point out that this is very useful – we know that more than one elephant made the prints because the apostrophe comes after the *s*. Do another conversion exercise. Look for apostrophes in what you are reading. (Don't get side-tracked to contraction apostrophes at this stage – just say *That's a different kind. We'll look at them soon.*) Give the class another list with mixed single and plural owners and fire questions at them (*The horses' field – One horse or more, Scott? The bee's knees – one bee or more, Rosie?*)

There are, of course, complications over collective nouns, irregular plural nouns and names ending in *s* and the most able children might investigate these. But keep it as simple as possible for most of the class just now.

● Tackle contraction apostrophes when you are sure that everyone is clear about the possessives. Children will be quite familiar with *don't, can't* and so on but may put the apostrophes in the wrong places. List 2 of high frequency words for Year 4 and 5 includes *can't, didn't, don't* and *I'm* so these words will probably be on display in your classroom and may be used as starting points. Another starting point is to write a sentence on the computer in full and contracted form so that the children can see how the contracted version is shorter as well as sounding more normal and less formal.

We are going to the sea. We have got to be there early and I shall have to take a picnic. I cannot take drink in a glass bottle. I am going to sit next to Josie. We're going to the sea. We've got to be there early and I'll have to take a picnic. I can't take drink in a glass bottle. I'm going to sit next to Josie.

Once again, this use of the apostrophe is in children's natural speech form – they've been using it all their lives and, if you teach it systematically, they can incorporate it in their writing without too many problems.

Grammar

⊘ Children's appreciation of grammar and syntax may be developed partly through prediction exercises such as those in which sentences are left incomplete and children either have to select a word from a choice of three or four, or have to create their own endings. The latter allows for an element of creativity and might be developed into a group activity in which children each produce incomplete sentences for others to complete.

⊘ The use of Cloze work should also encourage an awareness of grammar and syntax, particularly if it is undertaken as a paired or small-group activity with discussion being encouraged. Cloze work can take several forms with words taken out randomly, particular parts of speech removed, or key words removed. Provide passages which encourage discussion and which do not have only one possible answer and have children share their answers with other groups to promote discussion. Avoid removing words from the first one or two sentences so that children have a chance to get into the text first.

Tenses

A common problem in children's writing at this stage is that they change tenses during a single piece of writing. Many early reading books include a lot of text in the present tense, while more advanced stories are generally written in the past tense. This may lead to later confusion.

⊘ Try showing the class a passage in which the verbs have been covered up and ask them, first of all, to suggest what the verbs might be and then to put them into the correct tense. By including speech within the text, you can ensure that there are examples of past, present and future tenses. Do not be afraid to use the terms 'past', 'present' and 'future' or the word 'tense'. Year 4 children are generally quite capable of understanding such vocabulary, if it is explained to them through comprehensible examples.

Handwriting

● By the end of Year 4, children should be able to write in legible, joined handwriting and should be able to hold pens and pencils correctly. Some children may not yet be forming letters correctly. It is particularly important to identify such problems at this stage, since continued misforming will inhibit joining of letters and lead to frustration for children, as well as poor presentation. Tactile exercises which involve tracing letters in sand, or copying letters which have crosses to mark their starting points, may help to reinforce correct letter formation.

● You should check that they are using correct left–right orientation and that they are all aware of where on the page they should begin to write. Some children may be encountering problems at this stage and an inability to present work well may inhibit some children from writing at length. A sympathetic approach from you will help to reassure such children and, where appropriate, allowing them to use the word processor will enable them to produce work which allows readers to appreciate the content of their writing without being put off by the presentation.

● Some children may be experiencing problems because of left-handedness. Always make sure that left-handers sit to the left of right-handers, so that they are not constantly knocking each other. Check that left-handed children have developed a comfortable writing position. The paper may be angled up to 45 degrees with the top right-hand corner nearer to the child than the top left. Left-handed children may also hold pencils between 2.5 and 4cm from the tip to enable them to see their writing.

Assessment

Year 4 is, then, a year in which children will have further developed their understanding of the reciprocal nature of reading and writing and will continue to draw upon the knowledge of language which they gain from their reading and their speaking and listening to enhance and develop their writing. They should experience an increasingly broad diet of reading and writing and should be afforded lots of opportunities to discuss the nature and variety of literature.

What should they know?

By the end of Year 4 children should know the following things:
- the function of full stops, capital letters, speech marks and question marks in sentences;
- how to use apostrophes;
- how to structure a sentence so that it is grammatically correct;
- the importance of careful presentation for their audiences for speaking and writing;
- how to use their knowledge of the alphabet to find information;
- an increasingly wide range of graphemes, blends and digraphs;
- that they should plan, draft and edit some of their writing to check for mistakes and to improve and refine it.

What should they be able to do?

They should be able to:
- communicate ideas confidently;
- identify the main points in texts and in discussions;
- listen carefully to discussions;
- adapt their speech to the needs of the listener;
- show some awareness of standard English and when it is used;
- read a range of texts fluently and accurately;
- read independently using semantic, syntactic and graphophonic strategies to help them to establish meaning;
- write imaginatively and clearly;
- adapt their writing to meet the needs of the reader;
- join letters and write legibly;
- use full stops, commas and question marks accurately;
- spell common polysyllabic words accurately.

What should they have experienced?

They should have:
- read and listened to a range of different genres in both fiction and non-fiction;
- read independently and in groups;
- written in a variety of styles for real audiences;
- had opportunities to talk about their work in groups and to the whole class;
- continued to develop a positive attitude to literacy;
- worked in and helped to create a stimulating and 'literate' classroom;
- continued to develop an awareness of the possibilities which are open to them as literate people.

In order to assess children's progress, you can make use of informal observation and conversation with children. This could take place during quiet reading periods and might be part of a reading conference between you and the child. You could ask the child to read to you during this conference, but there should also be discussion about features of the literature being read and about the child's reading generally. It is not sufficient simply to listen to a child reading if one is to build up a picture of his overall reading ability. As OFSTED reported in 1996: 'Listening to children read is a necessary but far from sufficient element in the teaching and learning of reading. It was most successful when it was diagnostic and related to an effective recording system designed to correct children's errors through planned sequences of work.'

In addition to listening to children reading, you should look for opportunities to observe and make notes upon the children's approaches to reading when they are choosing books, reading independently, or reading in other areas of the curriculum. The notes could include the following.

Reference to the children's choices of reading materials

- Do they look carefully at a range of books before choosing one to read?
- What kind of books do they tend to prefer?
- Are they able to find books on the subjects in which they are interested?
- Which features of books do they look at when choosing their reading? For example, do they look at the cover, the illustrations, the publisher's blurb or the contents page?

Reference to behaviour during independent reading

- Do they concentrate on what they are reading?
- Are they constantly changing their books?
- Do they become absorbed in their reading?
- Are they easily distracted?
- Do they talk about what they are reading?

Reference to the children's abilities to cope with reading across the curriculum

- Can they follow instructions on worksheets?
- Can they read for information using an index and contents page?
- Can they make use of reference books?
- Can they skim and scan text to find information?
- In mathematics, is their progress affected when problems are set out in words rather than figures?
- Can they make use of information technology without being hampered by their reading abilities?

Mathematics
including Numeracy Hour

The teaching and learning opportunities that you provide children with in Year 4 build upon the mathematical foundations established in Year 3. It is here that children continue to apply the pure mathematics (mathematical knowledge, skills and understanding) which they have learned in Year 3 and in Key Stage 1 to real-life, problem-solving investigations.

Children also need to continue to develop a firm understanding of new mathematical concepts and make the necessary connections between the mathematical experiences they encounter. That is, between:

- mathematical symbols: 'x', '÷';
- mathematical language: *property*, *circumference*, *imperial*;
- pictures: recognize that $\frac{5}{10}$ or $\frac{1}{2}$ is shaded;

- concrete situations: *Three quarters of our class like cheese and onion crisps. How many children do not like cheese and onion crisps?*

The teaching and learning objectives contained in this chapter show progression throughout Year 4. It is about 'what' mathematics to teach. So often children's learning is led by the activity rather than the learning intention that underpins the activity.

It is hoped that what follows will enable you to identify where children are in their stages of development and where best to develop these further in the future.

Language

While still developing the vast range of skills, knowledge and understanding learned from previous learning objectives, children are being exposed to new mathematical concepts of ever-increasing difficulty. While you need to accept children's early mathematical vocabulary, you should now help them to develop more formal mathematical language. For example, when learning about multiplication, children may first use terms such as 'lots of', 'sets of', and 'groups of' but, at this age, they should move on to the more formal language of multiplication such as 'times', 'multiplied by' and 'product'.

When children are asked to talk about what they are doing and thinking in mathematics, they not only show you how much they understand, but they also clarify and develop their own understanding.

Encourage the children to talk about their experiences and make the necessary connections between the language, pictures, symbols and concrete situations they encounter in their learning.

You need to be continually asking questions that will help children:

- make connections in mathematics: *If you know what $\frac{1}{4}$ of 12 is ,what do you think $\frac{3}{4}$ of 12 equals? How does the solution to that problem help you to solve this question?*

- develop a greater understanding of the learning objective: *What have you learned from the investigation you have just undertaken?*
- make new discoveries in mathematics: *What have you done so far?*
- apply their mathematical knowledge to other contexts: *If you know that 3 x 6 = 18, what do you think the area of a shape with sides 6cm, 6cm, 3cm and 3cm is?*

Estimation and approximation

Development of the ability to estimate and approximate should be a regular component of the mathematics programme in all classes. It is important that children are provided with the opportunities to estimate a 'rough answer' to a problem, and approximate the 'range' an answer is likely to occur within. Only through practical activities aimed at developing their estimation and approximation techniques will they be able to develop a 'feel for numbers' and assess whether an answer is reasonable or not.

Estimation and approximation skills also play an important role in the ability of children to measure with understanding. They should be continually exposed to real-life situations to develop these skills.

As children develop, encourage them to estimate as close to the actual answer as possible.

Do they still need apparatus?

Children need to develop their initial understanding of mathematical concepts through the manipulation of concrete materials in everyday contexts that are relevant and practical to their own experiences. Such experiences enable children to 'see and touch' the mathematics they are engaging in.

There does, however, come a time when children are ready to move away from manipulating concrete apparatus and begin to internalize their understanding and develop more sophisticated 'mental mathematics' strategies.

The time of when to remove the concrete apparatus is a difficult one to determine and it varies enormously from one child to another. Unfortunately, children don't give off a signal when this 'internalization' has occurred. It is only through probing questions (*You have just shown me that if you have 3 groups of blocks with 5 blocks in each group, you will have 15 blocks altogether. Let's see what happens when we add another group of 5. Can you tell me what 4 groups of 5 are?*) and discussions with the children that you can begin to ascertain that it is no longer appropriate for children to be working only with concrete apparatus.

There will be times when children will need to return to using appropriate concrete apparatus, for example, when you introduce a new concept, and such materials should be available for children to use when and where appropriate.

The Numeracy Hour

During the Numeracy Hour, all the children should be working on mathematics at the same time for the whole period. The mathematics you do in the Numeracy Hour will not be part of a general theme or integrated work but is focused on teaching specific mathematical concepts and methods.

You will be spending most of the time directly teaching and questioning the class. Children should spend approximately half of their time in a direct teaching relationship with you and the rest of the time working independently either in groups, pairs or individually.

Each lesson should follow the following structure.

Oral work and mental calculation (about 5–10 minutes)
Aimed at:
- developing mental fluency in previously taught concepts/methods and developing children's oral skills (whole class).

Main teaching and pupil activities (about 30–40 minutes)
Aimed at:
● introducing children to new mathematical concepts/methods (whole class, group); or
● consolidating previously taught concepts/methods (whole class, group); and
● providing children with opportunities to practise, consolidate, use and apply taught mathematical concepts/methods (groups, pairs, individuals).

Plenary (about 10–15 minutes)
Aimed at:
● drawing together the main teaching points of the lesson (whole class).

Children's recording

When introducing a new mathematics topic in Year 4, the emphasis should be on consolidating children's mental and written methods and talking about mathematics. By Year 4 they should be able to record their results confidently using both their own methods of recording and the more conventional mathematical recording techniques.

What should they be able to do?

By the end of Year 4, children should have had appropriate and sufficient experiences to help them in the following key areas. **The statement 'Children should' refers to the majority of children within the year group.**

Key area: Using and applying mathematics

You need to provide children with opportunities to:
● use and apply mathematical knowledge, skills and understanding, that have been previously taught, practised and consolidated, in problem-solving situations;
● acquire knowledge, skills and understandings through 'real-life', meaningful, problem-solving investigations.

So often children in Key Stage 2 experience real difficulties in solving mathematical problems. This may stem from a lack of mathematical knowledge or a failure to apply existing knowledge. However, these difficulties may also have nothing to do with children's mathematical understanding; rather it is often more to do with far more fundamental issues such as lack of confidence, an inability to persevere and failure to be motivated.

In Year 4, give children the opportunity to apply their mathematical knowledge, skills and understandings in an environment which both motivates them and promotes the self-confidence and perseverance they will need later to solve more sophisticated and challenging investigations.

Making and monitoring decisions to solve problems

Children should be able to:
● select and use materials and mathematics appropriate for a particular task;
● develop their own strategies for working through a problem;
● understand the ways of working through a problem;
● begin to organize and plan their work;
● look for ways of overcoming problems;
● develop different mathematical approaches to a problem;
● begin to make decisions;
● realize that results can vary according to the rule used;
● check results.

Developing mathematical language and forms of communication

Children should be able to:

- understand and use appropriate mathematical language;
- discuss mathematical work and begin to explain their thinking;
- use and interpret mathematical information and relate it to a range of situations;
- represent their work in a variety of mathematical forms.

Developing mathematical reasoning

Children should be able to:

- make and test predictions and statements about patterns and relationships;
- make a simple rule;
- understand a general statement;
- investigate statements and predictions by finding and trying out examples.

Key area: Number

Children should be given opportunities to develop both their own and standard methods of working; mentally, orally and in the written form; in a variety of contexts, using a range of practical resources.

In order to ensure that children receive a broad and balanced range of experiences, you need to provide your class with activities that employ the following tools:

- concrete materials;
- mental mathematics;
- paper and pencil;
- information technology.

Developing an understanding of place value and extending the number system

Children should be able to:

- count forwards to 10 000 and beyond from any given number;
- count backwards from 10 000 and beyond from any given number;
- recognize, read, write and order numbers to 10 000 and beyond;
- recognize written number names to 10 000;
- know what each digit in a number represents and partition a number into thousands, hundreds, tens and units (ThHTU);
- say the number that is 1, 10, 100, or 1 000 more or less than any whole number;
- use ordinal numbers;
- compare two numbers saying which is more or less and giving a number which lies between them;
- make sensible estimates and approximates of at least 500 objects;
- round any two- or three-digit number to the nearest 10 or 100.

Money

Children should be able to:

- recognize the value of all coins and notes;
- use all four operations to solve word problems involving money;
- convert pounds to pence and vice versa.

Fractions

Children should be able to:

- recognize fractions that are several parts of a whole, for example $\frac{2}{3}$ and $\frac{5}{6}$;
- recognize simple mixed numbers, such as $5\frac{1}{2}$;
- recognize equivalence between simple fractions;

- know that $\frac{1}{2}$ is more than $\frac{1}{4}$ and less than $\frac{3}{4}$;
- know that a number like $4\frac{1}{2}$ lies half way between 4 and 5;
- begin to relate fractions to division, for example $\frac{1}{4}$ is equivalent to $\div$ 4;
- find fractions such as $\frac{1}{2}, \frac{1}{3}, \frac{1}{4}, \frac{1}{5}, \frac{1}{10}$ of a single-digit or two-digit number where the answer is still a whole number;
- find fractions such as $\frac{2}{3}, \frac{3}{4}, \frac{4}{5}$ of shapes.

Decimals

Children should be able to:
- use decimal notation for tenths;
- use decimal notation to two decimal places in the context of money and length;
- convert a sum of money, such as £32.45, to pence; or a length, such as 4.5 metres, to centimetres;
- order decimal amounts of money or a set of lengths expressed in metres to one decimal place;
- round a decimal to the nearest whole number.

Fractions and decimals

Children should be able to:
- recognize the equivalence between the decimal and fraction forms of one-half, one-quarter and one-tenth.

Negative numbers

Children should be able to:
- recognize negative numbers in context.

Understanding relationships between numbers and developing methods of computation

Patterns

Children should be able to:
- recognize and extend number sequences formed by counting from any number in steps of constant size;
- recognize and extend the number sequence beyond zero when counting backwards;
- recognize odd and even numbers up to 1 000;
- begin to recognize the outcomes of adding and subtracting pairs of odd and even numbers;
- recognize multiples of 2, 3, 4, 5, 10 and 100;
- know and apply simple tests of divisibility;
- recognize squares of numbers 1 to 10;
- recognize factors;
- recognize prime numbers;
- make generalizations and predictions about patterns;
- record observations.

Addition

Children should be able to:
- extend their understanding and use of the vocabulary associated with addition;
- understand the principles of the commutative and associative laws of addition;
- understand doubles of all numbers 1 to 50 and multiples of 10 to 500;
- begin to understand all number pairs that total 100;
- understand and use all the addition facts to 20;
- use knowledge of number facts and place value to add a pair of numbers mentally;
- use paper and pencil methods to record, explain and support partial mental methods involving HTU + HTU.

Subtraction

Children should be able to:

- extend their understanding and use of vocabulary associated with subtraction;
- understand that the principles of the commutative and associative laws do not apply to subtraction;
- understand and use all subtraction facts to 20;
- use knowledge of number facts and place value to subtract a pair of numbers mentally;
- use paper and pencil methods to record, explain and support partial mental methods involving HTU – HTU.

Addition and subtraction

Children should be able to:

- extend their understanding of the relationship between addition and subtraction;
- further develop mental strategies for addition and subtraction;
- further develop paper and pencil methods for calculations;
- solve problems involving addition and subtraction;
- choose the appropriate question when solving + and – problems.

Multiplication

Children should be able to:

- extend their understanding and use of the vocabulary associated with multiplication;
- understand the principles of the commutative, associative and distributive laws of multiplication;
- recall 2x, 3x, 4x, 5x and 10x multiplication tables;
- understand doubles of whole numbers to 50;
- know all the multiples of 10 to 500 and beyond;
- begin to recall 6x, 7x, 8x and 9x multiplication tables.

Division

Children should be able to:

- extend their understanding and use of the vocabulary associated with division;
- understand that the principles of the commutative, associative and distributive laws do not apply to division;
- understand the remainder expressed as a whole number;
- begin to understand the remainder expressed as a decimal;
- make sensible decisions about rounding up and down after division;
- understand halves of multiples of 10 to 100;
- recall division facts related to the 2x, 3x, 4x, 5x and 10x multiplication tables;
- develop an understanding of the division facts related to the 6x, 7x, 8x and 9x multiplication tables.

Multiplication and division

Children should be able to:

- extend their understanding of the relationship between multiplication and division;
- further develop mental strategies for multiplication and division;
- further develop paper and pencil methods for calculations;
- solve problems involving known multiplication and division facts;
- choose the appropriate operation when solving multiplication and division problems.

Mathematics

Solving numerical problems

Children should be able to:

● solve numerical problems involving known addition, subtraction, multiplication and division facts in the context of real-life, investigative problems involving: money, length, mass, volume and capacity, perimeter, area, time.

Key area: Shape, space and measures

Here, activities involving concrete apparatus provide opportunities for enabling children to develop their spatial and geometric skills, knowledge and understanding.

Understanding and using properties of shape

3-D solids

Children should be able to:

● extend their understanding and use of the vocabulary associated with 3-D solids;

● continue to recognize, name and describe the properties of 3-D solids including a tetrahedron, square-based pyramid;

● unfold cuboids, pyramids and prisms to identify their nets;

● identify the different nets of an opened cube;

● construct 3-D solids using various apparatus;

● sort known 3-D solids according to faces, edges and vertices.

2-D shapes

Children should be able to:

● extend their understanding and use of the vocabulary associated with 2-D shapes;

● continue to recognize and name 2-D shapes including quadrilateral and heptagon and regular and irregular polygons;

● construct polygons using appropriate apparatus;

● construct circles using appropriate apparatus;

● understand the relationship between the centre, radius, diameter and a semicircle and a quadrant.

Symmetry

Children should be able to:

● extend their understanding and use of the vocabulary associated with symmetry;

● recognize and sketch two or more lines of symmetry in a 2-D shape or pattern;

● sketch a reflection of a simple shape in a mirror line.

Understanding and using properties of position and movement

Position

Children should be able to:

● extend their understanding and use of the vocabulary associated with position;

● find the position of an object on a grid using co-ordinates;

● recognize the eight points on a compass.

Movement and angle

Children should be able to:

● extend their understanding and use of the vocabulary associated with movement and angle;

● make and measure clockwise and anti-clockwise turns, for example, SW to N;

● recognize the rotation of a 3-D shape after a turn through a right angle or half right angle;

● use a 45° and 60° set square to draw and measure angles of 90°, 60°, 45° and 30°.

Understanding and using measures

Length

Children should be able to:
- extend their understanding and use of the vocabulary associated with length;
- recognize the centimetre (cm), metre (m) and kilometre (km) lengths;
- estimate and measure to the nearest centimetre, metre and kilometre;
- recognize the need for a standard unit smaller than a centimetre;
- recognize the millimetre (mm) length;
- estimate and measure using millimetres;
- know the relationship between familiar units;
- know $\frac{1}{2}$, $\frac{1}{4}$ and $\frac{1}{10}$ of a kilometre and a metre;
- recognize the imperial measurement, mile;
- convert up to 1 000 centimetres to metres;
- choose and use the appropriate unit and measuring apparatus;
- record estimates and measurements;
- use the four operations to solve problems involving length.

Mass (weight)

In the National Curriculum for mathematics the term 'weight' no longer appears, but has been replaced by the term 'mass'. 'Weight', the amount of pull something exerts, is properly measured in newtons; 'mass', the amount of substance, is measured in grams.

Children should be able to:
- extend their understanding and use of the vocabulary associated with mass;
- recognize the gram (g) and kilogram (kg) measures;
- estimate and measure using grams and kilograms;
- know the relationship between familiar units;
- know $\frac{1}{2}$, $\frac{1}{4}$ and $\frac{1}{10}$ of a kilogram;
- choose and use the appropriate unit and measuring apparatus;
- record estimates and measurements;
- use the four operations to solve problems involving mass.

Volume and capacity

'Volume' is the measurement of space in a solid shape; 'capacity' is the amount of space something will hold.

Children should be able to:
- extend their understanding and use of the vocabulary associated with volume and capacity;
- recognize the litre (l) and millilitre (ml) measures;
- estimate and measure using litres and millilitres;
- know the relationship between familiar units;
- know $\frac{1}{2}$, $\frac{1}{4}$ and $\frac{1}{10}$ of a litre;
- introduce the imperial measurement, pint;
- choose and use the appropriate unit and measuring apparatus;
- record estimates and measurements;
- use the four operations to solve problems involving volume and capacity.

Perimeter

Children should be able to:
● measure and calculate the perimeter of rectangles and other simple shapes using counting methods and the standard unit, cm.

Area

Children should be able to:
● measure and calculate the area of rectangles and other simple shapes using counting methods and the standard unit, cm^2.

Time

Children should be able to:
● extend their understanding and use of the vocabulary associated with time;
● continue to tell the time on the hour, half hour and quarter hour using digital and analogue clocks;
● tell the time using digital and analogue clocks to the nearest minute;
● estimate and check time using seconds, minutes, hours;
● use am and pm;
● understand the notation 16:46;
● read a simple timetable and use this year's calendar;
● use the four operations to solve problems involving time.

Handling data

In Year 4, children need to formulate questions and use simple statistical methods. They should be given opportunities to access and collect data through purposeful enquiries. The use of computers should be encouraged as a source of interesting data and as a tool for representing data.

Collecting, representing and interpreting data

Children should be able to:
● collect, record, discuss and predict numerical data frequency tables;
● collect, record, discuss and predict numerical data using bar charts (involving intervals of 2, 5, 10 and 20);
● collect, record, discuss and predict numerical data using pictograms (with the symbol representing 2, 5, 10 or 20 units);
● collect, record, discuss and predict numerical data using a wider range of graphs;
● find the mode and median of a set of data.

Practical ideas

Numeracy Hour

All of the practical ideas which follow are suitable for using in the Numeracy Hour. If, for example, your objectives were:

▶ to consolidate children's understanding of the 6x table;

▶ to reintroduce mental calculation strategies for multiplication;

▶ to solve word problems involving the 6x table in a 'real-life' context;

then your Numeracy Hour could take the following pattern.

Oral work and mental calculation (10 minutes)

▶ Play 'Countdown' with the class (see page 62) (Numbers:10, 6, 8, 43; operations: x,+, −; target number: 81; answer: (6 x 8) + 43 − 10 = 81);

▶ ask individual children to discuss the strategies they used to arrive at the answer.

Main teaching and pupil activities (30 minutes)

▶ Remind children of some of the mental calculation strategies for multiplication (see page 59);

▶ pose a number of questions relating to the 6x table and ask individual children to work out the answer and discuss how they did it;

▶ pose questions involving the 6x table in 'real-life' contexts, asking individual children to work out the answer and discuss how they did it.

Plenary (10 minutes)

▶ Play Multiplication Bingo (see page 61) with the class, asking questions involving 6x table.

Making a start

The first activities under each main heading are particularly suitable for introducing the concept.

Assessment

Most of the activities can be effectively used for some form of assessment. However, those activities that have ☼ in the margin alongside them are particularly useful for assessment purposes.

Number

Place value

☼ Start from any given number and count round the room within the range 0–10 000 forwards and backwards in 10s, 100s and 1 000s.

● Display place value cards for a selection of numbers within the range 0–10 000 to familiarize children with place value.

> Th H T U
> **4 6 9 8**
>
> four thousand six hundred and ninety eight

Number charts and squares

Use a 10–1 000 chart or 100–10 000 chart.

● Identify the pattern that occurs in the columns and rows, for example, the pattern of 500s in the hundreds column and the pattern of 2000s in the thousands row.

100	200	300	400	**500**	600	700	800	900	1 000
1 100	1 200	1 300	1 400	**1 500**	1 600	1 700	1 800	1 900	2 000
2 100	2 200	2 300	2 400	**2 500**	2 600	2 700	2 800	2 900	3 000
3 100	3 200	3 300	3 400	**3 500**	3 600	3 700	3 800	3 900	4 000
4 100	4 200	4 300	4 400	**4 500**	4 600	4 700	4 800	4 900	5 000

● Ask children to complete an incomplete 10–1 000 square or 100–10 000 square.

100	200		400	500	600	700		900	1 000
1 100	1 200	1 300	1 400	1 500	1 600		1 800	1 900	2 000
	2 200	2 300	2 400	2 500		2 700	2 800		3 000
3 100	3 200		3 400		3 600		3 800	3 900	4 000

Variation: Ask children to complete an incomplete 10–1 000 square or 100–10 000 square following another pattern.

100	1 100	2 100		4 100	5 100		7 100	8 100	
200		2 200	3 200		5 200	6 200			9 200
		1 300	2 300		4 300		7 300		9 300
400	1 400		3 400		5 400		7 400		9 400
		2 500				6 500		8 500	

● Cover up a number or numbers and ask the children to identify the number(s) being covered.

● Give the children a completed 1–100 square, 10–1 000 square, 100–10 000 square jigsaw that they have to cut and put back together again.

100	200	300	400	500	600	700	800	900	1 100
1 100	1 200	1 300	1 400	1 500	1 600	1 700	1 800	1 900	2 000
2 100	2 200	2 300	2 400	2 500	2 600	2 700	2 800	2 900	3 000
3 100	3 200	3 300	3 400	3 500	3 600	3 700	3 800	3 900	4 000
4 100	4 200	4 300	4 400	4 500	4 600	4 700	4 800	4 900	5 000

✂

Variation: The children make their own 1–100 square, 10–1 000, 100–10 000 square jigsaw.

Number cards

✪ Use a selection of number cards in the 0–10 000 range.
Place a pack of a series of jumbled cards in order.
▷ Place all the cards with:
  1 ten in one pile;
  2 tens in one pile;
  3 tens in one pile, and so on.
▷ Place all the cards with:
  1 hundred in one pile;
  2 hundreds in one pile;
  3 hundreds in one pile, and so on.
▷ Remove a card from the pack and ask the children to name the missing card.

● Hand out a selection of number cards in the range 0–10 000 to the class. Ask two children to come out to the front and display their number cards, for example, 4 256 and 1 627. Ask the remainder of the class to stand up if they have a number which is in between 4 256 and 1 627. Repeat.

● Make three- four- and five-digit numbers using 0–10 number cards. For example, make the number 3 567. Discuss the value of the 3, 5, 6 and 7. *What is the value of the 5 in 3 567? How many 10s in 3 567?*

● Using a selection of three- four- and five-digit number cards ask the children to place them in order. For example: 475, 354, 243; or 2 646, 2 534, 2 756, 4 657; or 12 654, 34 657, 12 765, 87 470.

Thousands, hundreds, tens and units

Use Dienes apparatus or similar Base 10 material.
✪ Show three 1 000s, six 100s, seven 10s and four 1s to the class. *How much Base 10 material do I have altogether?* Count them with the class. (Three 1 000s, six 100s, seven 10s and four 1s = 3 674.) Ask a child to write the number 3 674 on the board. Repeat using other numbers to 10 000.

● Show 4 512 using the number cards, then ask a child to show the same number using Base 10 material.

● Ask children to compare the size of two numbers displayed using Base 10 material and written on the board as numerals: for example, 1 376 and 3 671. *Which number is larger/smaller? How can we tell?* Try with numbers such as 4 001 and 1 004, 4 741 and 4 471. *Hint:* An overhead projector is an excellent way to display Base 10 apparatus to the whole class.

● Ask a child to show 139 using Base 10 apparatus. Ask another child to add 10 to the 139 to make the number 149. Ask a third child to add another 10 to make the number 159. *What does 139 and 10 make? What does 149 and 10 make?* Discuss the pattern with the children: 139, 149, 159... 199. Extend to include numbers within the range 0–1 000, adding 100 each time; then to numbers within the range 0–10 000, adding 1 000 each time.

✪ Ask the children what is 1, 10, 100, 1 000, 10 000 **more** than any two-/three-/four-/five-digit number. For example, *What is 100 more than 67? What is 10 000 more than 4 178? What is 100 more than 15 037?*

✪ Ask the children what is:

◗ 1, 10, 100 **less** than any three-digit number (*What is 100 less than 537?*);

◗ 1, 10, 100, 1 000 **less** than any four-digit number (*What is 1 less than 9 000?*);

◗ 1, 10, 100, 1 000, 10 000 **less** than any five-digit number (*What is 10 000 less than 17 781?*). *Variation:* Display number cards or number name cards asking the same sort of question.

● Ask the children to name two numbers in the range 0–1 000. *Which number is more or less? Can you think of any number that lies between these two numbers?* Extend to include numbers in the range 0–10 000.

● Display cards showing the multiples of 10 (10, 20, 30, 40 … 100). Remove a card and ask children to identify the missing number. Jumble the cards and ask the children to put them in the correct order. Extend to include multiples of 100 and 1 000.

Matching game 0–1 000

Ask the children to shuffle a selection of about 30 0–1 000 number cards and corresponding number name cards together and play Pelmanism with them. *Variation:* Use a selection of 0–10 000 number cards and corresponding number name cards. Play Snap.

Calculator

Children should be able to:

◗ use the clear key, all four operation keys, the equals key and the decimal point to calculate with realistic data;

◗ select the correct key sequence to add, subtract, multiply or divide numbers;

◗ have a feel for the approximate size of an answer after a calculation;

◗ check a calculation by performing the inverse calculation;

◗ recognize simple decimal notation, such as $\frac{1}{2}$ = 0.5, $\frac{1}{4}$ = 0.25, $\frac{1}{3}$ = 0.33;

◗ recognize simple decimal notation involving money, for example £5.36 + £4.94 = £10.30 which is the same as 10.3;

◗ use the constant key for repeated addition, subtraction and repeated multiplication and division of a number by 10;

◗ understand a negative number output.

Estimation

● Encourage children to develop their estimation and approximation skills to about 500 by asking them questions such as:

How many words on this page?
How many books on these shelves?
How many bars in those railings?
How many days in the school year?
How many hours in a month?
How many weeks until the holidays?
How far is it in metres from the hall door to the front gate?
What is 169 + 245?
What is half of 376?
What is 89 multiplied by 6?

Ask them to explain how they arrived at their estimate. Then they can record their estimates and find the difference between the estimate and the actual answer.

Rounding

● Show children a number card in the range 0–99 and ask them to round it to the nearest 10. (54 rounded to the nearest 10 is 50.) Numbers ending in 5 should be rounded up.

● Show children a number card in the range 0–999 and ask them to round it to the nearest 100. (272 rounded to the nearest 100 is 300.)

● Ask children to round a two-digit number to the nearest 10 and a three-digit number to the nearest 100 without using cards.

Money

● Children should apply their knowledge of addition, subtraction, multiplication and division number facts to solve calculations involving money, finding totals and giving change. Ask children to bring in catalogues/newspaper advertisements and choose a selection of items to buy. *Can your friend tell you what the total cost of your choice would be? What change will you receive from £15?*

● Encourage children to use notes and coins in simple contexts adding, subtracting, multiplying and dividing as well as calculating with fractions. *What is the total of £8.50 and £5.70? If one tin of paint costs £5.24, how much do three tins cost? Fran is able to save 60p a week. She wants to buy a CD that costs £4.40. If she already has £1.50, how many weeks will it take to save enough money to buy it?*

● Teach children to convert pounds to pence and vice versa. Talk about place value. *How many pence in a pound?* (100) 100p + 67p = 167p. There are 167 pence in £1.67. Ask them to work out more examples. Then ask *How many pounds in 8,427 pence?* When you get the answer, write £84 on the board. *How many pence left over?* (27) Write '27' beside the £84 - £84.27.

Fractions

● Show a 2 x 5 grid. Colour five squares.

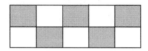

We have five out of ten squares coloured. Write $\frac{5}{10}$ on the board. Then say *I can colour the squares in a different way.*

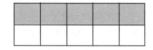

I have coloured five out of the ten squares a different way. What do you notice about the shape now? When you have the answer ('it's a half') you can explain that another way of saying $\frac{5}{10}$ is $\frac{1}{2}$. Show them that in $\frac{5}{10}$ there is one five in the 5 and two fives in the 10, $\frac{5}{10}$ making $\frac{1}{2}$.

● Ask the children to colour two-eighths and one-quarter of a 2 x 8 grid. *Are they the same? How do you know?* Repeat using other examples of simple equivalent fractions.

● Ask the children to ring two-tenths and one-fifth of the items in a drawn set of ten.

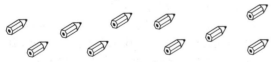

Repeat using other examples.

● After practical work of this kind, check that children know the equivalences between:
halves, quarters and eighths;
tenths and fifths;
thirds and sixths.
Children who have problems with doing this need to spend more time on practical work.

● Children need to recognize that one whole is made up of:
$\frac{4}{8} + \frac{4}{8}$;
$\frac{2}{3} + \frac{1}{3}$;
$\frac{2}{6} + \frac{4}{6}$ and so on.
Some children can do this mentally, but many will need to continue to colour in grids, segments of a circle and so on to be confident of calculations like these. They can fold a sheet of paper into eight parts and then cut it up and put it together again to prove that $\frac{4}{8}$ plus $\frac{4}{8}$ equals 1 but $\frac{4}{8}$ plus $\frac{3}{8}$ does not equal 1.

● Use concrete materials to show children the relationship between fractions and division. Divide:
▶ a rod of 8 cubes in half to show that, for example, $\frac{1}{2}$ of 8 is the same as 8 ÷ 2;
▶ a slice of bread into 4 to show that $\frac{1}{4}$ is the same as 1 ÷ 4;
▶ a pile of 12 buttons into 3 to show that $\frac{1}{3}$ is the same as 12 ÷ 3.

● Use fruit cut into pieces to help children recognize that:
▶ $\frac{1}{2}$ is more than $\frac{1}{4}$ and less than $\frac{3}{4}$;
▶ $4\frac{1}{2}$ lies between 4 and 5.

☼ Count on from 0 and back from 10 in halves and quarters. Then start at different points. *Jonathan, count on in quarters from $7\frac{1}{2}$ ... Susie, count back in halves from $5\frac{1}{2}$ ...*

● Make a number line showing wholes, halves, quarters, (see below). Add eighths. Make other number lines for wholes, thirds and sixths; wholes, fifths and tenths.

● Children need to be able to find fractions of numbers or quantities. Remind them that $\frac{1}{2}$ means that an object or group of objects is divided/shared equally between 2; $\frac{1}{4}$ into 4 equal parts, and so on. Use rods of interlocking cubes to demonstrate $\frac{1}{4}$ of 12, $\frac{1}{5}$ of 20 and so on. Extend by asking questions such as:

| 0 | $\frac{1}{4}$ | $\frac{2}{4}$ | $\frac{3}{4}$ | $\frac{4}{4}$ | $1\frac{1}{4}$ | $1\frac{2}{4}$ | $1\frac{3}{4}$ | $1\frac{4}{4}$ | $2\frac{1}{4}$ | $2\frac{2}{4}$ |
| | | $\frac{1}{2}$ | | 1 | | $1\frac{1}{2}$ | | 2 | | $2\frac{1}{2}$ |

What is $\frac{1}{10}$ of 100, 40, 600...?
What is $\frac{1}{5}$ of 20, 10, 60...?
What is $\frac{1}{4}$ of 16, 20, 40...?
What is $\frac{1}{10}$ of 70, 20, 50?
What is $\frac{1}{10}$, $\frac{1}{5}$, $\frac{1}{4}$, $\frac{1}{3}$, $\frac{1}{2}$ of £1/1 metre ...?
What fraction of £1 is 20p?
What fraction of 1 metre is 50 centimetres?
What fraction of this shape is that shape?

● Remind children that fractions are asking you to find a smaller group/amount from a larger group/amount. That, for example, $\frac{3}{4}$ is three parts of an object or a group of objects divided into four equal parts.

Decimals

● Explain to the class that decimals are based on the number 10. Ask them to cut up a whole sheet of paper into 10 equal pieces. *There are ten equal parts which make up a whole one. Each of the ten parts is smaller than the whole. We know*

0.1	0.1
0.1	0.1
0.1	0.1
0.1	0.1
0.1	0.1

we can write one part as a fraction, $\frac{1}{10}$, but we can also write one part as a decimal, 0.1. Add together the ten 0.1s to show 1.0. Two parts are written as 0.2. *How do we write six parts? What would that be as a fraction?*

● Explain that if we write 3.6 we mean that there are three whole units and six out of ten equal parts. It is the same as $\frac{36}{10}$. If $\frac{36}{10}$ is the same as 3.6, how would we write $\frac{74}{10}$? Repeat using other examples, such as $\frac{28}{10}$, $\frac{43}{10}$ and so on.

If $\frac{45}{10}$ written as a decimal is 4.5, how do we write $4\frac{1}{2}$ as a decimal? Use the paper divided into 10 to remind them that $\frac{5}{10}$ is a half. Ask them about $3\frac{1}{2}$, $9\frac{1}{2}$ and so on.

✪ Count from 0 in steps of one-tenth.

● Tell the children that $\frac{1}{4}$ is written as 0.25 as a decimal. Divide a sheet of paper into quarters and write 0.25 in each quarter.

Together with the class, add the four quarters (0.25 + 0.25 + 0.25 + 0.25 = 1.0). *If $\frac{1}{4}$ is 0.25, what do you think $\frac{3}{4}$ written as a decimal is?* (0.25+ 0.25 + 0.25 = 0.75).

0.25	0.25
0.25	0.25

● Talk about the value of the 4 and the 8 in 4.8, of the 2 and the 6 in 12.6 and so on.

✪ Start at 4.1 and count backwards in steps of 0.1. Repeat for other numbers.

● Point out that we use decimals all the time when using money. Revise with them the conversion of pounds to pence and vice versa (see page 52). Ask them to put in order amounts of money, smallest first. For example, £3, £3.99, 30p, 33p.

● Remind the children that there are 100cm in 1m. Ask them to put lengths in order, smallest first: 4.5m, 2.3m, 4.7m, 2.9m. Then ask them to convert the decimal figures into measures (2m 30cm and so on).

● Give children practice in converting measures into decimal notation:
❱ 150cm = 1m and 50 cm = 1.5m
(50cm is $\frac{1}{2}$ a metre; $\frac{1}{2}$ is written as 0.5);
❱ 1250cm = 12.5m;
❱ 95mm = 9.5cm;
❱ 4500g = 4.5kg.

● Ask children to show, using a calculator, that:
❱ $\frac{4}{5}$ is the same as 0.8
❱ $4.7 + \square = 6.8$.

● Remind children that decimals are based on the number 10 and that, when we round a number, we round it up to the nearest whole number if it is 0.5 or more ($\frac{5}{10}$), or down if it is less than 0.5. Ask the children to round decimals to the nearest whole number:
❱ 4.2 = 4;
❱ £4.76 = £5.00;
❱ 6.8m = 7m.

● In the context of word problems ask children to solve calculations involving mixed units, for example:
❱ 73p + £2.89 = $\square$;
❱ 3.5m + 20cm = $\square$;
❱ 6 kg + 250g = $\square$.

Fractions and decimals

✪ Matching game: the children shuffle a selection of fraction cards and corresponding decimal cards together and play Pelmanism or Snap with them.

✪ Ask the children to:
❱ write $\frac{4}{10}$, $\frac{1}{4}$, $\frac{3}{4}$ and $4\frac{1}{2}$ as decimal fractions;
❱ write 3.25, 6.75, 0.3 and 0.8 as fractions;
❱ express 4.7, 5.6, 7.0 in pounds and pence.

Negative numbers

● Discuss with the children the concept of negative numbers in familiar contexts such as temperature and on a calculator display. You could relate it to going up and down steps at the swimming baths with the waterline being 0 and steps below it being negative.

● Put a thermometer in a freezer then ask children to read the temperature, for example, –8°;

● Ask children which temperature is less: –3°C or –5°C?

☼ Check their understanding by asking them to write down all the whole numbers between –10 and 5 and to place a set of cards, –20 to 10, in order.

Methods of computation
Patterns
☼ Use a 10–1 000 multiples of 10 chart, and then a 100–10 000 multiples of 100 chart, to identify the patterns that occur in the columns and rows.

☼ Children count forwards and backwards in 1s, 10s and 100s from any two- or three-digit number.

☼ Children count forwards and backwards in 2s, 3s, 4s and 5s from any number up to/from 100.

Sequences
☼ Ask the children to describe and extend sequences, for example: 57, 64, 71, 78; 35, 31, 27, 23. *What is the rule?* Children make up their own and ask others to describe and extend the sequence.

☼ Children find the missing numbers in a sequence: □, 38, 41, 44,□, 50. *What is the rule?* Children make up their own and ask other children to describe and extend the sequence.

Odd and even
Revise odd and even numbers. Use one or two of the following activities to check that children are confident with them.

● Count round the room - even numbers clap their hands.

● Sort a pack of a random selection of 0–1 000 cards into odds and evens.

● Identify odd and even numbers on a 0–100 chart.

● Make an 'always' chart on which children can write what they've noticed about odd and even numbers. For example:
❱ the last number of an even number is always 0, 2, 4, 6, 8;
❱ the last number of an odd number is always 1, 3, 5, 7, 9;
❱ after 1, every second number is always odd;
❱ the numbers on both sides of an odd number are always even;
❱ if you add two odd numbers the answer is always even;
❱ if you add an odd and an even number the answer is always odd;
❱ the difference between two odd or two even numbers is always even;
❱ the difference between an odd and an even number is always odd;
❱ if you divide an odd number by an even number, you will always have a remainder.

☼ Children may need practice in continuing sequences involving odd and even numbers: 147, 149, 151, 153 …; 362, 364, 366, 368 …

☼ Children can test each other with questions like *What odd number comes before 574? What even number comes after 371?*

Multiples
☼ Identify the patterns in 2x, 5x, 10x multiplication on a 1–100 square. Children colour the multiples of various multiplication tables on the square. *What do you notice?*

☼ Children need to recognize multiples in the 2x, 3x, 4x, 5x, 10x tables. For example, *Ring all the numbers in the box divisible by 3.*

2	3	5	12	16	18	20	24

Which numbers in the box are also divisible by 6?

● Identify the patterns in 2x, 3x, 4x, 5x, 10x multiplication and related division facts. For example:

1 x 2 = 2	2 ÷ 2 = 1
2 x 2 = 4	4 ÷ 2 = 2
3 x 2 = 6	6 ÷ 2 = 3
4 x 2 = 8	8 ÷ 2 = 4
5 x 2 = 10	10 ÷ 2 = 5

● Discuss with the children the relationship between the various multiplication tables, 2x, 4x, 8x (4s are double 2s, 8s are double 4s); 3x, 6x, 9x (6s are double 3s, 9s are treble 3s); 5x, 10x (10s are double 5s).

● Teach children to recognize the multiples of 10, 100 and 1 000: 60 is a multiple of 10; 400 is a multiple of 10 and of 100; 9 000 is a multiple of 10, of 100 and of 1 000.

Tests of divisibility

● Ask children if they can devise rules about when whole numbers are divisible by:

  100 (if the last two digits are 00)
   10 (if the last digit is 0);
    5 (if the last digit is a 0 or 5);
    2 (if the last digit is a 0, 2, 4, 6 or 8);
    3 (if the sum of the digits is divisible by 3);
    4 (if the last two digits are divisible by 4).

Square numbers

Introduce square numbers using grids.

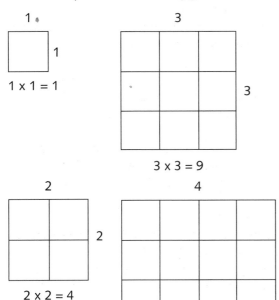

Can you discover the rule for square numbers? (When a number is multiplied by itself the answer is a square number, ie 1, 4, 9, 16, 25, 36, 49, 64, 81 and 100.) Introduce the children to the mathematical symbol ². *Can you draw a grid to show 7^2 and 10^2?* Ask children the value of 2^2, 5^2, 6^2, 8^2.

Factors

● Explain that 2 is a factor of 12 because 2 x 6 = 12. Therefore, 6 is also a factor of 12. Discuss with them what might be other factors of 12 (4 and 3: 4 x 3 = 12, and 12 and 1: 12 x 1 = 12). Together, establish that 12 has six factors: 1, 2, 3, 4, 6 and 12.

● Ask children to find all the factors of any number to 30 and beyond.

● Help children to recognize that:

  since 18 = 6 x 3
  then 5 x 18 =
       [5 x (6) x 3) =
       30 x 3 = 90

Addition
Mental strategies

Many Year 4 children still find crossing the 10s or 100s boundary difficult, (for example, 5 + 7 = ☐ ; 46 + 37 = ☐ ; 145 + 29 = ☐).

● Revise some mental strategies that will help them to solve these types of calculations easily and introduce more:

❱ start with the largest number first;
❱ count forward in repeated steps;
❱ know that 46 + 25 is the same as 25 + 46;
❱ count up through the next multiple of 10, 100 or 1 000;
❱ use two stages to add 9 (+10 − 1), 19 (+20 −1), 29 (+30 −1) and so on;
❱ use two stages to add 11 (+10 +1), 21 (+20 +1), 31 (+30 +1) and so on;
❱ know doubles, such as 6 + 6;
❱ know near doubles, based on doubles already known, 6 + 7 is one more than 6 + 6;
❱ partition 6, 7, or 8 into '5 and something':

       8   +   7
    (5 + 3) + (5 + 2)
    (5 + 5) + (3 + 2)
       10   +   5 = 15;

❱ partition into '10 and something':

       15   +   14
    (10 + 10) + (5 + 4)
       20   +   9 = 29;

❱ increase the largest number to the next multiple of 10 and add the remainder:

       8   +   3
    (8 + 2) +   1
       10   +   1 = 11;

❱ adding three or four small numbers: put the largest number first and/or find pairs totalling 9, 10 or 11;
❱ use patterns of similar calculations;
❱ use the relationship between addition and subtraction;
❱ use knowledge of number facts and place value to add a pair of numbers mentally.

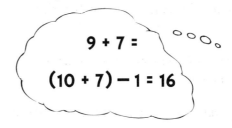

9 + 7 =

(10 + 7) − 1 = 16

Using the strategies

Teach the children to solve the following type of addition calculations using the mental calculation strategies mentioned above:

▶ addition of a single-digit number to any three-digit number without crossing the 10s boundary: 385 + 4 = ☐;

▶ addition of a two-digit number to a multiple of 100: 200 + 45 = ☐;

▶ addition of a two- or three-digit number to a multiple of 10, without crossing 100: 40 + 21 = ☐;

▶ addition of a pair of two-digit numbers, without crossing the 10s boundary or 100: 43 + 21 = ☐;

▶ addition of number facts to 20: 13 + 6 = ☐;

▶ addition of a two- or three-digit number to a multiple of 10, 100 or 1 000: 90 + 16 = ☐;

▶ find what must be added to a two- or three-digit number to make 100 or the next higher multiple of 100: 39 + ☐ = 100;

▶ addition of 10 to any two- or three-digit number, including crossing the 100s boundary: 94 + 10 = ☐;

▶ addition of a pair of multiples of 10, crossing 100: 40 + 80 = ☐;

▶ addition of a pair of multiples of 100, crossing 1 000: 400 + 700 = ☐;

▶ addition of a three-digit multiple of 10 to make the next higher multiple of 100: 440 + ☐ = 500;

▶ addition of a multiple of 10 to a two-digit number, crossing 100: 42 + 70 = ☐;

▶ addition of a pair of multiples of 100, crossing 1 000: 300 + 800 = ☐;

▶ addition of 100 to any three-digit number, without crossing 1 000: 576 + 100 = ☐;

▶ addition of a single-digit number to a two-digit number, crossing the 10s boundary: 75 + 8 = ☐;

▶ addition of a single-digit number to any three- or four-digit number, crossing the 10s boundary: 376 + 9 = ☐;

▶ addition of any pair of two-digit numbers crossing the 10s boundary: 63 + 29 = ☐;

▶ find what must be added to a four-digit multiple of 100 to make the next higher multiple of 1 000: 5 200 + ☐ = 6 000.

Paper and pencil

● Teach children to solve addition calculations using paper and pencil procedures to record, support and explain mental methods, building on established mental strategies. Encourage them to discuss and compare their methods.

● When setting out columns, show that units line up under units, tens under tens, and so on. The following paper and pencil procedures should be encouraged for addition of:

▶ TU + TU not crossing the 10s boundary;

▶ TU + TU crossing the 10s boundary;

▶ HTU + TU not crossing the 10s boundary;

▶ HTU + TU crossing the 10s or 100s boundary or both;

▶ HTU + HTU not crossing the 10s or 100s boundary or both;

▶ HTU + HTU crossing the 10s or 100s boundary or both.

Method 1: Most significant digit first (one with greatest value):

254 +	636 +	462 +	608 +
28	91	59	175
——	——	——	——
200	600	400	700 ⎤ add
70	120	110	70 ⎬ mentally
12	7	11	13 ⎦ from top
——	——	——	——
282	727	521	783

Method 2: Crossing through a multiple of 100:

684 +
 47
———
700   (684 + 16) add 16 to get to a multiple of 100
 31   (47 – 16) leaves 31 to add on
———
731

Method 3: Adding the least significant digits first and preparing for 'carrying', leading to 'carrying' below the line:

386 +	386 +	239 +	482 +	465 +
45	45	45	45	58
——	——	——	——	——
11	421	284	527	523
120	11	——	——	——
300	——	1	1	11
——	431			
431				

Number line

● Working on a number line helps children who are having problems with addition.

For example: 45 + 6 =

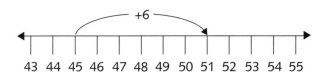

● 67 + 5 =
   (67 + 3) + 2 =
   70 + 2 =

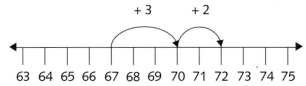

● The 'empty' number line:
   67 + 14 =

Base 10 material

● 58 + 24 =

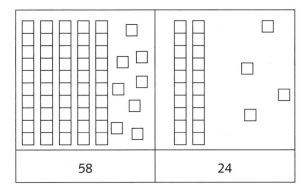

| 58 | 24 |

Add the 5 tens and 2 tens

Add the 8 units and 4 units

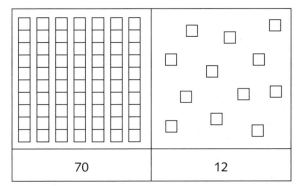

| 70 | 12 |

Exchange the 12 units for 1 tens and 2 units

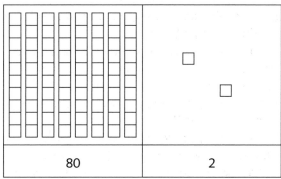

| 80 | 2 |

Subtraction

Mental strategies

Teach the children a range of mental strategies that will help them to solve subtraction calculations easily. For example:

◗ count backwards in repeated steps;

◗ if you know that 6 + 5 = 11 then you also know what 11 − 5 and 11 − 6 are, as all three calculations involve the same three numbers (5, 6, 11);

◗ find a small difference by counting up from the smaller to the larger number: 304 − 298 = ;

◗ use two stages to subtract 9 (−10 +1), 19 (−20 +1), 29 (−30 +1);

◗ use two stages to subtract 11 (−10 −1), 21 (−20 − 1), 31 (− 30 −1);

◗ decrease the largest number to the next multiple of 10 and subtract the remainder, for example:
   74 − 6
   (74 − 4) − 2
   70 − 2 = 68;

◗ use patterns of similar calculations;

◗ use the relationship between addition and subtraction;

◗ use knowledge of number facts and place value to subtract a pair of numbers mentally.

Using the strategies

Teach the children to solve subtraction calculations like those examples following using the mental calculation strategies above:

◗ subtraction of a single-digit number from any three-digit number without crossing the 10s boundary.

◗ subtraction of a single-digit number from a multiple of 100 or 1 000;

◗ subtraction of a pair of two-digit numbers, without crossing the 10s boundary or 100;

◗ subtraction number facts to 20;

◗ subtraction of a multiple of 10 from a two- or three-digit number, without crossing the 100s boundary;

◗ subtraction of 10 from any two- or three-digit number, including crossing the 100s boundary.

Mathematics

- subtraction of a pair of multiples of 10, crossing 100;
- subtraction of a multiple of 10 from a two-digit number, crossing 100;
- subtraction of a pair of multiples of 100, crossing 1 000;
- subtraction of 100 from any three-digit number,
- subtracting a single-digit number from a 'teens' number, crossing the 10s boundary;
- subtracting a single-digit number from a three- or four-digit number, crossing the 10s boundary;
- find the difference between a pair of numbers lying either side of a multiple of 1 000:

  for example, 7 005 − 6 979 = □;

- subtraction of any pair of two-digit numbers, crossing the 10s boundary.

Paper and pencil

Teach the children to solve subtraction calculations using paper and pencil procedures to record, support and explain mental methods, building on established mental strategies. Encourage them to discuss and compare their methods.

The following paper and pencil procedures should be encouraged for subtraction of:

HTU − TU and HTU − HTU crossing the 10s boundary or the 100s boundary of both.

Method 1: Counting on (complementary addition):

```
643 −
 75
    5   from 75 to 80
   20   from 80 to 100
  500   from 100 to 600
   40   from 600 to 640
    3   from 640 to 643
  ───
  568
```

Method 2: Crossing down through a multiple of 100:

```
643 − 75 =
  600   (600 − 43)
 − 32   (75 − 43)
  ───
  568
```

Method 3: Approximating by taking away 100:

```
643 − 75 =
  543   (643 − 100)
 + 25   (10 − 75)
  ───
  568
```

Method 4: Decomposition:

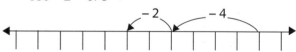

```
 643   = 600 + 40 +  3
 − 75        − 70 +  5

       = 600 + 30 + 13    adjusting from
            − 70 +  5     T to U

       = 500 + 130 + 13   adjusting from
            −  70 +  5     H to T

    500 +  60 +  8  = 568
```

Number line

- 83 − 4 = 79

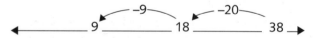

73 74 75 76 77 78 79 80 81 82 83 84 85

- 684 − 6 =
  (684 − 4) − 2 =
  680 − 2 = 678

673 674 675 676 677 678 679 680 681 682 683 684 685

- The 'empty' number line. For example,

38 − 29 =

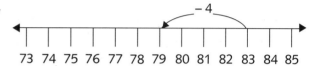

Base 10 material

- Use Base 10 material to consolidate work on subtraction. For example:

65 − 28 =

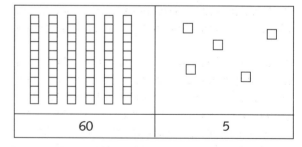

| 60 | 5 |

Change one ten for 10 units.

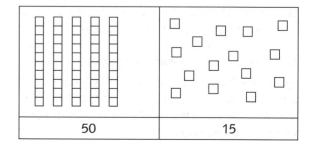

| 50 | 15 |

Remove 20   Remove 8

| 20 | 8 |

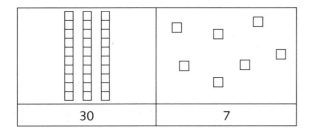

| 30 | 7 |

Relationship

Teach children that knowing one of the relationships between addition and subtraction means that you also know the other three. For example:

36 + 27 = 63
27 + 36 = 63
63 – 36 = 27
63 – 27 = 36

Multiplication
Vocabulary

Revise the vocabulary associated with multiplication: *multiplication, multiply, times, groups of, lots of, sets of, product, multiple.* For example, 3 times 4; 3 multiplied by 4; Multiply 3 by 4. *Is 12 a multiple of 4? 3 lots of 4. What is the product of 3 and 4?*

Revising multiplication

✪ Count around the classroom in 2s, 3s, 4s, 5s and 10s. Use a number line or 1-100 chart if necessary.

● Give one child a tower of six cubes. *How many towers are there?* (one). *How many cubes are there in each tower?* (six). Write and say, 1 x 6 = 6. Give a second child another tower of six cubes. *How many towers are there?* (2). *How many cubes are there in each tower?* (6). Write and say, 2 x 6 = 12. Continue this process, with the children telling you what to write, until ten children are each holding a tower of six cubes. Recite together the 6x tables.

● Repeat the same process for introducing the 7x, 8x, 9x multiplication facts. Use other appropriate apparatus, such as buttons, counters, children and so on, until you are confident that the children understand the concept.

Mental strategies

Teach children a range of mental strategies that will help them to solve multiplication calculations easily. For example:
▶ to multiply a number by 10/100, shift its digits one/two places to the left;
▶ use doubling, starting from known facts (such as 8 x 4 is double 4 x 4);
▶ double any two-digit number by doubling the 10s first;
▶ use closely related facts (multiply by 9 or 11 by multiplying by 10 and adjusting; add facts from the 2x and 4x tables to work out the 6x tables);
▶ partition: 25 x 4 = (20 x 4) + (5 x 4);
▶ use the relationship between multiplication and division;
▶ use knowledge of number facts and place value to multiply by 2, 3, 4, 5, 6, 7, 8, 9, 10, 100, 1 000. For example:

8 x 24 =
8 x 20 = 160
8 x 4 = 32
160 + 32 = 192.

Using the strategies

Teach the following type of multiplication calculations using the mental calculation strategies above:
▶ multiply a two- or three-digit number by 10 or 100: 38 x □ = 3 800;
▶ double any multiple of 5 up to 100: 65 x 2 = □;
▶ consolidate multiplication facts for the 2x, 3x, 4x, 5x, 10x tables: 6 x 4 = □;
▶ begin to know multiplication facts for 6x, 7x, 8x, 9x tables: 7 x □ = 56;
▶ consolidate multiplication of a two-digit multiple of 10 by 2, 3, 4, 5 or 10 and begin to multiply by 6, 7, 8 and 9: 60 x □ = 180;
▶ multiply a two-digit number by 2, 3, 4, or 5, crossing the 10s boundary: 54 x □ = 162.

Paper and pencil

Teach children to solve multiplication calculations using paper and pencil procedures to record, support and explain mental methods, building on established mental strategies. Encourage them to discuss and compare their methods.

The following paper and pencil procedures should be encouraged for multiplication of TU x U.

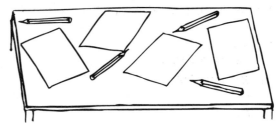

Method 1: Partitioning: using the standard algorithm:

$$18 \times 6 =$$

```
   18
 × 6
 ———
   60   (10 × 6)
   48   (8 × 6)
 ———
  108
```

Method 2: Area method, partitioning:

$$18 \times 6 =$$

×	10	8	
6	60	48	= 108

Method 3: Doubling and halving:
$$18 \times 6 =$$
$$36 \times 3 = 108$$

Laws

● Children need to understand and use, when appropriate, the principles (but not the names) of the commutative, associative and distributive laws as they apply to multiplication:

Commutative law: 13 × 4 = 4 × 13;

Associative law: 16 × 6 = 16 × (3 × 2) or (16 × 3) × 2;

Distributive law: 14 × 6 = (10 + 4) × 6 = (10 × 6) + (4 × 6) = 60 + 24 = 84.

● Make sure the children understand that, for example:

◗ adding 15 fives together is the same as 15 × 5 or 5 × 15;

◗ the product must be greater than either number;

◗ multiplication by 1 always leaves the number unchanged;

◗ multiplication by 0 always leaves the answer as 0;

◗ multiplication is the inverse of division.

Division

Vocabulary

Revise the vocabulary associated with division: *division, divide, share, divided by*. For example, *Share 12 between 3; 12 divided by 3; Divide 12 by 3. How many 3s in 12? Is 3 a multiple of 12?*

Revising division

● Re-introduce division. Count out 35 cubes in front of the class. *We are going to share these thirty-five cubes evenly among seven children. How many do you think they will each have?* Choose the seven children and give one cube to each of them, then another, and so on. *How many cubes do each of you have?* (five). *Thirty-five shared among seven is five.* Write and say, 35 ÷ 7 = 5.

● Repeat, if necessary, using other examples of division facts from the 2x, 3x, 4x, 5x, 6x, 7x, 8x, 9x and 10x tables.

● The same process can be used later to develop an understanding of the concept of remainders by using a number of cubes that will not divide equally.

Mental strategies

Teach children a range of mental strategies that will help them to solve division calculations easily:

◗ use halving, starting from known facts (such as find quarters by halving halves);

◗ use the relationship between multiplication and division;

◗ use knowledge of number facts and place value to divide by 2, 3, 4, 5, 6, 7, 8, 9, 10, 100, 1 000.

Using the strategies

Teach children to solve the following type of division calculations using the mental calculation strategies above:

◗ divide a four-digit multiple of 1 000 by 100 or 10: 6 000 ÷ 100 = □ ;

◗ halve a multiple of 10 to 200: 160 ÷ 2 = □;

◗ consolidate division facts related to the 2x, 3x, 4x, 5x, 10x tables: 32 ÷ □ = 8;

◗ begin to know the division facts related to the 6x, 7x, 8x, 9x tables: □ ÷ 7 = 8.

Paper and pencil

Teach children to solve division calculations using paper and pencil procedures to record, support and explain mental methods, building on established mental strategies. Encourage them to discuss and compare their methods.

The following paper and pencil procedures should be encouraged for division of TU ÷ U.

Method 1: Using repeated subtraction:

$$72 \div 4$$

```
    72
  − 40   (4 × 10)
  ———
    32
  − 32   (4 × 8)
  ———
     0    = 18
```

$56 \div 3$

$$\begin{array}{r} 56 \\ -\ 30 \quad (3 \times 10) \\ \hline 26 \\ -\ 24 \quad (3 \times 8) \\ \hline 2 \end{array}$$

= 18 remainder 2

Method 2: Using the standard algorithm, developed from repeated subtraction:

$108 \div 6$

$$\begin{array}{r} 18 \\ 6\ )\ 108 \\ -\ 60 \quad (6 \times 10) \\ \hline 48 \\ -\ 48 \quad (6 \times 8) \\ \hline \end{array}$$

= 18

Laws

Make sure children understand that, unlike multiplication, division cannot be carried out in any order, for example, $3 \times 4 = 4 \times 3$, but $12 \div 3 \neq 3 \div 12$.

Remainder

Make sure children understand remainders (see page 60), when to round up or down after division and what to do with a remainder.

They should be able to:
▶ give a remainder as a whole number: $45 \div 4 = 11$ remainder 1; $467 \div 100 = 4$ remainder 67;
▶ begin to give a remainder as a decimal fraction when dividing by 10 or 2: $45 \div 10 = 4.5$; $21 \div 2 = 10.5$;
▶ begin to give a remainder as a decimal fraction when dividing pounds and pence;
▶ find the remainder when dividing with a calculator;
▶ round decimals to the nearest whole number: 4.2 is between 4 and 5, but nearer to 4;
▶ decide what to do about a remainder after division and round up or down accordingly.

The four rules

☺ Ask: *How many ways can you make 284? You must find examples that include +, −, x and ÷, fractions, decimals and one-, two- and three-digit numbers.*
Variation: any number to 1 000.

☺ Use flash cards with addition, subtraction, multiplication or division number facts to produce instant recall of number facts.

● Ask children to write and discuss examples of addition, subtraction, multiplication or division facts in real contexts.

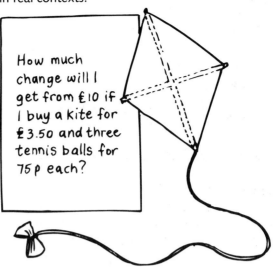

How much change will I get from £10 if I buy a kite for £3.50 and three tennis balls for 75p each?

Addition bingo

Children write down any 16 numbers from, say, 30 to 60 on a 4x4 grid. Present addition statements in a variety of ways:
▶ two number cards to be added together;
▶ orally: *Twenty-three add nine equals ...?*;
▶ throw two dice with high numbers, call out the numbers, and ask the children to add the numbers together;
▶ as a problem to solve: *Sarah had 36p and was given another 15p. How much has she altogether?*

Children work out the answer and, if they have that number on their grid, they cross it out. *Bingo!* is called when a child has crossed out any four numbers that are together vertically, horizontally or diagonally. You can go on until someone has crossed out all of his/her numbers.
Variations: Play Subtraction/Multiplication/Division Bingo.

Today's number

☺ Have a number of the day: when challenged at odd moments during the day, children have to give number statements for this number using any operation or computational method they can that hasn't already been used.

20 questions

☺ Give the children 20 quick-fire addition, subtraction, multiplication and division questions orally using a range of appropriate mathematical vocabulary. Ask them to write down the answer only. Repeat the next day. *Did you get them all finished? How many did you get correct today/yesterday?* (If you want to have differentiated questions, do this with a group while the others do the next activity.)

Mathematics

Beat the clock

☺ Give the children a strip of paper containing 20 simple calculations. (You can differentiate by giving different tasks to different groups.) Ask the children to complete it in a specified time (four minutes, perhaps). Repeat the next day. *Did you get them all finished? How many did you get correct today/yesterday?*

Countdown

☺ Work out a calculation involving known number facts and operations, for example, (8 x 6) + 43 – 10 = 81. Don't tell the children – keep it to yourself! Write the numbers 10, 8, 43 and 6 on the board. Tell the children that using only each of these numbers once only, in any order, and using some or all of the four operations, they have to reach the total 81. Children can make up their own examples and test them on each other. Ask them to find alternative ways of reaching the total.

Four corners

☺ Ask the children to find the four corner numbers which total the centre number. *Can you find six different ways to make 678 using four numbers?* Change the centre number. Change the square to a triangle, pentagon and so on.

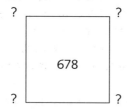

Solving numerical problems

Give children experience of applying their knowledge of number in a variety of written problems in contexts involving money, length, mass, volume and capacity, perimeter, area and time.

Shape, space and measures
Properties of shape

3-D solids

● Show children a tetrahedron. Name and label it. Discuss its properties in relation to faces, edges and vertices. Repeat this for a square-based pyramid. *Who can do the same for a cuboid, cylinder, sphere, pyramid, cone, prism and a hemisphere?*

● Children can identify cubes, cuboids, cylinders, spheres, pyramids, cones, prisms, hemispheres, tetrahedrons and square-based pyramids in pictures,

drawings and in the environment. Make posters (Our Pyramid Collection) on which children can stick appropriate pictures they have found and/or set up a display of real objects.

☺ Play *What Am I?* Children describe the attributes of a shape/object and the class have to try and identify it.

● Children pull apart boxes of various shapes (including cuboids, pyramids and prisms) and reassemble them. *What do you notice about the shape of the different nets? What 2-D shapes are the prism/pyramid made from? Are there different nets for the same 3-D solid?*
Variation: Children pull apart boxes of various shapes, trace around their net on to a sheet of card, cut around the net and assemble the shape.

● Ask the children to make a net for an opened cube. *How many different nets can you make?*

● The children construct 3-D solids using various construction materials, including paper. (You will find the nets in most maths schemes.)

☺ Children sort a collection of 3-D solids and everyday objects according to faces, edges and vertices. For example, objects with:
▶ 6 faces, 12 edges, 8 vertices;
▶ no vertices;
▶ 3 faces;
▶ 5 faces, 8 edges, 5 vertices.

2-D shapes

● Draw a quadrilateral on the board or large sheet of paper. Name and label it. Discuss its properties in relation to sides and corners. Repeat for a heptagon and regular and irregular polygons. Repeat to consolidate children's understanding of regular and irregular squares, rectangles, triangles, circles, hexagons, pentagons, octagons. ('Irregular' squares are on one point, 'irregular' circles are elipses.)

☺ Ask the children to identify regular and irregular squares, rectangles, triangles, circles, hexagons, pentagons, octagons, polygons, quadrilaterals and heptagons in pictures, drawings and in the environment. Make posters and/or displays.

● Children construct and draw regular and irregular polygons using appropriate apparatus (pencils, compasses, rulers, dotty paper and geoboards). They should now be drawing with increasing accuracy.

- ⟩ pentagon (a 5-sided polygon);
- ⟩ hexagon (a 6-sided polygon);
- ⟩ heptagon (a 7-sided polygon);
- ⟩ octagon (an 8-sided polygon);
- ⟩ nonagon (a 9-sided polygon);
- ⟩ decagon (a 10-sided polygon);
- ⟩ dodecagon (a 12-sided polygon).

● Children construct circles using cups, cylinders, compasses and other appropriate apparatus, with increasing accuracy. Make sure they have good quality compasses and teach them to keep the pointed leg of the compass still and completely vertical. The pencil should be sharp and the pressure on the pencil leg constant but not too hard.

● Make sure children know the following parts of a circle: centre, radius, diameter, semicircle, quadrant.

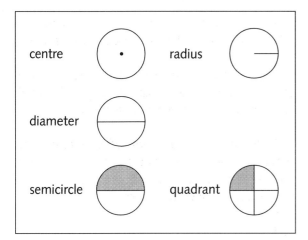

☼ Children sort a collection of 2D shapes (regular and irregular) according to faces, edges and corners.

Matching game

Children shuffle a variety of 2D shape cards together (say, 4 x regular and irregular squares, rectangles, triangles, circles, hexagons, pentagons, octagons, polygons, quadrilaterals and heptagons) and play Pelmanism or Snap with them.

Variation: Have 1 x regular square, rectangle, triangle, circle, hexagon, pentagon, octagon and polygon picture cards, 1 x irregular square, rectangle, triangle, circle, hexagon, pentagon, octagon, polygons, quadrilaterals and heptagons and 2 x squares, rectangles, triangles, circles, hexagons, pentagons, octagons, polygons, quadrilaterals and heptagons label cards. Children have to match the picture card with the label card.

IT

Some children could draw the figures for these cards on the computer.

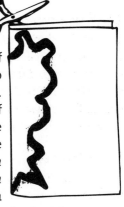

Symmetry

● Revise the concept of symmetry. Ask the children to make a symmetrical pattern. (They should fold a piece of paper in half, draw a shape around the fold, cut out the shape.) *Who can make a snowflake? Who can paint a symmetrical picture?* (Fold a piece of paper in half, paint a simple picture on one half, fold the sheet in half again, open out.)

 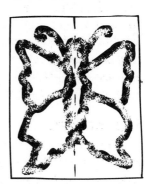

● Remind the children that:
- ⟩ the fold line divides the shape into two parts;
- ⟩ the two parts are the same - they are halves;
- ⟩ certain shapes have symmetry;
- ⟩ certain shapes are symmetrical;
- ⟩ the fold is called 'the line of symmetry'.

☼ The children make their own symmetrical shapes/ patterns involving two or more lines of symmetry.

● Children sketch the reflection of a simple irregular shape using a mirror.

☼ Children find examples of reflective symmetry in shapes and in the environment and check with a mirror to see if they have chosen shapes correctly.

Properties of position and movement

Position

● Revise the vocabulary to describe the position of an object, and encourage the children to use it:
- ⟩ in relation to themselves;
- ⟩ in relation to other subjects;
- ⟩ in describing models, pictures and diagrams.

For example: *near, close, far, to the left, to the right, in front of, behind, beside, next, next to, above, across, along, around, after, back to back, before,*

top, bottom, centre, down, up, far, forward, further, from, here, high, low, in, inside, into, first, last, middle, near, on, on to, on top of, outside, over, past, right over, around, round, side by side, there, through, turn, under, underneath, upside down, clockwise, anti-clockwise, grid, row, column, vertical, horizontal, diagonal, compass point, north (N), south (S), east (E), west (W), north east (NE), north west (NW), south east (SE) and south west (SW).

IT

Use a LOGO package/Roamer/Turtle to show position.

Co-ordinates

● Draw a 4x4 grid on the board or a large sheet of paper.

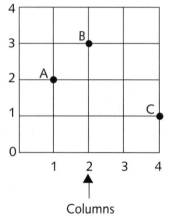

Discuss with the children the positions of the letters.
▶ Point A is 1 square along and 2 squares up. We write this as co-ordinates (1, 2);
▶ Point B is 2 squares along and 3 squares up. We write this as co-ordinates (2, 3);
▶ Point C is 4 squares along and 1 square up. We write this as co-ordinates (4, 1).
Tell the children that to find a point using co-ordinates we look *along* the columns and then *up* the rows. They can remember this by saying to themselves, *Along the hall then up the stairs.*

✪ Draw marks or letters on other locations on the grid. Ask individual children to find and name the location of the various marks/letters using co-ordinates.

✪ Give the children a worksheet with various marks/letters in a similar grid to the one above. Ask them to name the location of each of the various marks/letters using co-ordinates.

Direction

● Revise the direction compass. *What is it useful for?* Discuss how sometimes we need ways of explaining directions to other people or finding our

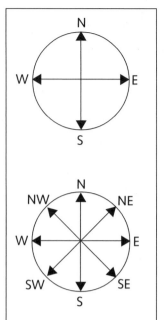

way. Draw a circle on the board. *Who can put in the four points of the compass? Who can remember the phrase that helps us to remember the order of the compass points?* (**N**ever **E**at **S**limy **W**orms.) *Have you made up a phrase of your own?*

✪ Add to the compass on the board to introduce north east (NE), north west (NW), south east (SE) and south west (SW).

Delete the drawing from the board and ask the children to draw a circle and put in the eight compass points.

✪ Give each pair of children a direction compass and describe how to use it. *Put the compass on a flat surface or hold it very still. The dark end of the needle will point to the north. Now move the compass round so the needle lines up with* [whatever marking your compasses have for magnetic north]. *Now your compass is ready to use.* When everyone is ready, ask *Who can point to the south/east/north west/south east?* and so on, to check that they are reading the compass correctly. Then go on to writing down objects in the classroom/playground that lie in each of the directions and completing worksheets that ask for the directions of school landmarks from a particular point to be filled in. Children can give directions to landmarks for friends to follow.

● Some schools have a compass painted on the playground. Use this, if you have one. If you don't, why not ask the head if one could be added? This would be a great stimulus to interest if the class believe it was done specially for them!

IT

Draw a large directional compass on a large sheet of paper and put a Roamer on it. Children have to move the Roamer towards various directions. For example, *Starting at north move the Roamer east, then south, then west and finally north.* Encourage children to describe the directions in which the Roamer is turning and travelling and to use vocabulary such as 'clockwise' and 'anti-clockwise'.

Movement and angle
Translation and rotations
🌑 Revise translations (movement in a straight line) and rotations (movement through a right angle or a half right angle) by asking children to trace round 3-D solids. They draw around the solid, rotate it or move it a little, draw around it again and repeat. *Variation:* Use two shapes.

✪ Children combine translations and rotations to create their own patterns.

IT
Use a LOGO package/Roamer/Turtle to draw various movement patterns including translations and rotations.

Right angles
🌑 Revise the concept of a right angle. Get the children to make a right angle tester. (Ask them to fold a sheet of paper in half and then in half again. Remind them that the corner measures a 'square corner'. They draw a small square in the corner.)

🌑 Ask individual children to go around the room and check for square corners. *What do we call a square corner?*

✪ Ask the children to find angles that are 'right angles' and those that are 'not right angles'. *Which are smaller than a right angle? Which are larger than a right angle?*

🌑 Using a clockface make and measure different angles of the hands. *At what time do the hands make a right angle?*

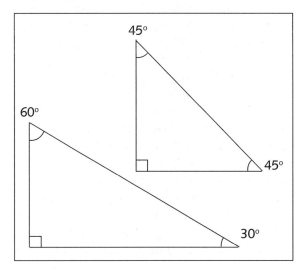

🌑 Show the children how to use a 45° and a 60° set square to draw and measure angles of 90°, 60°, 45° and 30°. (Line the set square up accurately and place the three middle fingers firmly on the base of the set square.)

Length
Centimetres and metres
🌑 Using a centimetre ruler and metre ruler establish that children are familiar with centimetres (cm) and metres (m).

✪ Working in pairs, children measure the length, height and distance of/between various objects/ people in and around the classroom using centimetre and metre rulers as appropriate. Tell them to:
❱ find objects of varying lengths (*Find something about 14cm long.*);
❱ estimate the length of objects before measuring them with the ruler;
❱ record both their estimates and actual measurements.
Discuss with the children the:
❱ differences between their estimates and actual measurements;
❱ concept of rounding measurements to the nearest centimetre.

🌑 Children find and make lists of objects that are:
❱ less than a centimetre;
❱ exactly a centimetre;
❱ more than a centimetre but less than a metre;
❱ exactly a metre;
❱ more than a metre.

Millimetres

● Discuss with the class the problems of measuring the length of a very small object in centimetres. Introduce the millimetre (mm) length.

☺ Ask children to measure and draw lengths involving centimetres and millimetres. (For example, the length and width of a book, the length of a pencil/card/their desk and so on.)

Kilometres

● Discuss with the class the best way of measuring the distance between the school and the nearest shops, where certain children live, the local police station, church and so on. Talk about the kilometre (km) length. Show the children a selection of maps which use kilometres.

● Using atlases, road maps, or any maps that show distances in kilometres, ask children to find out the distances between various locations. *How far is it to London in kilometres?*

Knowledge to check and use

● Make sure they know that:
◗ 1 metre = 100 centimetres;
◗ $\frac{1}{2}$ metre = 50 centimetres;
◗ $\frac{1}{4}$ metre = 25 centimetres;
◗ $\frac{1}{10}$ metre = 10 centimetres;
◗ 1 kilometre = 1 000 metres;
◗ $\frac{1}{2}$ kilometre = 500 metres;
◗ $\frac{1}{4}$ kilometre = 250 metres;
◗ $\frac{1}{10}$ kilometre = 100 metres.
You can throw questions (*How many metres in half a kilometre?*) at children at odd moments to test and reinforce their knowledge of these measurement facts and others mentioned in the section on mass. They can also play Snap and Pelmanism with cards showing equivalents.

● Give children opportunities to use the four operations to solve problems involving length using the standard measures, centimetres, metres, kilometres and millimetres.

Miles

Talk to the children about the imperial unit, the mile. You could start by asking them *Do your parents talk about kilometres? What do they use instead? Do the numbers on road signs tell us how many kilometres it is to the next town? What about the numbers on the speedometer in a car?* Tell them about the origin of the word mile. (A Roman measure of 1 000 paces). *Has anyone seen an old milestone?* Look at maps of all kinds which show distances in miles. *Do you think that when you are grown-up people will talk about distances in kilometres? What do they use in other countries?*

Mass (weight)
Grams and kilograms

● Remind the children of the standard measure, gram (g). Discuss with them the difficulty in measuring heavy items in grams. *What do we use instead?* Talk about the standard measure, kilogram (kg).

● Ask children, working in pairs, to weigh various objects in and around the classroom using both grams and kilograms. Encourage them to:
◗ find objects of varying masses: *Find something that weighs about 1 kilogram and 50 grams*;
◗ use a variety of weighing apparatus (balances, scales, dial scales);
◗ estimate the mass before weighing anything;
◗ record both their estimates and actual measurements;
◗ use measuring apparatus with increasing accuracy.
Discuss with the children the differences between their estimates and actual measurements.

● Children find and list objects that are:
◗ exactly or about 10 grams;
◗ exactly or about 50 grams;
◗ exactly or about 100 grams;
◗ exactly or about 500 grams;
◗ exactly or about a kilogram;
◗ more than a kilogram.

Check and use knowledge
● Use the standard weights that come with scales and question the children about equivalence. This is a one kilogram weight. *How many grams is that? Who can show me the weight that is half a kilogram? What about a quarter of a kilogram? This weight is a hundred grams - what part of a kilogram is that?*

● Give the class plenty of opportunities to use the four operations to solve problems involving mass using the standard measures, gram and kilogram.

Capacity
Litres and millilitres
● Show children some litre containers. *How much do you think these hold? Who can write 'litre' on the board? What is the short way of writing it?*

● Show the children a litre jug with millilitre calibrations. *What are these markings on the side of the jug? Who can write 'millilitre' on the board ? What is the short way of writing it? How many millilitres are there in one litre?* Make sure that everyone knows there are 1 000 millilitres in a litre. *Are there 1 000 marks on the side of the jug? Why not?*

✪ Working in pairs, children estimate how many litre measures and millilitres will be needed to fill various containers. They record their estimates and then find and record the actual measurements.

● Ask the children to find and make lists of containers that hold:
❱ exactly a litre;
❱ more than a litre;
❱ less than a litre.

● Ask children questions (see Mass on page 66) to make sure that they know that:
❱ 1 litre = 1 000 millilitres;
❱ $\frac{1}{2}$ litres = 500 millilitres;
❱ $\frac{1}{4}$ litres = 250 millilitres;
❱ $\frac{1}{10}$ litre = 100 millilitres.

● Give children opportunities to solve problems using the four operations involving capacity using the standard measures, litre and millilitre.

Pints
Mineral water and cola come in litre bottles. *What measures does milk come in?* (Pints.)
Talk about the imperial unit, the pint. Use a collection of pint containers including some that show litres as well. *How does the pint compare with the litre?*

Volume
Using boxes and containers of various sizes children estimate and then count how many cubes/beads/counters/marbles/and so on will fit into the boxes/containers. They should record their estimates and actual measurements.

Perimeter
● Introduce the children to the term 'perimeter'. Explain that perimeter means the distance all the way round the edge of something: the boundary. *Run your finger all the way round the perimeter of your desk.*

✪ Ask children to find out which of two or more large objects (table top, blackboard, door ...) has the greatest perimeter by measuring around their edges.

● *Can you estimate which of these large objects has the greatest perimeter?* The children then check their answer by measuring around the edges of the objects.

✪ Ask children to find the perimeter of various shapes marked out on a geoboard.

● Ask children to draw around shape tiles on to centimetre-squared paper and measure the perimeter. Explain to them that:
❱ whole squares count as one;
❱ half or more of a square counts as one;
❱ less than half a square does not count.
Encourage children to estimate, then measure and record their answers in centimetres.

Area
● *Who can remember what 'area' is ?* Establish that area means the amount of surface space an object has. Ask the children to find out which of two or more large, flat surfaces has the greatest area by covering them with various objects (coins, cubes, sheets of A4 paper, sheets of newspaper, post cards, squares, playing cards and so on) and then counting the objects.

● Ask children to estimate which of two or more large objects has the greatest area. They then check their answer by covering the surface with various objects and counting them.

✪ Ask children to find the area of various shapes marked out on a geoboard.

● Introduce the square centimetre and show the children that it can be written as 1 sq. cm or 1cm². Ask them to draw around shape tiles on to squared paper and count the enclosed squares to find the area of each tile. Explain to them that:

▶ whole squares count as one;

▶ half or more of a square counts as one;

▶ less than half a square does not count.

Encourage children to estimate, then measure by counting the squares, recording their answers in cm².

Time

● Use an analogue clock and a digital clock to check how many of the class are confident with telling the time. Start with o'clock. Then go on to half past. *Who can write the times on the board in analogue time? In digital time?* Reintroduce quarter past and quarter to. Then use worksheets to establish that everyone is able to use these times correctly.

● Some children may need further practical work to consolidate time-telling to this point. Others will be ready to revise five-minute intervals before going on to minute intervals.

Minute intervals

● Introduce the children to telling the time to the nearest minute using digital and analogue clocks.

▶ Set an analogue clock to 3 o'clock. Ask *What time does the clock show?*;

▶ Slowly move the big hand through seven minutes counting 1, 2, 3, 4, 5, 6, 7. Say *It now shows seven minutes after three. We say that as 'seven minutes past three'.*

▶ Write the time on the board in both analogue (7 minutes past 3) and digital (3:07) time.

▶ Slowly move the big hand through another nine minutes counting 8, 9, 10, 11, 12, 13, 14, 15, 16.

▶ Say *It now shows sixteen minutes after three. We say that as 'sixteen minutes past three'.*

▶ Write the time on the board in both analogue (sixteen minutes past three) and digital (3:16) time

▶ Continue with other minute intervals up to half past three.

▶ Explain to the children that 'a quarter past' is the same as 'fifteen minutes past', and 'half past' is the same as 'thirty minutes past'.

▶ Explain to the children that the big hand is now moving towards the next hour - four o'clock. - and that there are 30 minutes to go.

▶ Slowly move the big hand four minutes, counting 29, 28, 27, 26. Say *It now shows twenty-four minutes before four. We say that as 'twenty-four minutes to four'.*

▶ Write the time on the board in both analogue (24 minutes to four) and digital (3:36) time. Continue in five-minute intervals up to 4 o'clock. Show the children that 'quarter to' is the same as 'fifteen minutes to'.

✪ Set the time on a clock hidden from the children and give clues. For example, *The large hand is on the five and the small hand is just past the seven.* Children have to guess the time on the clock. They can repeat this activity in pairs.

Measuring time intervals

● Say *It is now twenty past three.* Set an analogue or digital clock at 3:20. Write 3:45 on the board. *How many minutes must pass before the clock shows 3:45?* Say: *We can count in fives, starting at twenty.* Point and say *twenty-five* – hold up one finger; *thirty* – hold up two fingers; *thirty-five* – hold up three fingers; *forty* – hold up four fingers; *forty-five* – hold up five fingers. Pointing to the five fingers count in 5s saying: *5, 10, 15, 20, 25.* Say *It takes twenty five minutes to pass from twenty past three to quarter to four.*

● Repeat using other time intervals and then using a digital clock.

● Children should have experience of working out time intervals using o'clock, half past, quarter to, quarter past and to the nearest minute.

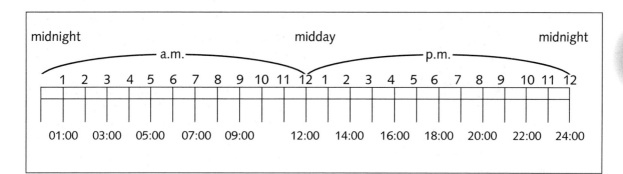

24-hour clock and am and pm

⬤ Introduce the children to the 24-hour clock and am and pm notation.

Show them a clock face displaying both the analogue and 24-hour clock together.

Count with them the hours from 1 to 12, then on to 13, 14… to reach 24 hours or midnight.

⬤ Introduce the children to the relationship between the 12-hour and 24-hour times using the diagram above.

⬤ Show and tell the time to the children using am and pm notation for the 12-hour clock. Read, write and say the time using 24-hour time, *3.00pm is 15:00 hours*.

⬤ Ask individual children to tell the time:
◗ using am and pm notation for the 12-hour clock;
◗ reading, writing and saying the time using 24-hour time.

☺ Provide children with opportunities to:
◗ use am and pm notation for the 12-hour clock;
◗ read, write and say the time in 24-hour time.
For example, they could:
◗ add the time to the date on their written work, in both 12-hour and 24-hour times;
◗ make a timetable (including evenings) for a day or a week showing times of activities in both forms.

☺ Using 12-hour and/or 24-hour and/or digital clocks show the children times (o'clock, half past, quarter to, quarter past and to the nearest minute) and ask them to identify the time using am and pm where appropriate. Ask children to show particular times on the clocks.

☺ Children can make their own 12-hour and/or 24-hour and/or digital clocks and use them to show various times (o'clock, half past, quarter to, quarter past and to the nearest

minute). They can take turns at testing each other's knowledge of times.

☺ Give children opportunities to:
◗ study bus, train, boat and air timetables to extract information;
◗ study this year's calendar to extract information: *What is the date of the second Tuesday in September? On what day does May 5th fall?*;
◗ use the four operations to solve problems involving time using o'clock, half past, quarter past, quarter to and minute intervals.

Time-matching game

☺ Children (in pairs or with up to four) shuffle together two different sets of time cards and play Pelmanism or Snap.
Variation: Children match three different sets of time cards.

Handling data

Collecting, representing and interpreting data

● Be aware while doing science/geography work of opportunities for creating graphs, bar graphs and pictograms.

Bar graphs

● Draw a blank bar graph on a large sheet of paper with, say, twenty-five rows and five columns. Discuss with the class the kind of music they enjoy and establish the five favourite singers/groups. Enter these on the horizontal axis. Ask each child to choose one of the five singers. *Hands up who chose [Singer 1]?* Together, count the number and a child can colour the corresponding number of squares on the graph while the activity is repeated for the other singers. When the graph is completed, ask questions that will enable the children to interpret it: *How many people liked [Singer 3]? Which singer was chosen five times? Who is our least favourite singer? Which singer is Top of Our Pops?*

● Collect larger data to show intervals of 5, 10 or 20 on the vertical axis. (For example, types of vehicles to pass the school in a certain time.) Encourage the children to collect their data using a tally. (See below – Pictograms.)

● Children make their own bar graphs (where the intervals increase by 2, 5, 10 or 20 using different contexts (such as kilometres to different places).

Pictograms

● Draw a pictogram on a large sheet of paper with, say, 15 rows. Title it *Our Favourite Television Characters*. Discuss with the children the concept of a tally as a quick form of record keeping and remind them, on the board, how four strokes are made and then a fifth is crossed through them. Ask them to keep a tally as each child names his/her favourite television character. *Do we all have the same numbers in our tallies?* Now a column can be drawn on the pictogram for each character and the numbers entered as pictures in the pictogram - each picture representing two. *What shall we do about odd numbers?* (Draw half the picture).

When the pictogram is completed ask questions that will enable the children to interpret it. *How many children like [character]? Which character do most children like? Which character do four children like?*

● Repeat the activity above. However this time use larger data and increase the intervals by 5, 10 or 20.

◐ Children make their own pictograms (where the intervals increase by 2, 5, 10 or 20) using other information.

● Ask children to interpret, discuss and make predictions from the data presented in a wide range of graphs, charts, lists and tables, for example in a newspaper, bus timetable or computer data.

IT

Children create block graphs and pictographs using a simple database package.

Mode and median

● Introduce the term 'mode' to the children. Explain that it means the value that occurs *most often* in a set of data. Find the mode using physical characteristics of the children (hair colour, eye colour, and so on).

◐ Find the mode of the data already collected, recorded and discussed in bar charts, pictograms and other graphs.

● Introduce the term 'median' to the children. Explain that it means the value that is *in the middle* of a set of data once the data has been sorted in order to show clearly the full range. Find the median by asking a group of children to stand in height order. Find the child (or two children) who is/are the median average. Repeat for median average age.

● Find the median of data already collected, recorded and discussed in bar charts, pictograms and other graphs.

Assessment

Children demonstrate the outcomes of their learning through speaking, writing, drawing and engaging in other activities.

A variety of assessment strategies is necessary if you are to have an understanding of where your children are in their learning and how best to develop that understanding further. Whatever assessment strategies you use, it is important to ensure that tasks are appropriate to the individual child and that they are directly related to the learning objectives. Remember that those activities marked with an ○ in the Practical ideas section are particularly suitable for assessment.

The levels of expectation suggested at the beginning of this chapter under the What should they be able to do? heading provide a comprehensive checklist for assessing your children's learning.

Science

Although the National Curriculum specifies what science must be taught at Key Stage 2, each school has to decide in which order it should be taught and make some choices.

The Orders for Key Stage 2 are divided up into 12 units of work to be taught over a 12-term period. It is not practical to deal here with every possible combination of units, so the following programme for Key Stage 2 is suggested:

	Autumn term	Spring term	Summer term
YEAR 3	**Unit 6** *Materials and their Properties* 1 Grouping and classifying materials	**Unit 11** *Physical Processes* 3 Light and sound	**Unit 3** *Life Processes and Living Things* 3 Green plants as organisms
YEAR 4	**Unit 7** *Materials and their Properties* 2 Changing materials	**Unit 9** *Physical Processes* 1 Electricity	**Unit 4** *Life Processes and Living Things* 4 Variation and classification
YEAR 5	**Unit 8** *Materials and their Properties* 3 Separating mixtures of materials	**Unit 12** *Physical Processes* 4 The Earth and beyond	**Unit 5** *Life Processes and Living Things* 5 Living things in their environment
YEAR 6	**Unit 10** *Physical Processes* 2 Forces and motion	**Unit 1** *Life Processes and Living Things* 1 Life processes	**Unit 2** *Life Processes and Living Things* 2 Humans as organisms (and health education)

(If your school has allocated the units differently, you may want to draw on the ideas in the other Key Stage 2 Yearbooks.)

This programme ensures that in each year every child will cover work within all three of the knowledge and understanding Attainment Targets.

Some units, such as Units 8, 10 and 12, are arguably more difficult to understand and so are included in Years 5 or 6. Similarly units which are easier for young children to understand, such as Unit 11, Light and Sound, have been placed earlier in Key Stage 2.

Units 3, 4 and 5 also contain a heavy workload. They are about plant growth, variation and classification and living things in their environment, and ideally need to be undertaken in the summer term so that outdoor work can be carried out when appropriate.

What should they be able to do?

The Statutory Orders for science are set down in four sections. When we examine these, it is easy to be lulled into believing that three sections dealing with knowledge and understanding put the emphasis on the content of science rather than the process. This notion is soon dispelled by the realization that *Experimental and Investigative Science* (Sc1) is regarded as having roughly equal importance to the other three science sections combined. Although it offers no facts to be learnt, Sc1 will only be achieved over a period of time – perhaps the whole of the primary school stage, or even longer. The aim is for children to develop an understanding of scientific phenomena through systematic and practical exploration and investigations.

The National Curriculum identifies three components within scientific investigations. They are: Planning experimental work, Obtaining evidence and Considering evidence.

Planning experimental work

Children have enquiring minds and are curious about everything around them. It comes naturally for them to try things out, to see how things work, to manipulate, to feel, to be curious, to ask questions and seek answers – exactly the attributes of a good scientist.

Planning includes asking questions and predicting. In this connection, it is important to provide plenty of opportunities for discussion between the children and between you and the children. Encourage the children to ask questions of the *Who? What? Where? When? Why? How many? How much? How far?* variety. By Year 4, they

should be having opportunities to identify questions that can be investigated and to plan and carry out their own investigations in which they have considered how to make each fair. In Year 4, some of these investigations will relate to contexts beyond the children's immediate experience, such as testing materials to see which would make the best damp-proof course for a house.

In Year 4, the children should also be able to identify the key factors that affect what is being investigated. In the case of an investigation into plant growth, for example, they should be able to suggest that temperature, light, water or fertilizer concentration may affect growth and suggest ways of setting up experiments to evaluate these factors.

Obtaining evidence

In Year 4 the children should be learning to carry out a fair test independently in contexts that include those that are less familiar. Encourage them to use all their senses to measure and record accurately. They should be making observations using equipment that is adequate for the task and suggesting suitable ways of measuring these. They should recognize that some situations require instruments that are more accurate and that it may be necessary to repeat observations. They should be recording their predictions and actual results using tables, charts and data files as well as informal notes.

Considering evidence

This includes interpreting the results of their investigations and evaluating the scientific evidence. Encourage your class to make comparisons, to look for patterns and to communicate their findings in a variety of ways. This gives them a great opportunity to share their thinking and to relate their understanding to scientific knowledge. In Year 4, the children's consideration of evidence will include presenting and interpreting charts, tables, pictograms, bar charts and line graphs. The majority of your class should be able to draw conclusions based on the evidence and, using datalogging, be able to recognize and explain any data that do not fit the trend. They should also be able to use a spreadsheet.

Knowledge and understanding

The three sections of the Programme of Study dealing with knowledge and understanding are *Life Processes and Living Things* (Sc2), *Materials and their Properties* (Sc3), and *Physical Processes* (Sc4). These are instantly recognizable as the biology, chemistry and physics of secondary school days. Remember that the Programmes of Study are not always intended to show progression, and the letters a, b, c, and so on do not always imply increasing complexity. It is also important to realize that the three Programmes of Study cannot be considered independently of the introduction to the National Curriculum or of *Experimental and Investigative Science* (Sc1).

Is there an Sc0?

There is a fifth area of the science curriculum which has no distinct title. Since it comes as an introduction to each Key Stage description, some people call this preliminary area 'Sc0'. It applies across *Experimental and Investigative Science*, *Life Processes and Living Things*, *Materials and their Properties*, and *Physical Processes*. It consists of five parts and, incidentally, highlights many important cross-curricular aspects of science. Year 4 provides opportunities to continue the introduction of the five components of Sc0.

1 **Systematic enquiry** includes giving opportunities for children to ask questions, use first-hand experience and simple secondary sources to obtain information, and also to use information technology.
2 **Science in everyday life** involves children relating their understanding of science to their own health and the environment.
3 **The nature of scientific ideas** is, amongst other things, an opportunity to look at the work of great scientists.
4 **Communication** is concerned with the special ways we record and communicate scientific understanding.
5 **Health and safety** is concerned with children following simple instructions to control the risks to themselves and to recognize hazards and risks when working with living things and materials.

Practical ideas

Making a start

There are many ways of introducing the three units (Units 4, 7 and 9) suggested for Year 4. The following are a few possibilities. Others are suggested in the Ideas bank on page 87.

Changing materials

● Show the children some wheat grains or maize seeds (corn) and some bread or cornflakes. Discuss what has happened to the raw materials in using them to make the end products.

● Ask the children to warm some playdough or Plasticine in their hands. Put some in the fridge. *What differences do you notice? How does the feel of the playdough or Plasticine change with temperature? What happens if the playdough or Plasticine is warmed again? Are the changes permanent?*

● Give the children some bread to examine with a hand lens. Put the bread in a freezer for a few hours or overnight. Carefully look at the bread again. *What has happened to it? Has it changed? Can the bread be turned back to the way it was?* Put the bread in a toaster. *What happens to the bread? Can the toasted bread be turned back to how it was originally?* (Toasting causes an irreversible chemical change in the bread.)

Electricity

Safety: Mains electricity is dangerous! Discuss these dangers with the children and remind them that they must not attempt any experiments or activities that use either mains electricity or devices that are connected to the mains.

Using electricity

Ask the children to bring to school toys or other portable devices that use battery electricity. Let them try out each one. Discuss what effect the electricity has in each of the devices.

Electricity in the home

Ask the children how many things in their home they can think of which use electricity. They should begin to appreciate that we use mains electricity for lighting, heating, cooking, cleaning, washing, keeping food cool, drying our hair, entertaining ourselves and many other things.

Sorting electrical appliances

Collect pictures of electrical appliances from magazines and catalogues. Let the children make sets of them, based perhaps on the different uses of the appliances or whether they are worked by battery or mains electricity.

Variation and classification

The variety of living things

Visit a zoo, wildlife park, botanical garden or the natural history section of a museum to give the children some indication of the living things on the Earth today. *How many ways can you find of grouping the living things you see?* Alternatively, collect, with the children, pictures of different animals cut from magazines. *How many ways can you find of grouping the animals?* If needs be, prompt them into classifying the animals by colour, size, what they have covering their bodies (feathers, hair, scales), how they move, what they eat, where they live, which make good pets. *Which methods of grouping animals work well? Which methods do not work well? Why?*

Developing key areas
Changing materials

The word 'material' is often used to mean 'fabric'. However, the *Concise Oxford Dictionary* defines material as 'matter from which a thing is made'. By this broad definition, which is that implied in Materials and their Properties, everything in the universe, including all living organisms, is made up of materials.

Most substances can exist in three different forms: as solids, liquids or gases. The change from one state to another is caused by heating or cooling, or by a change in pressure. For example, when water – a liquid, is heated, it forms a gas – water vapour (steam), and when it is cooled it becomes a solid – ice.

Ice-cubes

Put an ice-cube on a saucer and ask the children to watch it closely. *What is happening to the ice-cube? Why is it happening? What will happen next?* Can the children predict what will happen if ice-cubes are placed in different parts of the classroom? Can they suggest ways of slowing down the rate at which ice-cubes melt (apart from putting them in a refrigerator or freezer)? Wrap ice-cubes individually in similar thicknesses of different materials and compare the rates at which they melt. *What must we do to make sure this is a fair test? Which material is the best insulator of heat?*

Candle wax

Place a household candle in the centre of a large aluminium baking case filled with sand. Light the candle and ask the children to observe what happens as the flame heats the candle wax. Explain that the solid wax melts to become a liquid which, when hot, becomes gaseous and burns, giving off light, heat and smoke. You can let drops of the liquid wax fall on to a sheet of paper. The children will be able to see that, as the hot wax cools, it turns back into a solid again. *Is this a chemical or a physical change?* (The melting and solidifying of the wax is a physical change. The burning of some of the wax is a chemical change.)

Investigate other substances which melt when warmed and solidify when cooled, such as butter, lard and wax crayons.

More about burning a candle

Carefully stand a candle in a transparent dish of water. It can then be lit and a glass jar placed over it. Eventually the candle will go out. *What happens to the level of water in the jar?* (It rises.) *Why is this?* (While the candle was burning it used up some of the oxygen (or air) in the jar and the water rises to replace it.) *What will happen if we have two identical pieces of burning candle, one covered by a large jar and the other by a smaller jar?* (The candle in the smaller goes out first. Candles, in fact, go out before they have used up all the oxygen.)

Heating chocolate

Though the children will already be familiar with this activity, it is fun to do and will help to reinforce the solid–liquid–solid concept. Break a slab of chocolate into a clean bowl and stand the bowl in a pan of hot water. Heat the pan if necessary to melt the chocolate. So that everyone can have a taste, dip one end of some plain biscuits into the chocolate and lay them on foil or baking parchment to cool. Alternatively, stir some cornflakes or rice crispies into the chocolate, and then spoon them out into little mounds on the baking parchment and leave them to set. Before they eat the evidence, make sure the children have noted that solid chocolate melts to a liquid and returns to a solid when cooled again (a physical change).

Making jellies

With the help of an adult, the children could examine jelly cubes and then warm some of these up. Pour the liquid jelly into an ice-cube tray and put it in the freezer. After an hour or two, remove the jelly from the freezer and note what has happened. *Can the process be reversed?* (Yes.) The children might then investigate further by using different quantities and temperatures of water (no hotter than 65˚C) to make jellies. Ask them to make up jellies using different amounts of water. *What do you think will happen? Do you need hot water to make the jelly? Do the jelly cubes melt or dissolve? What is the difference between melting and dissolving?*

Dissolving

Let the children attempt to dissolve a teaspoon of salt, sugar, instant coffee, washing powder, sand, sawdust or wood shavings and crumbled cork in different beakers of cold water. If they work in pairs with a timer with a second hand, they can not only determine which of these materials dissolve (the salt, sugar, washing powder and instant coffee), but also how long each takes to do so. Introduce these terms: 'dissolve', 'solute' (the substance which dissolves), 'solvent' (the liquid a substance dissolves in), 'soluble', 'solution', 'insoluble'.

Solubility at different temperatures

Ask the children to predict what will happen to the solubility of soluble substances as the temperature of the water increases. They can repeat the previous

activity using the soluble substances, but this time they need to record the temperature of the water. Then supply them with some warmer water and ask them to repeat the experiment. Finally give them hot water (at 60–65°C) and get them to repeat the experiment. Can the class obtain enough results for each of the substances at different temperatures to be able to plot graphs for them? (The results should show increased solubility at the higher temperatures, although there will be differences from substance to substance.)

White substances

Put a teaspoon of bicarbonate of soda into a glass beaker, and in another a teaspoon of salt. Add a few drops of vinegar to each. *Are the two white substances the same?* (No, the salt simply dissolves in vinegar, while the bicarbonate of soda fizzes in a chemical reaction that produces the gas, carbon dioxide.)

Evaporation

Leave a saucer of water by an open window or on a radiator. Eventually the water will evaporate away (it turns into a gas – water vapour). Then challenge the children to devise experiments to test the conditions that affect evaporation. Ask questions such as *Does evaporation occur more quickly in a draught/in the open air/in a warm room/in a cold room?* Let them predict the answers and then test these conditions by measuring the amount of water each time and checking their experiment every hour or so to see any change in water level. *What happens when salt or sugar solution is left to evaporate? Does it all evaporate away?* (The water evaporates away but the salt or sugar is left behind.)

The water cycle

The water cycle is the process whereby the finite amount of water on Earth is recirculated, allowing us to use the same water over and over again.

During the water cycle, water evaporates from oceans, seas, lakes and other wet surfaces. High in the sky the water vapour cools and condenses to form clouds from which rain falls. The rain water collects in rivers which eventually flow into the oceans, seas and lakes.

● Demonstrate the stages in the water cycle by holding a long metal ladle, or a tablespoon tied to the end of a stick, in the steam coming from a kettle. The water vapour will condense on the cold ladle or spoon and water droplets will fall like rain so that they can be collected in a saucer or plate.

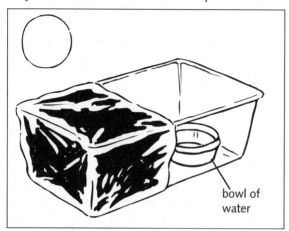

bowl of water

● Alternatively, make a simple model of the water cycle in a plastic aquarium. Place a dish of water at one end of the aquarium and cover that half of the aquarium with transparent plastic. Cover the other half with black plastic. Stand the aquarium on a sunny windowsill and examine the inside of the dark part from time to time. Some of the water in the dish will evaporate and the water vapour will condense on the cool surfaces of the black and transparent plastic. Discuss what is happening with the children. Because condensation forms in both parts of the aquarium it shows that it is the sun's heat, not the light, that causes evaporation.

Water vapour in the air

You can demonstrate that there is always water vapour in the air by cleaning the label off a metal can and filling the can with ice-cubes. Put a lid on the can and leave it to stand. Examine the outside of the can at intervals. *What do you see? Have the water droplets come from the ice-cubes in the can? How do you know? Where have the water droplets come from then?*

A model thermometer

A thermometer works because a liquid, like all materials, expands when it is heated and contracts when it is cooled. The higher the temperature, the more the liquid expands. Make a model thermometer from a clear glass or plastic bottle about 18cm high. Put water, coloured with red ink or food colouring, to a depth of about 3cm in the bottle. Soften a lump of clay or Plasticine by warming it in the hands or near a radiator, and then use it to seal a drinking straw in the neck of the bottle. The seal should be completely airtight and the drinking straw should reach down just below the surface of the water. Warm the model thermometer by wrapping your hands around it. Look carefully at the water in the drinking straw. *What do you notice?* Stand the bottle near a radiator. *What do you notice?* Stand the bottle in a bowl and pack ice-cubes around it. *What do you see? Can you explain how this model thermometer works?* Can the children suggest a way of calibrating the model thermometer?

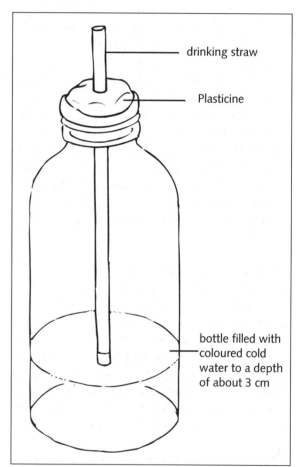

drinking straw

Plasticine

bottle filled with coloured cold water to a depth of about 3 cm

Changes caused by heat

Observe the changes that occur when a range of familiar food substances are heated. Make spoons out of aluminium foil and hold them in clothes pegs attached to 15cm lengths of dowel rod. As a source of heat, stand a short length of candle in the centre of an aluminium foil dish or metal baking tray containing sand, or use Plasticine to stand the candle upright.

Supervising strictly, let the children take it in turns to heat small amounts of sugar, salt, bread, flour, custard powder, baking powder, rice and raisins. Heat each substance until nothing else happens. Put the spoon on another metal dish of sand until it cools. Use a new aluminium foil spoon each time. Encourage the children to observe carefully and note what they see, hear or smell. Ask them to construct a table on which to record their results. *Which of the foods are changed by heating? Can we turn the heated food back to how it was originally?* (All of the substances listed, with the possible exception of the salt, will be changed by heating. Whether or not the salt changes depends upon the temperature of the flame. All the changes produced are permanent and are, therefore, examples of chemical changes.)

Why do iron and steel rust?

Iron, and most kinds of steel, quickly rust when they are exposed to moist air. This is a chemical change. Investigate why rusting occurs.

● Take two clean, shiny steel nails or screws. Suspend one nail or screw on a thread hanging from a pencil laid over a jar of cold water. Stand the other nail or screw by the side of the jar. Leave the nails or screws where they are for a few days. *What happens? Why do you think this is?*

● Now repeat the experiment, this time using two steel nails, one of which has been painted with gloss paint and allowed to dry. Hang both nails in a jar of cold water for a few days. *Can you see why iron often has to be painted? What does the paint do?* (Keeps air and water away from the iron or steel.)

● Now leave two more clean steel nails on a windowsill outside. Give one of the nails a thin coating of oil or Vaseline. Look at the nails after a week or so. *What difference do you see?*

● Bury a clean shiny steel nail in the garden. Mark the spot. Dig the nail up again after a few days. *What has happened to it?*

Chemical changes by living things

Yeast is a simple, plant-like organism, called a fungus. Yeast breaks down sugar for its energy, producing carbon dioxide and alcohol.

● Put the same amount of water (about four or five centimetres) in each of two deep, identical narrow-necked transparent plastic bottles. Add a teaspoon of sugar to the water in both bottles and shake them to dissolve the sugar. Then add a level teaspoon of yeast to one of the bottles. Stretch the necks of two identical balloons and fix them over the tops of the two bottles. Leave the bottles in a warm place for several hours. *What happens?* (The yeast breaks down the sugar and forms the gas, carbon dioxide, which inflates the balloon on that bottle slightly.) *Why did we need to have a bottle with just sugar in it?*

● The children can repeat the investigation using different amounts of sugar to see how this affects the amount of carbon dioxide produced. They can also carry out the experiment at different temperatures to see what effect this has. (The yeast cannot grow and multiply, and produce carbon dioxide, at high or very low temperatures.)

Electricity

Background information

An electrical generator or battery is like a pump, forcing an electric current along wires and cables. The harder the pump works, the greater the pressure and the more electricity will flow. Electrical pressure is termed 'voltage', and measured in 'volts'. Electricity from the power station usually travels at 400 000 volts. The voltage is then reduced by 'transformers' before use. Most domestic electricity supplies in the UK are 240 volts, while a torch battery gives only 1.5 volts. 'Watts' is a measure of the power or energy supplied or used in a second. Finally, 'amps' measure the quantity of electricity flowing in a second.

Batteries produce an electric current by means of a chemical reaction. However, there is no difference between the electricity that comes from a power station generator and that which comes from a cell or battery. Electricity is not stored in the battery; the chemicals within the battery react and cause a flow of electricity when wires are connected to it. Car batteries and other rechargeable batteries produce electricity in the same way as an ordinary battery.

Simple circuits

Revise the work done on circuits in Key Stage 1 by letting the children create simple circuits using a single bulb in a holder, a battery and wires, without and with a simple switch. Show them what happens when extra bulbs are added to the circuit. With the simplest arrangement of wires, the more bulbs that share a battery, the dimmer the light from each bulb will be. Then try adding additional batteries to the original circuit. In this case, the light from a single bulb will be much brighter and the bulb will burn out unless the circuit is quickly disconnected.

Circuits without wires

Ask the children to find as many ways as they can of lighting a 1.5 or 1.25 volt torch bulb with a 1.5 volt cell ('battery') without using wires. Let them invent circuits that use any materials or objects they wish from the collection you provide. You could include scissors, a coat hanger, wire paperclips, keys, coins, knives, forks and spoons, and a metal can. Also include non-metal objects so that the children can find out that some materials conduct electricity and some do not. They can make a table of *Conductors* and *Non-conductors* and draw the electrical circuits which work.

Electrical messages

The children can use simple circuits containing a switch and a torch bulb or buzzer to pass messages to each other using the Morse code.

Torch bulbs

Ask the children to examine carefully torch bulbs held against a white background, using a magnifying glass. Discuss the meanings of any numbers or letters stamped on the bulbs. *Which part of the bulb lights up? Do you know why this happens?* (See below.)

A model light bulb

Make a model light bulb to illustrate how the filament in a bulb becomes hot and therefore gives off light. Set up the circuit shown in the illustration below using a battery, two wires and a thin piece of fuse wire or a thin strand of wire wool. (If you are using wire wool, you must supervise this experiment carefully as the wire wool may catch fire briefly. If not, it will certainly get hot.) Wrap the fuse wire or wire wool around a pencil to create a coil. Pass the ends of the coil through, or down the sides of a cork, or grip the piece of fuse wire or wire wool between two crocodile clips.

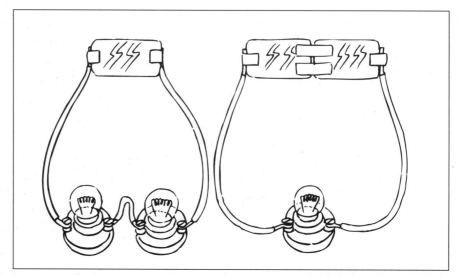

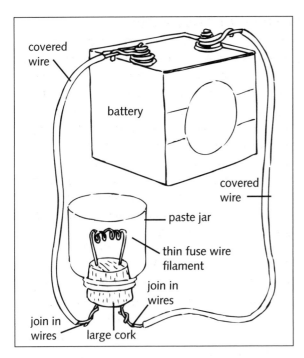

The reason for the filament getting hot is that the thin piece of wire creates a higher resistance for the electricity which then has to push harder. This causes the wire to heat up and, in a real light bulb, to produce light. The inert gas in a real light bulb prevents the wire from burning away too quickly. An electric fire or electric cooker uses the same principle.

Switches

The children can design and make their own simple switches. *Can you design a switch which will show when it is raining outside or when someone has stepped on a doormat, or a greetings card which lights up when it is opened? Can you make switches that do other things?*

Dimmer switches

● Talk to the children about the use of dimmer switches. Explain that they are used to vary the brightness of lights. Tell them they can make a dimmer switch of their own, using the 'lead' (really graphite) from a pencil. Provide the children with lead pencils that have been cut in half lengthways. Ask them to connect the pencil point to a battery, using a wire and a crocodile clip. A second crocodile clip should be connected to the end of a wire from a bulb in a holder. Now ask the children to touch the mid-point of the pencil 'lead' with the second crocodile clip, then to bring the clip closer to the pencil point. *What is happening to the light bulb? What do you think would happen if the clip was moved further away from the pencil point? Can you explain what is happening?* (The resistance of the 'lead' increases as its length increases, and the bulb is less bright.)

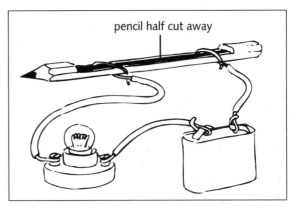

pencil half cut away

● If you don't want to split pencils lengthways, you could build up a collection of lead pencils, all the same kind, but of different lengths and sharpened at both ends. Touch (do not clip) the crocodile clips on both ends of the pencil and see how the brightness of the torch bulb varies. If a rheostat is available, use this for another demonstration of how a dimmer switch works. Attach the rheostat to a circuit containing a torch bulb and battery and move the sliding contact to make the bulb brighter and

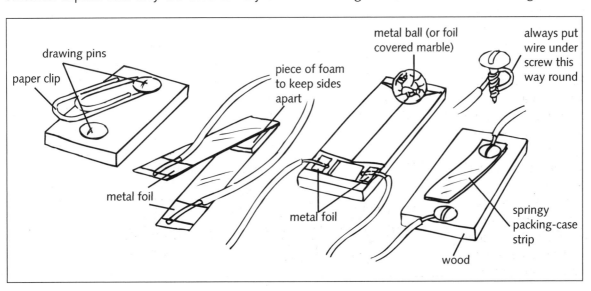

dimmer. *Do you know why this happens?* (The rheostat consists of a coil of wire, and the slider varies the length of the coil the electricity has to flow through. The greater the length of the coil in the circuit, the greater the resistance and the dimmer the bulb.)

Torches

● Make a collection of electric torches. Ask the children to examine them and try them out without taking them apart. *Make a drawing to show what you think is inside the torch*. This will provide an opportunity for you to assess whether or not they have understood how the wires, batteries, bulb and switch in a simple circuit are connected. Then let the children carefully dismantle a torch to see whether their ideas were correct.

● Use an enlarged photocopy of the illustration below for the children to examine and see how one type of torch works. Can they make their own working model torch using torch batteries and a suitable bulb, wire or paperclips, cardboard tubes and card backed with metal foil for a reflector?

Electromagnets

Passing an electric current through a coil of wire surrounding a soft iron bar produces a very useful

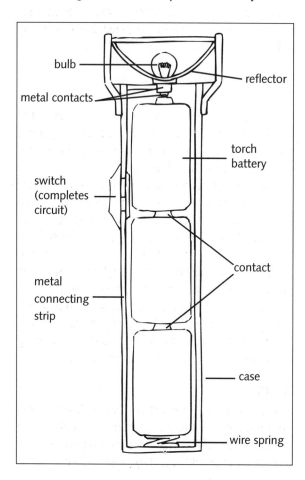

kind of magnet called an 'electromagnet'. When an electric current passes through the wire, the iron bar acts as a magnet. When the current is switched off, the iron is no longer a magnet. Electromagnets are used for sorting iron, steel, cobalt and nickel from other metals. They are also used in electric bells, telephones, electric clocks, loudspeakers, television sets, radios and electric motors.

● Make an electromagnet from a large iron nail or iron coach bolt. Wind a thin piece of insulated wire neatly and evenly around the nail or bolt. Strip the insulation from the two ends of the wire and connect it up to a battery and switch. When the switch is in the 'on' position, the nail or bolt will be a magnet. Find out which objects and materials are attracted to the electromagnet when it is switched on.

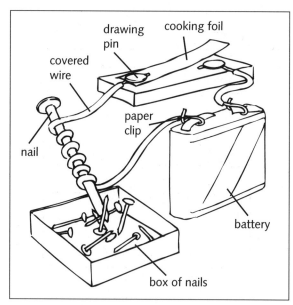

● Let the children make electromagnets, using the same kinds of nails or bolts, but with an increasing number of turns of wire (say 10, 20, 30, 40 and 50) around the iron core. *Does this have an effect on the strength of the magnet? How can we tell?* (They could count how many paperclips or small steel tacks the magnet will pick up each time.) Plot the results on a graph. (Do not use an electromagnet for prolonged periods of time, otherwise the battery will quickly become flat).

Drawing circuits

Electrical circuits can be represented by drawings, but it is often quicker and easier to use symbols to represent the various components of a circuit and then to use straight lines to represent the wires. Some commonly used symbols are shown in the illustration below:

● Set up a simple circuit with a bulb, battery and switch, joined by three pieces of wire. (Ensure that the electrical components are working before the

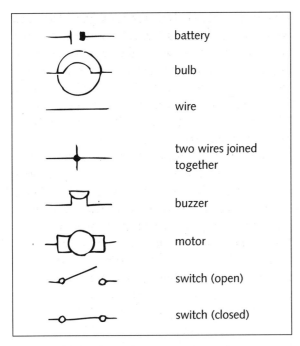

	battery
	bulb
	wire
	two wires joined together
	buzzer
	motor
	switch (open)
	switch (closed)

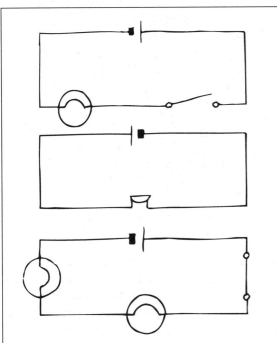

start of the activity.) When the circuit has been set up, draw the circuit diagram with the switch shown in the open or 'off' position. Turn the switch in the real circuit to the closed or 'on' position and ask the children to draw the circuit.

● Now replace the real torch bulb with, first of all, a buzzer and then a small electric motor. Ask the children to draw the appropriate circuit diagram in each case. Then go on to construct circuits containing more than one bulb and more than one battery and ask the children to draw the circuit diagrams for these. Instead of drawing the circuits by hand, the children could use a simple computer drawing package to make their circuit diagrams.

Technical terms

Ask the children to find out what the word 'voltage' means. Let them examine various electrical appliances (NOT while they are connected to the mains) or advertisements for electrical appliances, as well as torch bulbs and batteries to see what voltages these objects require or provide. The children will probably also come across the term 'watts' or 'wattage' on, for example light bulbs and electric motors.

Variation and classification

There are about a million kinds of animals and more than 343,000 different kinds of plants living on the Earth today. To make it easier to study such a vast collection of living things, scientists arrange them in order, grouping together those resembling each other in important details. This is called 'classification'.

Animals

The animal kingdom is split into two big groups.

The animals with a backbone inside their bodies are known as 'vertebrates' and include mammals, birds, reptiles, amphibians and fishes.

Then there is the great array of animals without such a backbone, the 'invertebrates'. These include octopuses, slugs, snails, lobsters, crabs, butterflies, moths, spiders and many minute creatures visible only with the microscope.

Plants

The other large main group of living things is the plant kingdom. Plants fall into two broad groups: those that reproduce with seeds and those that reproduce by means of spores.

The seed plants are again in two broad groups. There are plants which reproduce their seeds inside cones; these are the 'conifers'. The other group of seed plants are the 'flowering plants'. These bear flowers which contain reproductive organs that produce seeds inside fruits. The flowering plants include herbaceous plants, grasses, sedges and rushes, and all shrubs and trees apart from conifers. The spore-bearing plants include ferns, mosses, liverworts, fungi, lichens, and algae (including seaweeds and many simple pondweeds).

Keys

A key is a series of questions which leads to the identification of individual plants or animals or related groups of plants and animals. Before children can use even simple keys they need to have studied

a number of plants and animals separately and to have some idea of the various ways in which these organisms can be arranged in groups or sets. It is best to begin work on keys with a very restricted group of organisms which have either been collected by you or which the children have collected in a very restricted part of a habitat (such as in leaf litter or under logs or stones).

Vertebrates and invertebrates

Provide the children with a large collection of pictures of animals, including both vertebrates and invertebrates. Include pictures of some of the animals which often cause confusion, such as a crab or lobster (invertebrates), a snail (invertebrate), a tortoise (vertebrate) and a snake (vertebrate). Explain to the children the difference between vertebrates and invertebrates. *Can you sort the pictures into these two kinds of animal?* Discuss which pictures caused them problems, and why.

An invertebrate hunt

Search the school grounds and the outsides of buildings, looking in crevices, under wood and stones, in tussocks of grass and other places for invertebrate animals. Carefully collect one animal

of each kind. Do not handle the animals but use a small brush and a plastic spoon to transfer them to transparent collecting pots. Encourage the children to examine their 'finds' carefully, using a hand lens if needs be. They should note how many parts the animals have to their bodies, how many legs, wings, their colour and so on. Identify the animals as far as possible, and then make a key to enable a friend to separate five of them. When the children have finished examining them, return the animals, unharmed, to where they were found. Later give the children the key below to help them identify some of the main invertebrate groups.

Classification key

Using this key takes a little practice. Tell the children to start with the first point and read parts a) and b) carefully. If part a) fits, it will tell them where to go next (for example, 'see 2'). If part b) fits it will tell them to go some other place (for example, 'see 4').

Guess the animal

Write the names of well-known vertebrate and invertebrate animals on sticky-back labels. Stick a label on each child's back without letting him or her read it. The group mingles. The children must guess

Classification Key

1	a) Soft bodies and no legs	*see 2*	**5**	a) Body flattened, two legs per segment	*Centipedes*
	b) Hard bodies and legs	*see 4*		b) Body cylindrical, four legs per segment	*Millipedes*
2	a) Long bodies divided into rings or segments	*Earthworms*	**6**	a) Seven pairs of legs, body grey or steely blue	*Woodlice*
	b) Body not divided into rings or segments	*see 3*		b) Fewer than seven pairs of legs	*see 7*
3	a) Four tentacles with a shell outside the body	*Snails*	**7**	a) Four pairs of legs	*see 8*
	b) Four tentacles with no outside shell	*Slugs*		b) Three pairs of legs and a body in three parts	*Insects*
4	a) Body with more than fourteen legs	*see 5*	**8**	a) Body divided into two parts	*Spiders*
	b) Body with fourteen legs or less	*see 6*		b) Body not divided, legs extremely long and hair-like	*Harvestmen*

which animals they are by asking each person one question about the animal. The questions must be answerable by 'Yes' or 'No'. *How long does it take before everyone in the group has guessed their animal? Which questions were most helpful?*

A mammal database

The children work in groups of two or three. Provide them with reference books and ask them to choose five mammals to study. Encourage them to write down the features they are going to investigate for their chosen mammals: body covering, size, whether it produces live babies or lays eggs, how many young it has at a time, where it is mainly found (land, water or in the air), whether it is warm-blooded or cold-blooded and so on. When their data is complete they can enter it on a computer database and produce a printout. The other groups of children can do the same thing. When several groups of children have compiled their data, compare all the printouts and discuss ways in which the databases can be amalgamated. When this has been done, the children can access the data and produce sub-groups of mammals, for example those that live in water or which feed mainly on plant materials. They can also produce block graphs and pie charts of their data.

Plant-spotting and sorting

Safety: Be careful to ask the children about any allergies they know they have before handling plants. Wash the hands thoroughly afterwards even if gloves have been worn.

Take the children on a plant-spotting tour of the school grounds or a local park or piece of waste ground. Look for cultivated and wild plants. Look for any unusual places where plants are growing, such as on walls and the trunks of trees. Try to find some of the smaller plants such as mosses, fungi, lichens and algae, as well as observing the larger ones such as trees. Make copies of the chart below so that the children can use the key to try to identify the group to which each of their finds belongs.

This key, together with some careful observation, will help you to classify plants. Remember that some plants may not have flowers or fruits at the time you examine them.

Variable plants

Take the children to see plants in a range of natural habitats. Ask them to make lists of the plants which grow in dry places, wet places, in the sun and in the shade. Encourage the children to compare these different plants. *What do the plants growing in the*

1	a) Simple, without obvious roots, stems or leaves	see 2	5	a) Tiny, upright, with 'leaves' growing right round the stem	Moss
	b) With roots, stems and leaves	see 4		b) Small, flat, ribbon-shaped, found in very damp, shady places	Liverwort
2	a) Simple, red, green or brown, growing in water or very damp places	Alga	6	a) Green, on land, with 'fronds' (tightly-coiled, feathery leaves when young, unfold in spring), grows up to 2m tall, has spores under the fronds	Fern
	b) If (a) does not fit	see 3		b) Leafy, stems bearing buds, flowers, fruits or cones in season	see 7
3	a) Brown, yellow, red or white, on land	Fungus	7	a) Seeds are in cones, not fruits	Conifer (Gymnosperm)
	b) Simple, dry, crusty, found on rocks, trees and buildings	Lichen		b) Flowers and seeds in a fruit	Flowering plant (Angiosperm)
4	a) Small, on land, up to 8cm tall, may have tiny capsules on stalks	see 5			
	b) If (a) does not fit	see 6			

shade all have in common? Do the plants growing in wet places differ from those growing in dry areas? If the same species of plant can be found growing in two contrasting habitats, such as sun and shade or wet and dry, let the children take measurements to see if there are important differences in, for example, the size of the leaves, number of flowers, or lengths of stems of the plants in the two areas.

Plant roots

In order to help the children recognize similarities and differences among plants, let them make a collection of different roots. They should wash the roots carefully and then examine them, with a hand lens if necessary, sorting the roots into two groups: fibrous roots, which look like lengths of thread; and taproots, which have a large main root with smaller side branches. *Are any of the roots swollen because they are storing food? Can we eat any kind of roots?* Ask the children to compare the lengths of the roots they have collected. *How long is the longest root? Are fibrous roots generally shorter than taproots, or is there no obvious difference?* They can record their results in tables, block graphs or pie charts.

Sorting plants

Make a collection of plants, or pictures of plants. Let the children work in groups. Ask one child in the group to divide the plants into two sets based on an observable feature but without telling the others which feature has been chosen. The remaining children have to see if they can work out the feature that divides the two groups. Then let the other members of the group take their turn to use different criteria to divide the plants into two or more sets for the others to determine. (Link this with work on sets in maths.)

Sorting fruits and seeds

Make a collection of fruits and seeds, including fruit stones, pips, bird or hamster seed and a variety of nuts. Let the children sort the seeds by size, shape, colour, texture and any other criteria they can come up with.

Grouping tree leaves

Make a collection of tree leaves and let the children examine the leaves for differences. They can look for differences in size, shape, colour and vein pattern. Look for leaves with different kinds of edge and also for rough leaves, smooth leaves, hairy leaves

and prickly leaves. Be careful with leaves that sting. Ask the children to prepare a key to identify, say, five leaves of their choice.

 Ideas bank

Make your own candles

It is instructive for children to make their own candles. The materials can be bought from craft shops and some hardware stores. However, be sure they melt the wax in a can or basin contained in a bowl of hot water, and not over a flame or hot-plate. Warn them that spilled wax can cause painful burns and that melted wax poured into the sink can block it. If, under continued supervision, the children light their candles, they can see further examples of both physical and chemical changes.

Tea bag tests

Investigate the effect of samples of water at different temperatures on tea bags. Provide three transparent containers, adding 200ml of cold water to one, 200ml of warm water to the second and 200ml of hand-hot water to the third. Add a tea bag to each. Leave for three minutes and stir each one once. Let the children write a description of the changes that occur in each container. *Why is there a difference?* (The higher the temperature the more the water particles are moving and the more tea dissolves.) Can the children devise a *Which*-style test to compare the solubility of different brands of tea bag? *What else is important besides the solubility of the tea?* (Taste, but this is not something children can test easily because of the need for boiling water.)

Sugar samples

Can the children devise a fair experiment to compare the solubility of granulated sugar, caster sugar, coffee or preserving sugar and sugar cubes at different temperatures?

Bobbing raisins

Pour a glass of fresh, carbonated drink, such as lemonade, or sparkling mineral water. These drinks all contain carbon dioxide gas dissolved under pressure and this gas starts to rise as bubbles as soon as the drink is poured. *What do you see? What are the bubbles made of? Why do they rise up?* Now drop two or three raisins into the drink. *What is happening? Why is this?* (The raisins sink, but gas bubbles soon stick to their rough surfaces. The bubbles buoy the raisins to the surface. At the surface, some of the bubbles burst and the raisins sink again. The raisins may then pick up more bubbles and rise to the surface again.)

A collection of batteries

Make a collection of batteries and display these in the classroom. Discuss what each kind of battery is commonly used for.

Safety: Some 'dead' batteries tend to leak chemicals which are poisonous. Beware also of the tiny 'button' batteries used in watches and some calculators and cameras as these can easily be swallowed. In both cases, it is advisable to display these batteries in sealed, transparent plastic containers or behind transparent sticky-backed plastic.

Michael Faraday

Ask the children to find out more about the life and work of Michael Faraday, whose discoveries paved the way for the production of electricity on a large scale. Make sure that you have appropriate books or software available. You could give each group of children a different list of questions to research and pitch the questions at appropriate levels for the group.

Electrical models

Ask the children to design and make working models that incorporate a battery-powered light such as a cardboard-box house, a model lighthouse, a model theatre, or a face with an illuminated nose. *What model can you design and make which incorporates a battery-powered buzzer?*

Saving electricity

Electricity is expensive to produce and most present-day forms of electricity production pollute the atmosphere. Discuss with the children how we could use less electricity and so save money and reduce pollution.

A tree database

Construct a database of the trees in the local area. While doing this you can teach the children the name of each tree species. They could also record the measurements and features of each individual tree.

Recording birds

Set up a bird table in the school grounds, together with a shallow dish of water. Keep the bird table well stocked with food (table scraps, nuts, seeds, but *not* salted peanuts or desiccated coconut).

Keep daily records of the number of birds of each species visiting the table. Ask the children to take careful note of the features of five common birds that visit the school grounds to feed or bathe. Let them work in pairs to make a key to separate five of the common bird visitors. They should then exchange their key with another pair of children and test the keys out on the birds they see in the school grounds.

Assessment

When you have finished the work with your Year 4 class, you will have a good idea as to whether the children enjoyed the topics and which style of teaching was most effective. You should also be able to judge how much the children have learned. Now is the time to evaluate each topic against the criteria with which you started.

What do they know?

There is no set list of facts they should know, but all the children should have gained something, even if that something varies from child to child. In Year 4 you might expect eight- to nine-year-olds to know:

- that there is a wide variety of living things (Sc2);
- that there are various ways of grouping or classifying living things (Sc2);
- that keys can help us to identify living things in the local environment (Sc2);
- that heating some materials causes changes which can be reversed by cooling (Sc3);
- that heating some materials causes changes which cannot be reversed by cooling (Sc3);
- that changes which occur as a result of burning cannot be reversed (Sc3);
- that when materials are mixed, changes may occur (Sc3);
- that temperature is a measure of how hot or cold things are (Sc3);
- that a thermometer is used to measure temperature (Sc3);
- that evaporation and condensation are natural processes in the water cycle (Sc3);
- that a complete circuit is needed to make electrical devices work (Sc4);
- that switches can be used to control electrical devices (Sc4);
- that some materials conduct electricity, while others, known as insulators, do not (Sc4);
- that the current in an electrical circuit can be varied (Sc4);
- that electrical circuits can be represented by drawings and diagrams (Sc4).

What can they do?

They should be able to:
- describe objects and materials (Sc1);
- describe things that happen (Sc1);
- identify a number of questions which can be investigated, in familiar and less familiar situations (Sc1);
- identify the key factors that affect what is being investigated (Sc1);
- recognize the need for a fair test (Sc1);
- change one factor and observe or measure the effect whilst keeping other factors the same, and know that this allows a fair test or comparison to be made (Sc1);
- explain what a prediction is and how it differs from a guess (Sc1);
- make predictions based upon relevant prior knowledge (Sc1);
- suggest what observations should be made and suitable ways of measuring these (Sc1);
- record their predictions and results (Sc1);
- present their findings using charts, pictograms, bar charts, line graphs and data files (Sc1);
- provide explanations for observations and simple patterns in recorded measurements, and relate these to scientific knowledge (Sc1);
- recognize and explain any data that does not fit the trend (Sc1);
- suggest improvements to investigations (Sc1).

What have they experienced?

They should have:
- examined a variety of plants and animals;
- used simple keys to identify plants and animals;
- handled a variety of materials;
- investigated a variety of methods of changing materials;
- investigated ways of varying the current in an electrical circuit;
- drawn electrical circuit diagrams;
- carried out simple experiments under guidance;
- devised their own simple fair experiments under guidance.

How have they made their knowledge public?

They should have discussed their work with others and displayed their work through drawings, models, charts, graphs and tables. They should also have produced clear written accounts of their various observations, activities, discoveries and conclusions.

History

It is not very difficult to interest a nine-year-old in history because, properly taught, it is not a dull subject. There is nothing that is more interesting than people and Year 4 children soon become fascinated when learning about the lives of human beings living in a different time and culture. Drawing on the history suggested in the National Curriculum for Key Stage 2 children, you will find stories that are full of fascinating people, romance, adventure and derring-do. And what nine-year-old does not love a good story?

Currently, primary teachers are expected to study history chosen from the National Curriculum 'study units' – although the compulsion to do so has been relaxed. For Key Stage 2 these are:

- Romans, Anglo-Saxons and Vikings in Britain
- Life in Tudor Times
- Victorian Britain *or* Britain since 1930
- Ancient Greece
- Local history
- A past non-European society

Schools can decide for themselves in which order to teach these units but, in practice, many opt for teaching history chronologically. This is a simple strategy and has a logic that is easy to follow. Few schools choose to do more than one unit in Year 3, so the most likely topic that you will be assigned in Year 4 is Life in Tudor Times.

History skills and concepts cannot be separated from content, therefore many of the practical activities given in this chapter have been linked to the teaching of the Tudors. If you have been assigned a different unit by your school, do not worry: general principles still apply; expectations and assessment will be exactly the same; and even the activities will usually adapt to fit a different topic. (Check whether or not your particular history unit has been dealt with in one of the other Yearbooks.)

The Programme of Study for *Life in Tudor Times* suggests that children should be taught: about some of the major events and personalities, including monarchs, and the way of life of people at different levels of society in Tudor times.

a   Henry VIII and the break with Rome
b   exploration overseas
c   Elizabeth I and the Armada (1588)
d   Court life
e   ways of life in town and country
f   arts and architecture including Shakespeare. (The National Curriculum, DFE, 1995)

Key areas

When studying any historical topic, children will have to tackle the essential elements of history itself which are usefully defined in the National Curriculum as:

- Chronology
- Range and depth of historical understanding
- Interpretations of history
- Historical enquiry
- Organization and communication

Some of these elements should be taught during every topic and all of them over the key stage.

What should they be able to do?

Year 4s are truly juniors. Gone are the insecurities associated with children in transit from Key Stage 1 to Key Stage 2 and, although they may not yet be top dogs, they confidently know who they are. History now not only has meaning, it has context as well, because children have acquired a body of knowledge, albeit small, into which new historical learning can be fitted.

Developmental changes from one year to another have slowed down and year-by-year development tends to be less dramatic in Key Stage 2 than in Key Stage 1. Although there may be a huge divide between a Year 3 and a Year 6 child, progress between Year 3 and Year 4 is far less marked.

Bearing in mind that individual differences can make nonsense of statistical generalizations, here is a guide as to what most of your class should be able to do and understand in relation to the key areas of the subject.

Key area: Chronology

Year 4s will certainly know and broadly understand a few period labels such as 'The Tudors', but individual experiences will vary. Much, indeed the majority, of the children's historical knowledge will have been gained outside school, but school will have begun to have its effect. The quality of their education to date should by now be visible.

At this age children are quite capable of using precise time terms, and even a few dates, accurately and appropriately if they have been taught properly. Common time words pose little difficulty and children can generally place events in their own lives in their proper temporal context. 'I went on holiday last year' now means just that, not 'any time before yesterday'.

Key area: Range and depth of historical understanding

The children's factual knowledge will depend partly upon whether they saw that programme about Egyptian mummies on TV last night and partly on the history that they have been taught. With a little prodding, they should be able to recall in some detail information they have learned previously. Refreshing their memory is a worthwhile exercise because, although Year 4s can recognize changes and continuities between past periods and their own, their ability to do so depends on knowledge and their ability to recall it. Year 4 is a good year in which to build up their body of knowledge – most children of this age are still insatiably curious and eager to please and to learn.

Examination and analysis of past events can be more searching than previously but still remains fact-based. Year 4s will not usually make abstract hypotheses about why events happened but they will understand and argue about events at what Piaget called a 'concrete operational' level. They will, for example, readily tease out the practical reasons why the Armada failed but they will not be able to cope with the religious and political reasoning surrounding the changes brought about by the Reformation.

Key area: Interpretations of history

By and large, children of this age clearly distinguish the past from the present, and consequently will know when the past is being represented in books and on film. This is partly the result of maturation and partly because their experience of studying the past has introduced them to stories and the most frequently encountered stereotypical images of the past. When they see an exhibition of medieval armour they know that it relates to real events and real people who lived long ago. Year 4 are sufficiently secure in their knowledge of what constitutes 'nowadays' to – at the very least – recognize what does not belong there.

Children will have visited museums, they will have seen the past recreated on film and on television (they are likely to have watched a school's history broadcast), they will have handled history books and they will almost always know history when they see it. Whether or not they will, or are able to, make judgements about the quality and honesty of these representations of the past, is a debatable point. There is little research evidence to help us, but clearly the ability to make valid judgements will depend heavily on prior knowledge as well as on intellectual maturity.

Key area: Historical enquiry

Year 4 children will utter the words 'That's not true!' and 'I don't believe that!' – phrases rarely heard up to now. They can readily cope with the notion of proving something and indeed with the idea that the past has to be proved. However, the idea that the past only exists because of the evidence is too difficult for young children to grasp. But Year 4 children who have been well taught will ask 'How do we know?'. More able reflective children may start to ask more probing questions about the stories and the evidence that they encounter.

Given a historical artefact most children will still respond with simple observations ('It's metal' or 'It's heavy') but they are gaining an improving facility to go beyond this: 'I think they must have been very small people in those days because these ceilings are too low for my dad.'

The evidence that they handle should still be predominantly non-literary but there are, exceptionally, accessible documents and exceptional children. Never underestimate children's ability to tease information from evidence, even if that evidence appears beyond them. Nine-year-olds will achieve most if they are given the language to think with and the time to do so.

Key area: Organization and communication

Children's ability to record and present work progresses steadily through the junior school but, in Year 4, there are not generally the marked changes that the maturation surge brings in Year 3. Writing should have settled down in size and, depending on how thorough and consistent the teaching has been, a neat joined hand will be apparent. IT skills should also be present now and most children will be able to present their work using word processors in ways that go beyond typing lines of text to ways that involve more complex presentations using pictures and borders.

History is a literary subject and the need to communicate history provides opportunity and purpose for children's writing in Year 4. But children of nine should also use options other than writing. Watch them in the playground as they act out the Battle of Bosworth in a fantasy that has its roots in the lesson learned in the classroom. Year 4s enjoy acting and assembly presentations and these are wonderful vehicles for communicating history.

Children's ability to communicate will depend very largely on their ability in English, but they should be able to tell a story in which can be identified the beginning, the middle and the end, and increasingly this should be done in writing.

Practical ideas

🏛 Making a start

Questions to answer

It is a good idea to map out broadly the ground that you hope to cover in your history project, but initially you will almost certainly put too much on your map. This will get you thinking about the topic, but is not very effective planning. Take a red pen to your 'map' and cut it until you have reduced it considerably, preferably to a few straightforward questions. From the questions, you should identify the direct teaching that you are going to do, then the activities related to this that the children are going to do. Some people prefer to start with the key elements and then go to the activities, but you have a better chance of stimulating enthusiasm and motivating the children if you start from your teaching and the children's activities. When you have a clear idea of these, simply check that some of the key elements are covered by them. If not, you will need to change some of your activities.

Tudor questions

🌑 If we take Life in Tudor Times as our example, the key questions might be: *Who were the Tudors? What happened in Tudor times? What was it like to live in those days?*

You can then sub-divide them, perhaps into questions for groups of children to investigate for themselves. For example:

What was it like to live in those days?
▶ *Was it the same for everybody?*
▶ *What kind of houses did they live in?*
▶ *How did they dress?*
▶ *What food did they eat?*
▶ *How did they enjoy themselves?*
▶ *What happened when they were ill?*
▶ *Did they go to school?*
and so on.

🌑 Involve the children in making the list of questions and in helping to select the ones to answer. You must not do everything. The questions themselves make an excellent activity for inclusion as part of Literacy Hour. Give a small group of children a question and a few

relevant books and the task of recording all the facts that they can find relating to the question. They can go further by discussing their findings and putting the information in an order of importance agreed by the group. Clearly there are many extensions and variations to this strategy.

Displays

Armed with your general plan and eager to launch into the project using the bright idea that you have had for grabbing the interest of your class, you only have one thing left to do. Prepare your resources. You must turn your classroom, or a corner of it, into a veritable Aladdin's cave of fascinating books and pictures, maps and artefacts. (See Resources on page 97.) Make sure that at least part of your display is interactive – demanding some response on the part of the children. A detective mystery perhaps. *Why did the Armada fail?* Give evidence, documents, maps and pictures. Invite the children to make up their own minds.

Starting points

You still have to decide how you are actually going to start the project in the classroom after your planning is complete. There is no single way of doing this, but you should stick to the principle of pitching straight in to the particular and the unique – a story, a film, a picture, an object, a visit or a person. Avoid general introductions to the topic or rambling thumbnail historical sketches of the period. Start by making them sit up and take notice.

● Tell the story of the battle of Bosworth as if you had witnessed the battle itself. No need to go to any great lengths to dress for the part, but a simple hessian cape will help you and the children to suspend disbelief.

● Start with a picture. There are many splendid examples to choose from, for example, portraits of Elizabeth, Henry VIII and so on; Field of the Cloth of Gold; the Armada; the sinking of the *Mary Rose*. Interrogate the picture as evidence and draw up a list of questions to answer.

● Bring into the classroom a variety of foods that only became available from the New World as a result of Tudor exploration, for example, apricots, potatoes, pepper, tomatoes, melons. Show on a map where produce such as lemons, coffee, cinnamon, bananas, cloves, maize and silk came from. Teach about the voyages of exploration. (Read extracts from *Hakluyt: Voyages and Discoveries*, Penguin.)

● Show a video – a period piece or educational broadcast. BBC Landmarks produced a programme on the Armada but you could also consider non-educational videos such as *Elizabeth I* (starring

Glenda Jackson). Give children one question to consider while they watch. It could be a very general one such as *In what period is this story set?*, but warn them that you will expect them to give evidence to support their answer. Discuss afterwards.

● Bring in some mystery objects (even one will do) obtained from the museum service. Play guessing games. Pass the objects around – every child has to make one observation.

● Year 4 children have not been taught a great deal of history so don't be afraid of trying out a few ideas on them that may seem old hat to you. Have they made a classroom frieze or a timeline?

Developing key areas

The ideas below are presented very briefly – adopt those that appeal to you and apply your imagination to them. For most ideas it is assumed that you will have taught the children about the events mentioned or they will have researched them.

General

● Make a giant comic strip of the main events during the reign of a Tudor monarch.

● *What is a hero/heroine?* Select one – Ralegh, say (his name was never spelled Raleigh during his lifetime) – and get the children to collect facts about his life from as many reference books as you can muster. They should write each fact on a small card. Have a display sheet 'Was Ralegh a hero?' and ask them to pin their cards under the most appropriate of three headings: Good/Bad/Neither. Have a debate about whether, on the balance of the evidence, he was a hero. You could use the facts to make a cartoon strip of your subject's life.

Battles

● Produce a news report about the Field of the Cloth of Gold based upon the famous painting of the scene by an unknown artist in the Royal collection at Hampton Court.

● Recreate the Battle of Bosworth or the Armada on tape, making your own sound effects. Use globes and maps to plot the route of the Armada. *Where did it sail from? Where did the action take place? Where did it go?*

Exploration

● Get the children to prepare an expedition to America. Work in groups to produce lists of stores, implements, clothes, games and so on. They could draw the objects and make a collage of the drawings for display. (A visit to the *Mary Rose* or the replica of the *Golden Hind* would make an excellent follow-up.)

● Construct a model of a Tudor ship. Use two or three tables as the backbone and build up the sides and decks using card and paper. Involve the children in the planning. They will invariably come up with some good ideas (and bad ones!). The ship will dominate the classroom and can be used as the focus for all sorts of work about the period.

● Replicate a captain's cabin in the corner of the classroom. Base it on evidence (pictures or visits to the *Mary Rose* or National Maritime Museum).

● Ask the children to research a day in the life of a sailor. They should list as many jobs as you can that would have to be done on board ship, and could produce a sailor's work rota for a day.

● Teach the children about compasses and navigation instruments. Make maps of the night sky showing the Plough and other easily seen constellations. *How can we find out from the stars where north is?* Find the lines of latitude and longitude on a globe or map then give the children references to pinpoint. Make compasses by magnetizing a needle and learn how to 'box' it.

● Use globes and maps to plot exploration routes. Refer to contemporary maps of the world (printed in many textbooks). Drake's round the world trip: Plymouth–North Africa–Sierra Leone–Atlantic–Brazil–Cape Horn–Peruvian coast–California–Pacific Ocean–Spice Islands (Moluccas)–Indian Ocean–Cape of Good Hope–Plymouth.

Tudors at home

● The food available on a Tudor table was governed mainly by the seasons and religion (meat was not eaten on Fridays). Investigate Tudor diet; you might even taste some Tudor food – there are simple recipes available. (A short guide is *Food and Cooking in 16th Century Britain*, Peter Brears, English Heritage.) For example, you can make crystallized rose petals using carefully washed petals coated with a thin layer of egg white and sprinkled with caster sugar. After they have dried they can be eaten.

● Create a Tudor kitchen in the classroom set up for preserving, salting, pickling, drying.

● Listen to Tudor music such as Thomas Tallis, William Byrd, Orlando Gibbons, John Taverner (not Tavener the modern composer). Use it as a stimulus for creative writing, dance (try a galliard – a spirited dance in pairs in triple time), or to launch an investigation into Tudor instruments. Recorders gradually became more popular than lutes in Tudor times so, if your class are learning the recorder, you could try some contemporary tunes.

● Examine the symmetrical patterns of knot gardens. Visit one, create one, design one. Look at other symmetrical patterns, axes of symmetry and so on. (A good maths scheme will give you plenty of ideas.)

Language

● Note what is different about Tudor language by examining the Authorized Version of the Bible or the Book of Common Prayer (compare them with modern versions), or a Shakespearean text.

● Make up conversations using some Tudor speech patterns. You can have fun with an anachronistic scene. Or you could conduct a PE lesson in Tudorese.

❖ Verbs: use the simplest form. 'I eat bread' not 'I am eating bread'; 'She maketh' not 'She is making'.

To have: *I have, thou hast, he hath, we/they have.*
To be: *I am, thou art, he is, we are, they be.*
To do: *I do, thou doest, he doth, we/they do.*
To come: *I come, thou comest, he/we/they cometh.*

To say: *I say, thou sayest, he saith, we/they say.* Avoid modern contractions (don't, can't). For example, say *Touch me not.*

❖ Pronouns: use 'It is' not 'It's'. 'Who', 'which' and 'that' are almost interchangeable.

Authentic words: *Whereas, whereat, whither, whence, whosoever, lest, likeas, perchance, yonder, therein.*

Causes

Debate causes and mysteries: for example, *Why did the* Mary Rose *sink?* Present the children with careful selections of evidence to work with.

Drama and presentations

● Do a Tudor assembly using Tudor music and 'Tudorese'. Let the children present the work that they have done, explain what they have learned, or, if you are ambitious, act out scenes from the period. The scenes could be simple domestic or rural craft scenes, you don't have to recreate Flodden field using an overhead projector and a PE bench (although no doubt somebody has).

● Record a museum tape guide to a collection of Tudor artefacts or pictures.

● Dramatize a Tudor scene. You could start with a famous picture such as the Bermondsey Wedding or Henry VIII's departure from Dover to go to the Field of the Cloth of Gold . Mime or act out incidents

portrayed in these complex scenes. Children could write dialogue to match the action. The less able could be given a copy of the picture with added speech bubbles which they could complete with appropriate words. Children can choose a figure in the picture and write about what happened to that person before and after the time of the picture.

● Act out a short scene from a Shakespearean play, for example the witches in *Macbeth*.

Leftovers

Make a large display of all that the Tudors have bequeathed us. Use photographs and drawings, artefacts and books. Think of the physical remnants of the age (buildings and objects) as well as art and literature. Think about how the Tudors changed our land and, indeed, the world.

Resources

● There are many suitable books for children on the Tudor period and it is worth considering using sets of the pupil books produced by publishers to service the needs of National Curriculum history (see Collins, Ginn and Longman). Reference books abound. Use as much visual material as you can, especially slides. Portraits are a splendid source for studies of the Tudors and many are available in slide form (from the National Portrait Gallery). Artefacts can usually be borrowed from your local museum or library as part of a schools loan service or can be handled in the museums themselves. Reproductions and facsimiles can be purchased from suppliers such as 'History in Evidence' and 'Past Times'.

● A number of well-known historic sites and museums are particularly rich in Tudor artefacts and, even if you are unable to go there, they are worth contacting because they often have school resource packs, books and guides that are excellent value for money. It would be a great pity not to take advantage of the superb national resources on this period and you should try to take your class to one of the major Tudor sites. Failing that, look for a relevant local visit – everywhere has somewhere.

Sites to consider

Mary Rose (Portsmouth); Southsea Castle; Tower of London; National Maritime Museum; Globe Theatre (Southbank reconstruction) and the *Golden Hind* nearby; National Portrait Gallery; Museum of London; Bosworth Field, (Leicestershire).

Outdoor collections of buildings: Singleton (Chichester); Avoncroft (Bromsgrove).

Numerous towns and villages have Tudor buildings and historic connections: Stratford upon Avon; Warwick; York; Chiddingstone (Kent); Lacock (Wiltshire); Lavenham (Suffolk).

Among the many wonderful houses worth visiting are: Hampton Court; Hardwick Hall (Derbyshire); Montacute (Somerset); Little Moreton Hall (Cheshire); Knole (Kent); Kentwell Hall (Suffolk); Shibden Hall (Halifax); Speke Hall (Liverpool); Tudor House (Southampton).

Music, videos, software

Other resources that you might consider are music, videos and computer software. Check the latest catalogues of leading suppliers as, like book lists, lists of these resources can date quite quickly.

Videos worth seeking: Landmarks series (BBC TV); *How We Used to Live* (Yorkshire TV); *Timelines: Tudor and Stuart Times* (Granada Television); *A Tudor Interlude* (Academy Television, 104 Kirkstall Road, Leeds); *Shakespeare: the Animated Tales* (BBC Educational Publishing).

Computer software is sometimes produced to accompany a TV series, for example, Landmarks. Check the schedules and the catalogues. One of the most comprehensive software catalogues is produced by AVP, School Hill Centre, Chepstow, Gwent, NP6 5PH (01291 625439).

Fiction

Historical fiction is to be highly recommended as a way of capturing children's imagination (we need our imagination to understand the truth about the past), but the stories must be good stories first and a means of instruction second. The best way to use fiction is to read to the class – young children can have difficulties in reading some historical fiction. Be selective. Consider the following:

Stories of Shakespeare, Ian Serraillier, OUP.
Shakespeare Stories, Leon Garfield, Puffin.
Sir Francis Drake and his Daring Deeds, Roy Gerrard, Puffin (A humorous picture book).
The Ghost of Thomas Kempe, Penelope Lively, Heinemann. (Not set in the past but well-researched connections to the past and a captivating book for 9-year-olds.).
Cue for Treason: Popinjay Stairs, Geoffrey Treece, Puffin.
Brother Dusty Feet, Rosemary Sutcliff, Red Fox.
The Queen Elizabeth Story, Rosemary Sutcliff.
Fireships Away, H T Sulton.

Representative of a number of stories that involve some kind of time travel experience are:
The Children of Green Knowe, Lucy Boston, Puffin;
A Traveller in Time, Alison Uttley, Puffin.

Assessment

Apart from records required to be sent to the next teacher you will need to be able to report to parents on children's progress in the subject. There are no SATs in history or formal assessments, but the National Curriculum does provide level descriptors to help guide your assessment of the children's work and understanding of the subject. Expectations given at the start of this chapter take account of these level descriptors and can be used as a measure against which to assess children's general progress.

You may wish to note children's knowledge of this (or another) particular topic. First ask yourself: *What do they know? What can they do? What have they experienced?*

What do they know?

For this study unit you might check children's knowledge of the following things.
● Main events and dates. (Can they use the term 'Tudor period' correctly? Do they know the dates of the Armada; the Field of the Cloth of Gold; Battle of Bosworth (1588; 1520; 1485) and/or other major events you have studied? Can they place the Tudor monarchs in the correct time order?).
● Major historical figures. (Elizabeth I, Henry VIII, Ralegh, Drake and so on).

What can they do?

They should be able to:
● explain simply the reasons why some key events happened (why the Armada failed, why the voyages of discovery took place);
● recognize stereotypical period images and artefacts correctly (identify a Tudor monarch, a Tudor house or ship);
● identify correctly on a map America, Spain, the Spice islands.

What have they experienced?

They should have:
● examined a range of evidence, especially pictures;
● experienced some simulations of Tudor life (eaten food to a Tudor recipe, visited a Tudor house, listened to Tudor music, or dressed in Tudor-style clothes).

Geography

During Key Stage 2 the children continue to learn about places, including their local area. They compare this with contrasting localities of a similar size, which might be within or beyond the UK, perhaps in Europe. They also learn about more distant localities in less developed countries.

Key Stage 2 children investigate aspects of their immediate and wider environment, including settlements, rivers, weather and environmental change, or other themes particularly appropriate to their school. These studies are about real places, near and far, large and small. Within these place and thematic studies the children extend their geographical skills, particularly by using maps and pictures in context, by collecting and handling data, and developing their research skills as they access relevant geographical information from a range of sources including books and IT.

Your school will have chosen the places and themes to be studied, and decided in which years they will be covered. Your geography curriculum should provide opportunities for children to 'revisit' themes and localities, reinforcing and extending their geographical knowledge and understanding.

It is not possible to deal here with every combination of topic so the following content structure has been adopted. (You may want to draw on ideas from the other Yearbooks if your school has allocated topics differently.)

Year 3:   Skills, enquiry
          Place: Local (urban), Local (rural), Topical
          Theme: Settlement (major), River (minor)

Year 4:   Skills, enquiry
          Place: Contrast (UK), Less developed country (urban), Topical
          Theme: River (major), Weather (minor)

Year 5:   Skills, enquiry
          Place: Contrast (EU), Less developed country (rural), Topical
          Theme: Weather (major), Environmental Change (minor)

Year 6:   Skills, enquiry
          Place: Local (revisit), Less developed country (contrast), Topical
          Theme: Environmental Change (major), Settlement (minor)

Whichever model your school has chosen, there are four fundamental key areas of geography in which your children should be progressing:

- Ability to undertake geographical enquiry and use geographical skills.
- Knowledge and understanding of places.
- Knowledge and understanding of geographical patterns and processes.
- Knowledge and understanding of environmental relationships and issues.

What should they be able to do?

In Year 4 the children should continue to make progress in the four key areas of geography. To facilitate this you should provide spatial experiences, opportunities for them to observe, describe, compare, explain human and physical geographical features, identify patterns, processes and relationships, and investigate issues with a geographical dimension, in a variety of locations. These activities may be in designated geography lessons or in topic or thematic work in which the geography is explicitly identified and planned.

Key area: geographical enquiry and use of skills

The children should develop and extend their ability to:
● understand and use appropriate geographical vocabulary;
● ask and respond to geographical questions about places and environmental topics on the basis of tasks you set;
● offer their own ideas about geographical situations;
● make, record, communicate and compare their own observations about places and environments from first-hand experience, practical activities and secondary sources such as photographs, videos and CD-ROMs;
● collect, record and represent information or measurements pictorially and graphically, and begin to analyse or explain it;
● carry out simple enquiries by undertaking fieldwork tasks and activities, supported by you, using simple equipment (such as a stop watch, anemometer) and secondary sources (such as atlases, maps, diagrams and electronic sources);
● begin to identify the resources they need for an enquiry, including accessing the World Wide Web.

Key area: Places: features, characteristics, contrasts and relationships

Year 4 children should be able to recognize, describe, compare, express views about and record:
● the main physical (for example, landscape, weather, vegetation) and human (for example, industry, transport features) features of their local area and other localities they study, using appropriate geographical terminology;
● the distinctive characters of different places such as an industrial sector of a town, an agricultural village;
● that places change on a range of time scales, for example seasonal changes, including weather and tourism, buildings built and demolished;
● that buildings and land are used for a variety of purposes, for example, industry, recreation;
● the significance of location: why features are where they are, why things happen where they do, for example, in-town and out-of-town shopping centres;
● similarities and differences between the places they visit and study, comparing and contrasting localities and offering explanations, for example, between a UK and a tropical seaside resort.

Key area: Patterns and physical and human processes

The children should make observations and respond to questions about:
● where things are, such as industrial sites adjacent to motorways and railways;
● physical (natural) and human processes: explain why things are like they are, for example, travel-to-work journeys and transport provision;
● the pattern of where features are, for example, drainage networks, streams flowing downhill into a river.

Key area: Environmental relationships and issues

They should begin to:
● express and account for their own views about physical and/or human features of their environment, recognizing that other people may have different views;
● recognize that their environment changes and that people affect it, for example, by noise and air pollution from traffic;
● recognize and describe how the quality of the environment can be maintained and improved. These aspects are looked at in more detail in Practical ideas.

Practical ideas

Developing key areas
Enquiry and use of skills
Geographical vocabulary

Practise and extend children's geographical vocabulary, introducing specialist terminology for the features, patterns and processes met with in place and thematic studies.

● Make word lists, for example of features associated with rivers and weather, then use the words to label photographs.

● Make word lists from topical, place or theme pictures, but also ask the children to give each picture a title, to encourage them to look at the picture as a whole as well as at its parts, and to generalize.

● Make alphabet lists, selecting a theme (for example Rivers), and encouraging children to find the name of one for each letter of the alphabet, Amazon, Brahmaputra, Colorado and so on, increasing locational knowledge by marking them on an appropriate map.

● Use classifications and hierarchies (for example, houses, flats, bungalows and so on are found in residential areas, which can be urban, suburban or rural, in cities, towns, villages).

Photographs
Field sketching

Field sketching is an important geographical skill which can be learned in the classroom before being used outdoors. Children should make field sketches from photographs.

To introduce this, project a picture on to a whiteboard or large sheet of paper, or use tracing paper or acetate over a large picture. Draw in the key lines, for example the skyline, outline of buildings, fields, roads, people; label or colour in the blocks; make a key if necessary. Omit detail.

Now ask for children to try this. Provide them with an A4 photograph (or photocopy) in a plastic wallet, and washable felt pens. Alternatively, tracing paper may be used. A photocopy of their field sketch enables children to complete the labelling of features, identification of land use, colouring and key.

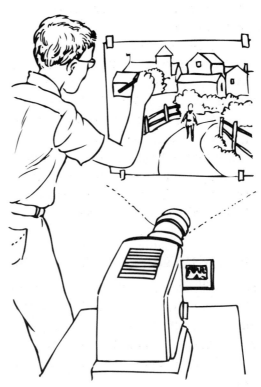

Questioning pictures

When looking at photographs, ask the children different types of question: concrete (*What can you see?*); descriptive (*What are the people doing?*); speculative (*Where are they going?*); reasoning (*Why are they dressed in these clothes?*); evaluative (*Is this a good place to live?*); problem solving (*How could these people get here?*).

● Ask children to write geographical questions around a photograph. Encourage their visualization by asking them to extend a photograph, drawing what is beyond its limits, or to complete a photograph in which you have blocked out the centre.

Oblique and vertical aerial photographs

● Ask the children to identify the human and physical features in aerial photographs, using correct geographical vocabulary. They can make a field sketch from the photograph (see above).

● Ask them to match the aerial photograph to an appropriate map, orientating the latter appropriately; ask them to identify landmarks on the aerial photograph and plan a route to visit them, marking the route on the map.

● They can compare oblique and vertical aerial photographs, perhaps of the school or local area. *What is similar/different about them?* Then they can compare each photograph with a map and mark what each shows on the map. *Do they cover the same area?*

Using maps

Use a wide range of plans, maps, atlases and globes (for example, sketch maps, pictorial maps, different scales, road and world atlases, political and physical globes) whenever appropriate, in as many contexts as possible, to locate places. Use:

◗ maps to locate places: being studied (comment on 'nesting': county, city or town, district, neighbourhood); in the news (have a topical event map on the wall, with newspaper cuttings and photographs); to be/that have been visited (colour the route on a photocopy, to identify 'shape', distance, direction relative to school);

◗ maps to relate to photographs of places;

◗ maps to help answer questions. *How will/could/ did we get to X? How many different ways could we get from A to B? How long will it take? How much will it cost?* (use with timetables and combine with work in mathematics);

◗ maps to carry out geographical enquiries;

◗ atlases to develop research skills (index);

◗ globes to recognize continents, countries, northern and southern hemispheres, Equator, North and South Poles, latitude and longitude; explain day and night, and begin to explain seasons and climate.

Making maps

Provide opportunities for groups of children to make large-scale maps or representations – and for individual children to draw freehand maps or representations – of localities being studied and of journeys undertaken within the local area (perhaps to the library or swimming pool), of directions for friends to special places, of journeys further afield (for example a school trip), or from stories (help them to visualize the location of a story).

● Encourage the children to make a sketch map for recording data. For example when exploring an issue such as 'How can we improve the use of the playground?', they could start by recording (on their own sketch maps) how the playground is used.

Topical geography

Each week find an item in the national or local press that has a geographical flavour, such as extreme weather, an environmental threat or a political event. Use it as text for Literacy Hour, for discussion and to develop geographical general knowledge, interest and understanding. If appropriate, use it for a small-scale geographical enquiry. (It doesn't need to be a half-term's topic!)

Geographical facts

Introduce some new geographical facts each week – names of high mountains, long rivers, 'nestings' (for example, the Thames is an English river with its source in the Cotswolds in the county of Gloucestershire, which flows 210 miles, 338 kilometres, eastwards through six counties and London, entering the North Sea at Tilbury, just downstream from Greater London). Encourage the children to find the river in an atlas, to name the six counties, and to find similar information for another river which they can then give to friends to follow up. You could develop this into your own version of Geographical Trivial Pursuits, again developing children's geographical general knowledge, while introducing or reinforcing geographical vocabulary.

IT

Use appropriate software, including some familiar software at a higher level, such as *My World*: *Make a Town*, *Weather Mapper*.

Encourage children to use the Internet and other electronic sources, including exchanging ideas and information with other schools at home and abroad through fax, e-mail and telephone.

Places

UK contrasting locality enquiry

Rather than carry out an encyclopaedic study of one place, you may consider that it is more important to study aspects of a contrasting locality and to compare it with aspects of the children's own locality, encouraging more in-depth geographical thinking and learning. By Year 4, through observation and description, the children will have become increasingly knowledgeable about their own locality and the people within it, and will be beginning to understand how it functions.

● Provide opportunities for them to compare their own locality with a contrasting locality, identifying similarities and differences. You may have chosen a

locality for a variety of reasons: one with which you are familiar, one that has some connections with your locality (perhaps the next place along the motorway or local river), one that shares some common factor (for example, another holiday resort). What is important is that there are significant contrasts.

● Unless the locality is near enough for the children to visit, you will be using secondary sources, especially maps and photographs, practising some of the skills outlined above. You may select a focus for the study (for example, economic activity, communications, settlement, land use) which will give it depth, rather than breadth, and enable you to reinforce geographical skills and enquiry in different contexts.

● Consider both cognitive aspects (human and physical features, routeways and landmarks, morphology, function, aspects of character) which will be the same for each person, and affective aspects ('feel', preferences, experiences, memories, values, familial connections) which will be different for each person. Collectively the cognitive and affective contribute to a child's 'sense of place'.

Asking and answering questions

● By Year 4 you will be increasingly encouraging the children to ask and seek answers to their own geographical questions. Before you begin a contrasting locality study, ask the children *What do you already know about this place?* and *What are you interested in finding out about it?* Respect and use their answers to the latter to give both structure to your study and extra motivation to the children. Help them to consider how they can find out, and how to set up an enquiry.

Nevertheless, in Year 4 geographical questions from you about localities (and themes) could still form the framework for the enquiry. Extend the children's geographical thinking beyond 'observe and describe', encourage them to 'compare', recognizing similarities and differences, to 'explain' their observations and to look for patterns (in location, spatial arrangement, economic activity).

● In studying a contrasting locality (and other places) you could use the question framework introduced in earlier Yearbooks and extended in the table below. Progression is achieved through the depth of the children's geographical understanding and thinking. (It is not sufficient to require the same type of geographical work, and same level of geographical thinking as previously, but in a different locality!)

Question	Skill or concept	Response
What is it? *What is it like?*	Observation, description locality.	Identify the main human behaviour and physical features, describe the morphology of the contrasting locality.
Where is it?	Location, distance, direction.	The address of the locality, it's relationship to the children's local area (distance, direction) and to major physical and human features (such as an upland village, a 'silicon valley', the centre of an historic old town).
What sort of place is it?	Categorization, classification.	Compare it explicitly with the children's local area and other localities they have studied or know.
Is it like any other places you know?	Comparison, similarity and difference.	Find and describe (using maps, timetables, pictures and words) routes to the locality, including distance, time, cost.
How could we get there?	Communications, time, cost.	Encourage the children to plan a visit to the locality and implement if possible!
Why is it like it is?	Hypothesis, speculation.	Begin to consider how and why a place develops in a certain way, and at a certain place (such as a fishing village or riverside town).

If the children are able to visit the place, or if you know it well and have suitable resources/evidence the children could consider:

Question	Skill or concept	Response
Is this place changing? How?	Continuity and change, dynamics, time, spatial process, development.	Recognize that places change – they are dynamic. Find out about recent or proposed changes (for example in the local press). Are changes similar to those in the local area happening here?
Why do you think it is changing?	Cause and consequence, power (economic, social, political) in the sense of who or what has the power to sanction or cause change?	Begin to look for explanations, for example, why shops or factories are closing.

From the experience of a visit, or from secondary sources, encourage the children to consider, while comparing with their own locality:

Question	Skill or concept	Response
What do you feel about it? Do you like it?	Opinion, values, attitude.	Recognize particular likes and dislikes, and give reasons for these preferences.
What would it be like to live/work here?	Empathy.	Give opinions and justify them.
What gives this place its character? What's special about this place?	Generalization.	Begin to consider that places have a character of their own, and what that character is for this particular locality, compared with their own.

These are challenging questions but Year 4 children will be able to meet them. They make cognitive and affective demands on the children, who will be learning about the morphology (the features, shape, form, structure) of the place, and also developing a 'sense of place'. This is about their own unique experience or interpretation of a place. They will be learning that everyone experiences, and thinks about, a place differently – there is not one 'right' answer or opinion. This will be reinforced as you introduce children to controversial geographical issues. (Later they will learn about consensus and decision-making processes.)

Hypothesis testing

Rather than use this question framework approach to enquiry, you may prefer to use the scientific approach of hypothesis testing, for example, *X is a better place to live/work in than Y*, with the children defining 'better'. Or you may like to pose one key question, for example, *Why do so many people go to Z for shopping/holidays?* or *Why did Company A build their new factory at B?*

Less developed country: urban enquiry

Year 4 children have an increasing awareness of the wider world. You may choose to focus their enquiry on a locality in an urban area in a less developed country, in the first instance. In doing this, you will avoid reinforcing what might be described as 'mud hut' stereotypes and the negative ideas children tend to hold, for example that all people in less developed countries suffer from disease, drought, war, famine and so on. Starting with an urban locality shows that, although there may well be poverty, there is also development and many of the features of a Western urban area.
● There are now many good resource packs to support an urban locality study. You may like to choose one that has a complementary rural pack, for later comparison. Examples include the Action Aid India and Kenya packs: *Bangalore and Chembakolli, Nairobi and Kapsakwony*, but there are others. The Oxfam *Big City* pack looks at several urban localities and raises interesting issues, particularly of identification. It is important to avoid the exotic, or tokenism, and to study the ordinary, everyday life experiences and environment of the local people – children are always interested in people! Encourage them to consider, in particular, the positive things about what it is like to live in this

locality, and to recognize the similarities with their own lives – the same basic needs of food, water, clothing, shelter, education and work.

● Use artefacts and visitors – people from, and people who have been to, the locality you are studying in order to enrich work from the photopacks.

● Whichever localities you choose, use the approaches to place study discussed above, combined with the ideas for using photographs and maps to develop geographical skills, with either the children or you identifying the key question to structure the enquiry.

Patterns and processes
Observing patterns

As children observe, describe, record, compare and begin to explain their observations, you will be developing the idea of geographical pattern and process. Encourage them to observe the patterns made by individual human and physical features and recognize associations between them, such as hotels along the seafront, car parks around shopping centres, concentration of significant buildings in urban centres, pattern of land use in the local area (residential, agricultural, industrial and so on), the pattern of bus routes through the local area, seasonal weather patterns.
● On appropriate scale maps ask the children to colour in, for example, different types of shops, sports facilities, hotels, different types of land-use, land above a certain height, streams and rivers, and encourage them to describe the distribution patterns, to explain 'why things are like that'.

Use events

Use topical and local events. Encourage children to identify and explain changes or short-duration events, for instance how and why the valley has flooded after heavy rain, how local shops have closed because of the new hypermarket, how building a new factory has produced more traffic on the nearby roads, how winter gale-damage and wind direction are related.

Environmental relationships and issues
Look again at the locality

Developing from their study of a contrasting locality, encourage children to reconsider how they feel about and value their own locality – what's good/

Primary teacher **YEARBOOKS**   **105**

not so good about it – and to reappraise its aesthetics and people's responsibilities. Help them to justify their opinions and appreciate other children's views which are different from their own. Help them to consider other people's opinions, for example some people might not like heavy traffic on the local roads, while others, such as shop-owners and hoteliers, might welcome it because it means more customers or visitors.

Local issues

Using local newspapers, identify local environmental issues. Identify the individuals or groups interested in the issue; discuss what their opinions might be – what 'side' are they on? Consider why they might think this way – what influences their perspective? Some people will agree, others disagree, so the key ideas of conflict and consensus begin to develop.

Global issues

Identify global environmental issues, using national press, television and the Internet. Use these for discussion and investigation, leading to informed role play. Begin to introduce children to controversial issues, such as the human impact of drought in part of an African country, or the human and physical impact of the development of a superquarry.

River study

An introductory or small-scale study was described in the Year 3 Yearbook. It introduced or reinforced the appropriate vocabulary, and checked the children's conceptual understanding of the movement of water in the environment.

Field study

For a more comprehensive river study, find a locality where the children can have access to the water! For safety try to use a small stream – it will show most of the features of a river, but on a small scale.
● Focus the investigation on questions. *How fast does the water flow? Does it all flow at the same speed? Which is the deepest/widest part of the stream? Are speed, depth and width related in any way?*

● Carry out investigations in the stream, using simple instruments to measure flow, depth and width. Encourage the children to design and use their own sheet to record the measurements. Transfer the measurements into diagrams, graphs,

maps as appropriate, possibly on the computer. Help the children to explain and communicate their observations. Check that the children know and can explain why the water is flowing and that it is flowing downhill, under gravity.

● In the course of making their recordings the children will make other observations: on flora and fauna; on the nature and pattern of material on the stream bed (fine material on the inside of bends or meanders); on the pattern of movement of material on the stream bed (the water flow is strongest on outside of meanders); on the pattern of water flow over large boulders in the stream bed; and many more. Encourage them to record and then try to explain these observations.

● While standing on the bank of a stream, encourage children to visualize more than just the section of stream they investigate – to begin to see the stream as a small part of a big river system. Ask questions like *Where has the water come from?* (upstream/rainfall/over and through ground flow), *Where is the water going to?* (downstream/ downhill/estuary/bigger river/sea and so on). Some children will respond to these two questions with 'the start/the end of the river'. Ask them, *If we walked to the start/end of the river, what would it be like? How would we know when we'd got there?*

● Encourage children to relate the movement of rainwater in the vicinity of their school to the movement of water in the vicinity of the stream. Compare flow down roofs and gutters to flow down valley slopes and streams.

In the classroom

● Make a collection of photographs (picture postcards are a useful, abundant source, but try to take a set of your own along the river into which

your fieldwork stream flows) to illustrate sources, mouths and other parts of rivers, in rural and urban settings, to use back in the classroom.

Activities include:

▶ match 'river' words to pictures;

▶ sequence features from source to mouth;

▶ find river(s) in an atlas and on an appropriate map;

▶ match photographs taken along your local river to a map and describe changes in the river, the surrounding scenery and the impact of human presence along the river;

▶ trace the whole course of the local river and its tributaries (including the stream visited);

▶ from OS maps or a road atlas, describe the pattern of the river system as a whole;

▶ identify settlements along the river, find out their population, and try to explain their location and size. All the time help children to make the difficult links between the scale of the stream and the scale of a river, and to begin to get some idea of the size of a river system or catchment area as a whole.

● Look in the local press for articles on issues associated with rivers and streams and use these to initiate an enquiry. There are often articles about flooding, pollution, bank 'improvement', wildlife, water extraction, diversion and so on.

Weather introductory study

Begin your Weather study with discussion and observation of how the weather affects children's lives – clothing, activities, holidays (time and destination) – and the lives of others, particularly farmers and other outdoor workers, here and around the world. In particular, consider the weather in distant localities being studied through the evidence of pictures and data from newspapers and global weather forecasts. Also make use of topical 'weather events' of local and global significance.

Small-scale activities

Introduce small-scale practical activities in the school and school grounds. This helps to familiarize the children with both the specific vocabulary and the instruments used to measure and record the weather. Identify a key question to investigate or a hypothesis to test.

These examples can be carried out for different periods.

● In one day or week:

Is the temperature the same everywhere in the playground/school grounds?

(Include below/at/well above ground-level)

Are some parts of the playground more/less windy than others?

How and why do shadows 'move' in the school grounds?

Is it warmer in the afternoon than in the morning?

● Twice a year (useful reinforcement):

There is more rain in January than in June.

● Over the school year:

Is January the coldest month or is July the warmest?

February is the windiest month.

● Short or long studies:

Some parts of the playground are always/never in the shade.

Some classrooms (or parts of the classroom or school) are warmer/draughtier/sunnier than others. Why?

Which is the most accurate weather forecast for our locality – the television or newspaper?

● In addition to introducing children to temperature, wind, sunshine, cloud cover, rain and other weathers, these enquiries all require measurement, recording and comparison (analysis) of weather data. Measurement will include the use of appropriate instruments (different types of thermometers; informal – size of puddles – and formal means of measuring rainfall; wind speed and direction; electronic probes and sensors). Recording might include the use of large-scale plans or maps of the school to locate measurement sites, and IT to handle the data. Encourage children to look for patterns and associations in the weather, for example, between wind direction and temperature, between cloud cover/type and rainfall.

Problem solving

Some key questions or hypotheses lead to more 'applied' weather study, requiring measurement, recording and analysis of weather data to solve a 'problem', adding purpose to relevance. For examples, *Which is the best place to put a new seat in the playground? Which is the best place to plant a new tree/put a new flower bed in the school grounds?*

The children need to define 'best' (for sitting at playtime, for tree and plant growth, perhaps) and having established their criteria, 'test' all relevant areas against them, probably by measuring, recording and mapping weather attributes for the school grounds.

Assessment

In Year 4 you will want to keep a simple record of the progress children are making.

What do they know?

Evidence will include their accurate use of geographical vocabulary to talk and write about the places and themes studied; their understanding of maps and geographical pictures, their increasing geographical general knowledge.

What can they do?

Evidence will include their use of geographical skills, their ability to ask and respond to geographical questions, the resources they can use to find information, give opinions, make comparisons and offer explanations.

What have they experienced?

This will include place and thematic studies, the geographical skills introduced, activities, and fieldwork (experiences outside the classroom).

How have they demonstrated their knowledge?

Evidence will include discussion, drawing, map-making and using, writing and practical activities.

What are they working towards?

What is the next conceptual, skills or enquiry stage?

Music

If music-making has been an integral part of classroom activities in the years leading to Year 4, then, having explored sounds thoroughly, the children will come to you with many valuable experiences, ready to move forward and to use their music-making in all parts of the curriculum. Year 4 is an exciting time, the elements having been explored in depth, and the creative work produced should be beginning to be more acceptable and recognizable. The National Curriculum suggests that children should 'make expressive use of the musical elements and show an awareness of phrase'. They should be able to sing songs 'in two parts and maintain independent instrumental lines with an awareness of other performers' and use 'musical symbols'. When listening, the children should be responding to the music, 'identifying changes in character and mood'. They should be beginning to evaluate their own work, beginning to recognize that music is affected by time and a place, be looking at different traditions and increasing their musical vocabulary.

The fourth year should be a consolidation of all the work that has gone before and a real movement forward towards the expectations of Year 5. At all levels, music should be seen as an important part of the whole curriculum, integrating wherever possible with other subjects, but still with an identity of its own.

Key areas: Listening, Composing, Performing, Appraising

A curriculum for music-making will always ask for sounds to be explored through listening, composing, performing and appraising and at times it is useful to look at the areas separately.

However, in a successful music session all four areas are in action at the same time. A music-maker will listen to sounds, discuss them, choose appropriate ones to place together in some order, move them around and will then perform them. This is as true at Year 4 as it is at university and should be encouraged at all times. These skills are involved in all the activities suggested here.

The activities will explore all the elements of music as suggested in the National Curriculum. These are: pitch, duration, dynamics, tempo, timbre, texture and structure.

What should they be able to do ?

Key element: Pitch

In Year 4, you should be able to assume that the majority of the children will know that pitch means sounds can be high and low. They will have explored these sounds with their voices, through body percussion and on tuned instruments. They should have used high and low sounds in their own compositions and will have experimented with sliding sounds and those moving by steps. A development to be explored is that sounds can also be moved in leaps.

Some children, mainly those who have specialist instrumental lessons, will have realized that all musical notes have special names. The letter names will have been seen on the classroom instruments and no doubt have been used in recording compositions, so this is a good time to reinforce this traditional notation with all children. Teachers who have a working knowledge of tonic sol-fa will also be increasing the children's repertoire of hand signs and symbols. The pentatonic or five-note scale should be being used freely in the children's compositions. There

should be much discussion of their own music and that of others, learning a variety of new words to add to their musical vocabulary.

Key element: Duration

By the beginning of Year 4, all children should know that there are different lengths for sounds: long and short. Most children should be able to group them in 2s, 3s and 4s. Word patterns and rhythms will have been explored many times and new ones can always be used as well as finding the pulse/beat of any piece of music. In Year 4, you should be beginning to teach the correct names for these long and short notes (minim, crotchet, quaver) and the children should know how long or short they are (2, 1, 1/2). Some children will also be ready to divide them up in equal sections (bar lines). The children should be using longer rhythms in their own compositions and you can encourage this by asking them to remember longer phrases of music when singing or playing together. Make sure the children see written music in song books and hymn books so that this notation becomes acceptable as the language used by other composers.

Key element: Dynamics

During Year 3, the children should have become very familiar with the sounds and signs associated with the dynamics of music – *p*, *f*, *pp*, *ff*, <, > – and should be beginning to know the musical terms for these. To these can be added *mp* (moderately soft) and *mf* (moderately loud). They should be creating short pieces that show their understanding of the signs and will be looking at how composers of the songs they sing and simple instrumental pieces they play have used these dynamics effectively. In their own music-making you should be encouraging them to make their pieces more colourful by using dynamic changes and they should listen to the music of famous composers to see how these can change the mood of the music. There should be much discussion about the dynamics of music and its effects.

Key element: Tempo

Over the years, the children's understanding of tempo should have progressed so that they know that music is not just slow or fast, but that it can get faster and move slower as directed by the conductor. The composer needs to give an indication of speed at the beginning of all pieces of music, and the children will be able to look out for these directions. To begin with, your class will be writing instructions such as 'slow' 'get faster' and 'slow down' for their compositions or, if they want to indicate a mood, they might use 'lively', 'calm', 'gently', 'with force'. Some children might notice that at the beginning of some music there are strange words. These are often in Italian and a music dictionary will give you the translations. If the children are interested, it is never too soon to teach these musical terms of tempo.

Key element: Timbre

The different timbres of voices and instruments from the children's natural environment should have been well explored by Year 4. A development of this will be to widen the children's horizons by introducing more attentive listening to specific instruments. Each orchestral instrument has a very special sound of its own and, in Year 4, you should be encouraging the children to pick out the new sounds. They should listen, discuss, have opinions about and in some cases, be choosing which they would like to play, if given the opportunity.

There are many recordings one could suggest to hear different sounds, but Benjamin Britten's *Young Person's Guide to the Orchestra* is still one of the best. Only listen in short bursts, and only then to one section of the orchestra. The children should also be continuing to discover a

wider range of sounds, which they can create on the available classroom instruments, to be used in their compositions to suggest special effects. Seize any opportunity of getting players of orchestral instruments to come into the class to demonstrate their instruments to the children.

Key element: Texture

As children have more musical experiences and make greater use of the elements, so they will be able to experiment and create a wider variety of textures. The National Curriculum suggests that they should be putting sounds together in different ways such as 'rhythm on rhythm', 'melody and accompaniment', 'parts that weave'. In previous years they will have been placing rhythms together (name scores), singing and playing songs with simple accompaniments and singing rounds, and they should continue to use these ideas. 'Parts that weave' can then be added to these; just like the threads of cotton in a tapestry, they use different sounds to create a finished piece of music. The children will need to discuss their work with others and should be forming opinions as to how or why a certain combination of sounds is the most successful.

Key element: Structure

In Year 4, the children should be constantly encouraged to create their own music, working individually, in pairs or as a small group. For each of these pieces they will need to use a specific structure. The National Curriculum suggests that these be 'rounds, questions and answers, repetition, phrases and ostinato (a musical pattern which repeats itself)'. In the earlier years they will have explored the idea of questions and answers and this should still be encouraged as it is a useful, simple structure to follow. They will also be singing rounds in Year 4, though they should be dividing up into more than two parts.

From early years they will have experienced the idea of repetition in songs and instrumental pieces and should be encouraged to continue using the form. During this year, they should discover how composers divide music into phrases and try to sing a phrase using controlled breathing. Any instrumentalists will already have been using phrasing and they could help the rest of the class to understand it. The idea of ostinato should also be more fully developed at this stage with children learning, remembering, creating and playing ostinatos as accompaniments to songs and their own compositions. Structure is all important and should be listened for and discussed in the works of others.

Practical ideas

Music-making can often look and sound very disorganized. In fact, the best results will always come from very careful organization, even if the preparation is very noisy. Decide just what it is you would like to achieve in a session (or group of sessions) and make a plan of linked starting activities and main group activities, always giving time at the end for performances and listening to one another. Some music-making will be in small groups, so plan your space well. Check on the availability of instruments and that they are complete and have beaters. If you are expecting the children to record their music, have paper available for both graphic and traditional notation as well as a tape recorder for the final results.

Time your sessions and keep stopping and starting small-group work, inviting children to perform. Check that some progress is being made (*How much have you done?*). Visit the groups, giving a helping hand when required, but generally stand back and watch as leaders emerge, instruments are chosen and creations develop. Encourage the children to discover for themselves, to make decisions, to create, to work in a team and then to perform.

Making a start

● Ask the children to imagine they are with you in a cave. What might they hear? Water rushing, drips on ledges, echoes. *What do you think will happen to your voice in a cave? Will the sound repeat? Will the sound die away?* With a small group of children, try to recreate the sounds of vocal echoes.

Remember to make the sounds get softer.
● Discuss reflections with the whole class. *How does a reflection change an image?* Clap a simple word pattern, such as 'Mirror mirror on the wall'. Can the children clap it the opposite way round – 'Wall the on mirror mirror'? Ask the children, in pairs, to clap reflections.

● Clap some names and addresses all together. Once the children have the idea of how to do this, ask them, in pairs, to clap names and addresses to each other in an AB structure. (One idea followed by another idea.)

● Sing rounds together, encouraging two- and three-part singing. Make sure everyone is involved and place your enthusiastic singers by your shy, reticent singers. When teaching rounds, make sure the whole tune is known before moving the children into parts. A & C Black's *Flying a Round* has an excellent selection of rounds for all abilities and to fit in with many classroom projects. Sing a line at a time with the children either copying you or, if you are not too confident, a tape.

Once they know a round, ask the children to sing the first line, think the second and come in together with the rest. This really tests if everyone knows the tune. Try again, missing out different lines.

● Ask the children to use instrumental sounds (timbre) to describe words. These might be 'wet', 'dripping', 'damp', 'darkness', 'bright'. *Which*

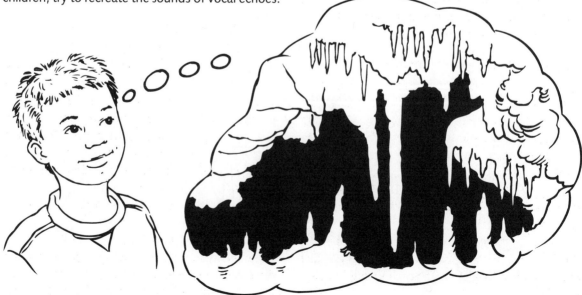

sounds might fit with the words? (Sliding sounds, short sharp sounds, sounds that do not ring, low, deep sounds, high light sounds.)

● Play 'Copy me' by using sounds that slide and sounds that move in step. Use either your voice, instruments or both.

● Ask the children, in pairs, to create opposite sounds, using either the voice or an instrument. Child A might make a sliding-down sound, Child B will slide up; high will be followed by low, downward steps will be followed by upward steps, upward leaps will be followed by leaps down. When Child A has run out of ideas, then the children should change over.

Introducing key elements

Leap and slide

With the children, think of animals that leap (kangaroo, lion, tiger, leopard, monkey) and slide (snake, alligator, crocodile, snail, worm). Give pairs of children the names of two contrasting animals as a starting point for some creative work based on sliding and leaping sounds.

Notes in order

Place the tuned percussion instruments in the centre of a circle of children, making sure everyone can see. Have a good look at each instrument and talk about it, looking particularly at the letter names on the bars/notes. They should be in alphabetical order. Listen together as someone plays up the notes and then down. *Do they sound in the correct order?* Take the notes off and ask a child to replace them, then play up and down. *Are they correct now?* Without letting the children see what you are doing, put two notes in the wrong order. *Who can hear which notes are wrong?*

Crotchets, quavers, minims

Make a lot of duration flash cards showing crotchets, quavers and minims (♩, ♪, 𝅗𝅥). Explain to the children that a composer needs to use extra tools other than just sounds if the music is to be passed down to others to play.

Show a flash card and play a note, counting carefully in your head – two for a minim, one for a crotchet and a half for a quaver. *Which do you think sounds the longest? The shortest?*

Place the flash cards in a line, in any order, on the floor in the centre of a circle of children. Can they clap what they see with you, moving from left to right?

Give a few flash cards to small groups of children and ask one child to place them in different orders so the others can clap them. Change the leaders frequently.

Tonic sol-fa

If you are happy to use tonic sol-fa, introduce a new note and hand sign for Lah.
Sing to the children:

Af-ter the storm				*rain- bows ap- pear*			
s	m	m	s	s	m	m	s

See all the col-ours				*when skies are clear*			
s	l	l	s	s	m	m	m

Can the children hear if the new sound is higher or lower than the others? Make up lots of tunes using the new notes and different words and invite the children to do the same.

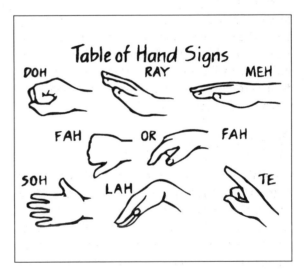

Table of Hand Signs

Pentatonic scale

● Many folk songs are based on the pentatonic or five-note scale. 'Amazing Grace' is one of these. Ask a small group of children to try to find the tune by starting on low D and moving to G B G B. This is the beginning. Once they have the tune, another child could play a repeating accompaniment (ostinato) just using the two notes of G and B. Teach the whole class the words, ask your instrumental group to accompany, the ostinato players to join in, and you have a ready-made piece for a school assembly.

● Use the pentatonic notes on a tuned percussion instrument for the children to create a piece of music where the notes weave. Pentatonic sound is very pleasant, so the weaving tunes will blend in with

each other. Working in groups of three, give each child one tuned instrument without the Fs and Bs and ask one child to play a repeating rhythm. The second child joins in with a different rhythm but one that will fit with it. The third child joins in when all is going well with a new rhythm. Ask them to listen carefully to each other. *Are the parts woven well together? Do they sound pleasing?* Since most schools have few tuned percussion instruments, this will be an activity to be explored in a spare moment by a few children.

Discovering instruments

Invite any willing instrumentalists to visit your classroom and give a short performance on their instrument. Try to involve any children who are having instrumental lessons. Give the class a chance to find out how the different instruments work. You could use Benjamin Britten's *Young Person's Guide to the Orchestra* to listen to the various sounds of the orchestral instruments. Only listen to one section at a time and ask specific questions for the children to respond to. *Put up your hand when you hear a flute. Which instrument in this family* (woodwind) *sounds lower than a flute? Which sounds higher?* The children should be able to distinguish the different timbres of the strings, woodwind, brass and percussion families.

Dance to the beat

Make up a simple repeating pattern and play it on a tambour. Invite different children to move rhythmically to the pattern, creating short dance patterns as used in line dancing and as seen in pop music videos. Agree, together, on a series of dance patterns to fit the tambour beat. Learn them together and dance around the school hall. The children will love to change the patterns and the movements.

Music links

Try to link your music-making, as often as possible, with your project work. Find appropriate songs, encourage the children to create topic-based pieces of music, help them to write poems and short stories to be either set to music in song or accompanied with background sounds. A machine theme, for example, could ask for clock songs ('Grandfather's Clock' or 'Big Clocks Tick Quite Slowly' in *Flying a Round*) and short pieces of music created by small groups of children using the voice, body percussion and instruments, focusing on the sounds that different machines make (clunk, click, burr, crash). Help the children to notate their work in either graphic notation (picture form) or traditional notation (C D E). Clock songs could also link to work on telling the time. You could all listen to some of Haydn's *Clock Symphony* or 'The Syncopated Clock' by Leroy Anderson. Select the ideas that work for your children, put them together and you have a sound base for a performance to other classes or the whole school.

Developing key elements

Music from other cultures

Invite any group of players from another culture to perform to the children. A group playing Indian music would bring with them a tambura (plays the ostinato) a tabla drum (plays the accompaniment) and a sitar (plays the tune). The Beatles used the flavour of Indian music in their recording 'Sergeant Pepper's Lonely Hearts Club Band' and the children might enjoy listening to a little of this. A group visiting you from Greece might bring a bouzouki (plays the tune) and a lyra (plays the drone or repeating sound). 'Zorba's Dance' by Mikis Theodorakis gives a true flavour of Greece.

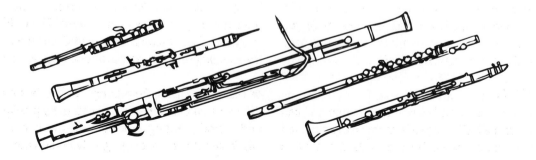

Looking at notation

Ask the children to look in their song books, hymn books and any music available to find and recognize the following musical notes:

They should also be asking why the notes are divided up into sections (bar lines). Explain that it makes music more manageable to do this and usually the sections all have the same number of beats (2, 3, 4). They could try mathematically to add up some of the notes in a bar to see if they all add up to the same, remembering that ♪♪ will make one beat.

Accompaniments

● Divide the class into small groups and give them the same four-line verse, an instrument set up in pentatonic scale (C D E G A) and an untuned instrument. Ask the groups first to clap the rhythm of the words, then create a tune, write it down, make up a simple accompaniment on the untuned instrument and, finally, to perform it to the class.

● Play and sing the round 'Row Your Boat' to a drone (repeating note) of Ds.

Body percussion signals

Use body percussion as signals to move children around the room. This will ensure that they are really listening to the sounds. Agree with the class that, say, one clap means stop, two clicks mean stand up, three knee slaps means turn around, four foot stamps means move forward. Use these signals to move groups through a series of obstacles.

Up and down

Sing with the children the carol 'Unto us a boy is born' and ask them to listen carefully to the music. The composer uses movement up and down very effectively . The folk song 'Early One Morning' uses this movement in a more flowing style. Find a copy of 'Goodnight Ladies' in the older song books and you will find the composer here begins the verse very slowly and then changes the tempo to quick as the chorus is sung. Have a good look with the class at the music of the songs you are singing. (An OHP or epidiascope is good for this.) *What do you notice about them? Which tunes move up and down? Do some move in steps?*

Bar lines

Use your duration flash cards to help the children find where the bar lines go in a rhythm. Use coloured straws as the bar lines. Put the cards in a random

rhythm in a line and read them from left to right. Decide to divide the beats into groups of three. Put the straws in the correct places. (You may have to move some cards to make sure that you have exactly three beats in a bar.) *Can you clap the rhythm?* It should fit in to a waltz time. Listen to any Strauss waltz to feel how the music is divided into threes.

Ideas bank

● With the children sitting in a circle, give each child a number between one and five – this is the number of beats they must clap. Begin with the person on your right clapping their beats, then the next person. Pass these varied number of sounds round the circle until it ends with you. Change the numbers and begin again.

● Make a card game and call it 'Instrumental Bingo'. Ask the children to draw or cut out pictures of orchestral instruments to glue on to an A5 card which has been divided like a bingo card. Record the sound of the orchestral instruments pictured (you could use very short extracts from *The Young Person's Guide to the Orchestra*). Play the tape and stop at random; players cover on the cards the instrument that has just been playing and the eventual winner becomes master of the tape.

● Play 'Add It On' by using a short spoken phrase, for example 'My mother went shopping', with the next person adding to it, for example 'and bought a [object of their choice]'. The next player repeats what has been said and adds another object. Each time the whole line has to be remembered. The children continue adding on until someone fails to remember the line. Now try the same idea but singing a line.

● Teach 'The Skye Boat Song' for the beauty of the words and the music, but also to help children understand phrasing. Ask them to try to sing the whole line (the phrase) using only one breath.

Assessment

The most important outcome of music-making with all children is that they should have enjoyed it. This should be extremely obvious at the end of a session since the children will be animated about what they have been doing as they move on to their next activity. However, there are many other observations to be made to help in your evaluation of the work they have done.

You should:
- encourage them to listen to sounds around them and the sounds they and others make on the instruments;
- ask for their opinion on all the music they hear;
- give them many opportunities to be creative in their music-making;
- let them perform as often as possible.

What can they do?

The children should be able to:
- listen attentively and collect sounds;
- recognize differences in sounds;
- recreate sounds;
- use sounds in a more structured way;
- respond through dance/drama and movement to sounds;
- discuss sounds;
- sing a wide variety of songs including two and three part rounds;
- play simple pieces on tuned and untuned instruments;
- play simple accompaniments;
- Have a greater awareness of pulse/beat;
- listen to longer pieces of music and remember them;
- use simple music terms in their discussions;
- use a form of graphic and traditional notation;
- use the letter names of notes to record and remember accompaniments as well as own compositions;
- use a pentatonic scale;
- use a wide variety of structures;
- discuss with growing confidence, using a music vocabulary.

Can they perform?

The music-making should be shared as much as possible with other children in the school, parents and friends. Everyone, not just the specialist performer, should be given a chance to perform. Look for abilities rather than disabilities – everyone can do something. Encourage those children who are having specialist lessons to demonstrate their skills to others by joining in whenever it is appropriate. School assemblies and school concerts should become a place for sharing successful activities.

Art

This year builds on the things which the children have explored and experienced in Year 3.

Experiences should cover the development of visual perception and the skills that are needed for investigation and making. The children should:

- record what has been experienced and imagined, expressing ideas with increasing confidence, representing chosen features of the world around them with developing accuracy;
- gather and use resources and materials and experiment with ideas in response to these;
- experiment, showing increasing control and using a range of tools, materials and techniques;
- reflect on and adapt work.

You should be introducing children to an increasing range of work by artists, designers and craftspeople. The children should:

- begin to recognize the work of artists, craftspeople and designers;
- begin to look at the intention and purpose behind works of art;
- begin to understand the historical and cultural context of works of art;
- respond to and evaluate their own art, craft and design and the art, craft and design of others, relating it to their own work.

What should they be able to do?

In Year 4, most children should develop control of an increasing range of materials and techniques. Most of them will have:

- experienced a range of graphic materials;
- experienced thick paint and watercolour;
- made prints, using found objects, press print, and possibly other methods;
- been introduced to collage, modelled and constructed in three dimensions;
- been introduced to the work of artists, craftspeople and designers.

Experimenting with new or unfamiliar tools and materials is still of paramount importance and you should enable children to make connections between this exploratory work and the finished product.

From about Year 4, children will become increasingly aware of reactions to their work from peers and adults. Unfortunately, you may find that this has the effect of making them less confident, so your encouragement is particularly important. It also helps to offer access to work by a range of artists and craftspeople which demonstrates that there is a variety of responses and that art is more than producing an accurate representation. Experiences in Year 4 should include:

- developing experience in the use of familiar tools and materials, and the introduction of new or more complex ways of working;
- continued work in the use pattern, texture, colour, line, tone, shape, form, space;
- visual communication and expression, using personal ideas and work from the imagination, stimulated by visits, events, stories, music and so on;
- developing their skill in the techniques of: drawing, painting, printing, collage, fabric work and work in three dimensions – working from memory and imagination;
- an introduction to imaginative and abstract images in the work of other artists, craftspeople and designers, including at least one example from a non-Western culture;
- opportunities to develop a vocabulary in art by talking about their own work and the work of others.

Children in Year 4 can take on increasing responsibility for organizing their own work.

Practical ideas

Working through the senses, particularly sight and touch, is of vital importance through all the stages. You should continue to develop the children's visual and tactile skills through increased opportunities to work from observation of real and interesting things brought into the classroom or through taking children outside to experience a place of visual or historical interest, locally or further afield. Ask open-ended questions and discuss what they have seen and discovered to stimulate interest and provide ideas and starting points which can be followed up in sketchbooks.

It is important that children at this age are given continuing opportunities and strategies for researching images and ideas from related books, videos and the computer so that they are informed and made aware through a variety of resources.

Starting points should sometimes be initiated by the child, coming from their own ideas and triggered by something they have read or an experience they have had. They should also be given the opportunity to work freely from their own ideas and imagination.

There should be opportunities for working on individual projects in art, in addition to working collaboratively or as a whole class.

Utilizing knowledge and experience which has been gained in Year 3, children in Year 4 should be encouraged to make choices and decisions about materials and the way in which they will respond to a challenge in two or three dimensions.

Continue to use graphics and painting computer software as another means of drawing, creating and changing patterns and exploring alternative combinations of colour by moving and dragging, cutting, copying and pasting. Children can produce their own drawings. Suitable software could include *RM Colour Magic*, *The Big Picture* and *Revelation 2*.

Making a start

Classroom environment

The whole classroom environment, from the pictures on the walls to the way in which the tools and materials are arranged and cared for, is part of the display and is a statement about the way in which children's work is viewed and valued. This, in fact, is a significant part of the teaching, and in Year 4 children should assume responsibility for organizing and maintaining the materials for art , craft and design.

A lively and rich learning environment where collections of visually exciting and tactile objects are brought in by the teacher and the children will stimulate curiosity and encourage an interest in, and response to, the world around. Encourage the children to be responsible for organizing and maintaining these collections. Written comments can usefully accompany the displays, particularly if they are presented in the form of a task or challenge. It is important that some displays are of work in three dimensions.

Tools and materials

Good quality tools and materials should be provided and children should be reminded of the need to care for them.

Brushes should be washed and stored with the bristles uppermost. Glue spreaders should be available for glue and stored away from the brushes. Water is best offered in shallow containers which are not easily knocked over. Paint, especially in readymix pots, can be quite an attractive feature if kept clean and stored tidily. Plastic sweetjars make good storage for coloured threads and small collage materials. These can also look attractive if the threads are sorted into colour families. The children can be similarly involved in sorting fabrics into small, open, plastic storage trays for future use in collage work or stitching activities. Flat trays also make good storage for watercolour boxes, packets of crayons or oil pastels. In Year 4 the children can be responsible for keeping the storage area tidy and can make labels, using the computer.

Images and artefacts as sources of ideas

● Encourage children to bring interesting objects and artefacts into the classroom themselves as this gives them a feeling of ownership. Additionally, collections of interesting items and artefacts can be borrowed from museums. These may relate specifically to a topic or theme and can be useful for extending children's experience. Through discussion, using open-ended questions, you can begin to help the children to discover the potential of images, artefacts and collections as a source of ideas for their own work.

If it is a picture, discuss the colours, the way the artist has worked, the mood and what is happening. If it is an artefact, ask them to look at the shape, colour and pattern and to consider and discuss the country of origin. If it is not valuable allow them to handle the object and encourage them to describe the design, shape and use. Initial responses could be recorded in a sketchbook using words and drawings. For example, items related to the theme of games might be brought in from a museum of childhood. These could be used for a variety of purposes. The children could respond by making a painting, drawing, print or collage, or by designing and making their own game.

Themes

Examples of themes offering potential for this age group could be:

● **Hobbies and pastimes**: surprisingly there are works of art which can be referred to in this context. Look at Renoir's *Luncheon of the Boating Party*, Degas' pictures of racehorses and ballet dancers, paintings of the circus by Seurat and by Chagall, Henri Rousseau's *Football Players*, Breughel's *Children's Games*, Cezanne's *The Card Players*. The following sections will refer to these themes and offer suggestions for working.

● **The elements**: there are many paintings to choose from which depict the elements. For example, you could look at Breughel's *Hunters in the Snow*, J M W

Turner's *A Shower* or *Buttermere Lake with Part of Crummock*, John Constable's *Salisbury Cathedral* or *Stonehenge with Rainbow*, Caspar David Friedrich's *Landscape with Rainbow*. Monet's *Cornstacks*, which is a series of paintings which he made in a variety of weather and light conditions, could also be useful. Link with work on weather in Geography (see page 107).

Developing key areas
Investigating and making

Expressive work based in real or imagined experiences and work from memory and imagination should all be offered in Year 4. Stories, music and drama are all good starting points and individual responses and ideas should be encouraged and shared.

Observational work from both natural and made forms and environments should be continued, for example, from pebbles, shells, feathers and other natural forms brought in by you or by children, or a collection of the items from the children's hobbies or favourite games. Exploration to find out what art tools and materials will do (sometimes through trial and error, and sometimes through guided discovery), combining materials and overlaying them, is an essential part of the art experience at all stages in children's development. It should be recognized and accepted as part of the process. You will also need to teach specific techniques .

Techniques

Drawing

● In Year 3, children should have had experience of the range of marks made with soft drawing pencils, charcoal, oil pastels, coloured chalks and so on. In Year 4, you can consolidate and extend this experience. Provide a range of graphic materials and encourage the children to experiment with them in their sketchbooks and to make informed choices about which is the appropriate material to use for the task. Linked to the theme of hobbies and pastimes, organize half the class to play games (board, dice or card games) and the other half to draw. Initially, the children could do a series of quick drawings in their sketchbooks and then straight afterwards do a drawing which gives an opportunity to use some of the effects which have been explored.

● Play some music, for example 'The Hebrides' (the overture also known as 'Fingal's Cave') by Mendelssohn or the 'Peer Gynt Suite', incidental music written by Grieg. Respond with pastels, charcoal or pencil. Try using paper in different sizes and shapes, for example a long strip of paper, or a circular piece. Listen to the music first and talk to the children before they work encouraging them to suggest different ways in which they could respond using the materials in a variety of ways and in combination. *What marks might you make if you heard a long continuous sound? What would you choose to make it with? Can you tell me why you would choose a ...?*

● Invite the children to bring in toys or sports equipment. They can then make large-scale observational drawings using charcoal and chalk on sugar paper.

Painting

● By Year 4, children should have had experiences of colour mixing and of different consistencies of paint. Linked to the theme of the elements, build on these experiences by working with cool and warm colours. In their sketchbooks suggest mixing a range of colours for a rainy day and a warm sunny day. Promote discussion about the reasons for choosing a particular range of colours. Talk also about how they feel on a rainy day and on a sunny day. This could develop into a figurative or an abstract painting.

● Look at Kandinsky's improvisations, semi-abstract paintings inspired by landscape painted in brilliant rainbow colours. Talk about the colours of the rainbow (ROYGBIV). *What is the difference between indigo and violet?* Children can then make their own rainbow paintings, representational or abstract.

● Linked to the theme of hobbies and pastimes, show the children a reproduction of Cezanne's *The Card Players*. Talk about the brush strokes (which are quite distinct). They could paint the upper part of someone playing a board game. You can combine this with a maths lesson so that the children being painted are genuinely playing a maths game rather than just posing. Pay particular attention to the way in which they put on the paint and the direction of the brush strokes. You could try mixing a little PVA

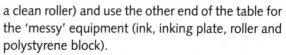

glue with the paint which could then be applied with a spatula or small piece of stiff card. Sketchbooks would be a good place to experiment with the technique before beginning on the picture. It is a good idea when working with thick paint to draw with chalk rather than pencil, as the chalk makes broader marks more compatible with larger brushes and thick paint.

Printing

● Develop the skills of press print. Use the small rectangular pieces of polystyrene as in Year 3, but the children can cut up the block so that it is in the shape of the object to be printed, for example just a boot kicking a ball. They can cut these shapes in the polystyrene with scissors or, under close supervision, with a hot wire. Note that the small polystyrene trays found in supermarkets are *not* suitable as the surface is usually sealed for hygienic reasons and this resists the paint. The type used for printing can be obtained from county supplies, and comes in square sheets which can easily be cut on the Rotatrim.

● Print-making can be a messy process unless it is done in a methodical way:

◗ Take a piece of black sugar paper and fold it into eight sections. The polystyrene block should be cut to fit into a section.

◗ Cover a table with paper. Keep clean things on one end of the table (the paper for printing on and

a clean roller) and use the other end of the table for the 'messy' equipment (ink, inking plate, roller and polystyrene block).

◗ Draw round the items of equipment when they are in position and ask the children to replace them in the drawn outline. This prevents ink, particularly from the roller, from getting everywhere.

◗ Tear some rectangles of newspaper larger than the printing block and place the block on the newspaper when inking up. The newspaper can then be thrown away leaving a clean space.

◗ Take a rectangle of perspex about A4 size and squeeze a small amount of white water-based printing ink at the top. Using the roller spread the ink up and down and from side to side. It should be thinly spread and have a suede-like appearance. Transfer the ink to the printing block using the inked-up roller.

◗ Pick up the inked block and place it ink side down on to the first section on the paper. Use a clean roller to roll on the back. Gently remove the block. Repeat this process for all sections.

● Colour mixing of the inks can be encouraged or the first image can be over-printed with another colour. It is probably more effective if the first colour is lighter in tone than the second but the children can experiment with this in their sketchbooks and talk about the results. When the print is dry, it can also be worked into, using oil pastels.

Collage

● Cover the tables with newspaper. Provide paper, scissors, glue and spreaders, and a selection of materials. Ask the children to create a games board for a blind person. Emphasize the feel of the collage pieces, for example black could be furry, white could be smooth. Use PVA glue which dries transparent.

● For a Weather theme, you could make a rainy/cold/frosty collage. Provide paper, scissors, glue and spreaders and a range of materials. The picture could be scanned into the computer and developed further using a paint programme. An example of this can be found in *Children's Art and the Computer* by K Mathieson (Hodder & Stoughton).

● Use collage for volcano pictures – perhaps on a black paper background.

Modelling

Challenge the children to work in pairs to design and make a 3-D game, for example, a marble run using tubes as runways. This can be combined with work in design and technology. The resulting game can then be painted using pattern and bright colours. This could possibly be based on the variety of patterns found in a collection of marbles.

Vocabulary

● Continue to build on previously learned vocabulary. Emphasize words like 'looking' and 'seeing', 'analysing', 'imagining', 'designing', and relate them to work in progress.

● Look at the drawings of Claes Oldenberg for his enormous soft sculptures. This would offer opportunities to discuss the ways in which he used drawing as a means of designing. Following on from this, involve the children in designing fantasy ideas based on observational drawings of everyday things.

● Generate opportunities to relate this and previously learned vocabulary to the work of artists, craftspeople and designers.

● Give the children opportunities to make links and comparisons between art and artefacts and their own work. Encourage them to express their feelings and support their views.

● Introduce the vocabulary relating to an extended range of art and design forms, 'mobiles' and 'mixed media', for example.

Sketchbooks

The National Curriculum suggests working with sketchbooks at KS2 and by Year 4 children should have developed a number of strategies for using them and be aware of a number of purposes, including experimenting with different tools and materials, recording observations, and developing ideas or designs.

For more information about how to make sketchbooks in different ways and use them effectively as a tool for learning, look at *Sketchbooks: Explore and Store,* by G Robinson (Hodder & Stoughton).

The elements of art

● Make opportunities for experimentation with the elements of art: line, colour, shape, pattern, texture, form. It is seldom that a work of art has only one element in its make up and children will usually be involved in working with several of the elements in one challenge or project. Look at volcanoes – Montserrat, for example. In this context you can explore line, texture and colour. Floods, waterfalls and caves would also offer a range of opportunities. The children can experiment in their sketchbooks.

● Encourage them to recognize the elements of art in the work of other artists, craftspeople and designers and to apply this knowledge to their own work; looking at colour and line in artists' work and responding to it by using it vigorously in their own to express feelings, for example. In Year 4, they can begin to analyse aspects of artists' work, comparing and contrasting materials, techniques and imagery.

Reviewing

Try to find time to sit alongside children so that they can talk about and evaluate their own work, finding something positive to say about it. From opportunities to discuss their work children will learn to reflect on it, to modify it and suggest new ideas. It is also an opportunity to reinforce vocabulary related, for example, to new experiences, elements, tools or techniques. Encourage the use of words to discuss, describe, analyse, compare, contrast, communicate and express feelings and thoughts naturally.

Knowledge and understanding

● In addition to books about individual artists, the following books are helpful as a general reference to get some idea of the range of artists' work available: *The Art Book, The Modern Art Book* and *The Pop Art Book,* all published by Phaidon. (*The Art Book* is now available cheaply in a small format volume.) Introduce the children to a range of different artists and to three-dimensional forms.

● If you know a lively local artist who would be willing to come into the classroom, this would be a great stimulus.

● The education departments of the main galleries in London are very helpful if you are planning a visit or want information about artists relating to a specific theme.

● Collect postcard reproductions (ask parents to contribute) in a photograph album and put it in the book corner.

● Encourage children to describe a variety of images and artefacts, to voice likes and dislikes and make choices about which they like best. This can take place through whole-class discussions, group work or spontaneously on an individual basis.

● Developing key areas
Recording from experience, observation and imagination

Remember that the children are not making an exact copy. They are looking intently and noticing things which they had not noticed before. They also feel challenged at this stage by an insistence on exact representation. However, looking is still a vital skill to be encouraged.

● Arrange a group of objects, for example jugs and pots, so that some are further away than others and are partly one behind the other. Talk about how this might be approached in a drawing by looking very hard at what can actually be seen. This could lead to interesting discussions about the Cubist artists, such as Braque and Picasso and the way they represented objects from more than one viewpoint.

● Talk about near, middle distance, far away. This can be done in conjunction with artists' paintings (those by Poussin, for example) in which distance is a feature. Take the children outside with their sketchbooks. Draw something far away, something nearer and something very close. Allow five minutes for each drawing. Come back into the classroom and use the drawings to make a composition.

● Use images of different sizes from magazines to create a collage which shows the way in which things appear smaller as they recede.

Evidence of success
The children should have developed:
❱ an ability to concentrate and observe carefully;
❱ an awareness of visual depth;
❱ an ability to use receding tones;
❱ a developing ability to extend and develop exploratory work from the sketchbook;
❱ an ability to select and make decisions.

Images and artefacts as sources of ideas

● Look at symbols and imagery relating to the elements.

● Investigate deities and figures from mythology relating to the elements, for example, the Aztec sun god; Surya, the Hindu sun god; Thor, god of thunder; Taru, the Hittite weather god (or the sun itself or the sun worshipped as a god). Zeus, the king of the gods in Greek mythology, was known to the Greeks as the weather god. Ask the children to imagine Zeus commanding the elements.

Evidence of success
The children should demonstrate:
❱ interest and motivation;
❱ a personal response;
❱ visual and tactile awareness;
❱ an ability to use descriptive vocabulary;
❱ inventiveness;
❱ an ability to use initial stimulus to generate ideas.

Tools, materials, techniques and the visual elements

● Ask the children to make observational drawings of things which move, for example animals, people involved in sport, their friends playing in the playground. Talk to them about how they will need to look hard, to remember the form, to draw quickly and to go on to another drawing when the subject moves. Remind them that the animal or person may well return to the same position enabling further drawing to take place.

● Ask the children to use drawing as a means of designing, creating fantasy images from their imagination. The designs can then be drawn with transfer crayons and ironed to transfer the image to fabric. These images can then be developed, either using a sewing machine with the feed-dog down or by hand stitching.

● With selected fabrics, recreate a picture or scene from close observation, or another stimulus such as emotions or thoughts.

● Make a rubbing, from bark for example, and recreate the rubbing using yarn.

● Model a figure or animal in movement. Use clay and base the sculpture on previous drawings of figures in movement. If you have access to a camera, the children could also take photographs. Remember that, in sculpture, visual information is needed for all sides of the object or figure.

Evidence of success

The children should demonstrate:
▶ a willingness to try new tools and techniques;
▶ a personal response and use of imagination;
▶ an ability to build on previous experience;
▶ involvement and concentration;
▶ manual dexterity in the manipulation of materials and threads;
▶ the use of appropriate descriptive and critical vocabulary;
▶ an ability to reflect on work done and make appropriate changes.

Artists, craftspeople and designers

● Build on the drawings which they have made from people or animals moving. Ask them to plan in their sketchbooks, a composition which would include moving figures or animals. Show them Degas' pictures of racehorses and ballet dancers. Look at Henri Rousseau's *Football Players* and Breughel's *Children's Games*.

● Show some examples of artists who have responded to the expressive nature of the elements, for example, look at Hiroshige's *The Wave*. The children could paint their own big wave pictures.

● Look at symbols which have been traditionally used for the weather. Design a weather vane using some of these. The children will also be involved in designing their own lettering for the points of the compass. You might even find that you have a craftsman in your area who makes these.

Evidence of success

The children should demonstrate:
▶ an ability to reflect on previous work and to make decisions about ways in which it can be extended and developed;
▶ an ability to choose from a range of possible tools and materials;
▶ a willingness to experiment;
▶ increasing knowledge of the work of a range of artists and craftspeople;
▶ an ability to apply the knowledge to make links with their own work.

Responding and describing

● Look at paintings of storms. Some of Turner's paintings of storms at sea or the expressionist seascapes of Emil Nolde which are full of brooding

and mood would be appropriate. Ask *What kind of weather/day/year is it? How can you tell? What would it feel like to be in the painting?* The children can experiment to find combinations of colours, marks and textures to create a feeling of storm. Try using different tools to create effects in paint – sponges, sticks, card, spatulas, fingers. Invent your own tool. The outcome of this could be a large, energetic storm painting or collage.

● Imagine what it would be like to be the rescuer or someone rescued by a lifeboat. Ask the children to describe the sounds and smells. Play Benjamin Britten's 'Sea Interludes', the storm sequence in Peter Grimes or Mendelssohn's 'Fingal's Cave', for example.

Talk to the children about the expressive use of materials. *What colours would you select? What textures would you choose? Would you use paint or collage or charcoal?*

Evidence of success
The children should demonstrate:
❱ an ability to experiment with tools and materials to create expressive marks;
❱ the use of previous experience of colour mixing;
❱ an ability to respond imaginatively;
❱ communication skills and art vocabulary;
❱ personal motivation and response;
❱ independent thinking.

Special occasions
Decorations
Introduce the children to mobiles. These could be linked to the work on the themes of Weather or Games. For example, mobiles based on rainbows, representational or abstract, or including players and equipment for a favourite sport. Probably the most difficult part of making a mobile is deciding how to suspend the component parts. Try using a small bound hoop, for example those used for lampshade-making. Linked to the work on the weather theme, various elements – cloud, rain (droplets hanging on thin cotton) rainbows and sun – could be designed by the children.

The children can work in small groups with each child taking responsibility for one element to produce a complete weather mobile.

Greeting cards
● The children can use pieces of work they have done in different media, or a new version, based on previous work, in an appropriate size. These look effective if mounted in a 'window' cut in the front of the card. Offer different sizes and colours of card for children to choose from.

● Birthday cards could relate to the recipient's favourite game or sport: a card cut in the shape of a ball, bat, racquet; a series of sketches of people playing the game; an aerial view. Encourage children to find new ways to use the theme to make an effective card.

● Children can choose collage, drawing, paint or print for cards with a seasonal weather theme. Ask *What colours will you choose?* Print enables them to produce a series of cards from one design.

● An image stitched from an observational drawing, mounted on a piece of card, with a message underneath, can be something a little different.

● Ask questions such as *Where will you put the message? What will you use to write it – coloured ink or crayon? Could you find a way of printing it? Or you might use the computer? Which font would you choose? Could you write a poem?*

● Or questions like: *How will you fold your card? Vertically? Horizontally? Can you find a new way to fold it? In three? Zig-zag? Can you make a pop-up card?*

● The children can print their own wrapping paper and design gift tags.

Display

Display is one of the ways in which we evaluate children's work.
● Try to involve the children as much as possible in making decisions about the way in which their work is displayed. They can use the computer to make simple labels for the display.

● Encourage the children to mount their own work.

● Try to include everybody's work in the display.

● Sometimes a 'pavement show', laying out the work on the hall floor, for example, or pinning it up quickly so that it can be celebrated and talked about immediately, is a valuable way of building on the children's experiences and making teaching points while the experience is still fresh in their minds. Involve the children in making positive observations about each other's work at this time. This helps the children to identify their developing skills and to use art-based vocabulary to describe them.

Assessment

In Year 4, children will be increasingly concerned about their drawings looking representational. You will need to take this into account when evaluating their work. It is important to respond sensitively to the questions they ask, the things they say, what they do and what they give us, whatever stage they are at. However, it is also important to discuss with them ways in which their work might develop using different methods and materials, for example, using print and textiles.

A vital consideration in any evaluation of outcomes in art is respect for personal and cultural identity, particularly as art should be instrumental in developing self-confidence. It is also important to develop positive attitudes to art through praise, help and encouragement. The beginnings of peer group evaluation are to be encouraged with an emphasis on the importance of positive comments. For example: *I like the way Liam has introduced mixed media into his work* or *I like the way in which this piece of work has developed into an abstract piece.*

It is possible to evaluate some of the following aspects of the children's art endeavours at this stage:

- How have they used what we have given them?
- What have they done and what are they trying to do?
- What evidence do you see of independent thinking and personal ideas?
- Have they begun to research for their own reference and resource materials?
- Have they been willing to experiment?
- Are they developing an increasing knowledge of how tools and materials behave?
- Have the materials been used in an imaginative way?
- Have they built on previous experience of colour mixing?
- Have they learned a new skill/technique?
- Are they beginning to experiment with combining techniques?
- Are they becoming more aware of art, artists, galleries?
- Have they learned about art from another country/culture/period?
- Are they growing more confident?
- Can they make a personal response?
- Are they motivated and involved?
- Can they work independently/co-operatively?
- Can they talk about their own and each others' work, using appropriate vocabulary?

Physical Education

Children in Year 4 need a wide variety of movement experiences on a regular basis to use and enjoy their rapidly growing movement confidence and competence. In most schools, however, PE is timetabled only two or three times a week, so you will need to decide when the six activity areas of PE are taught and for how long. You will need to ensure that you teach a balance of the three core activities (gymnastics, games and dance) throughout the year.

The length of each PE lesson may vary, but you would expect a minimum of 30 minutes' activity for each session. For the purposes of this chapter, it is assumed that one unit of work (approximately half a term) for athletics and outdoor and adventurous activities will be included in Year 4, although swimming may also be one of the activities which are included for your class.

Whatever their previous experience of PE, the majority of children will be keen and eager to please, but they will require a consistent, firm and supportive environment in order to use their energies in purposeful and positive ways. You will need to explain and establish your own special routine and arrangements for this area of the curriculum (changing, lining up and going to the hall or playground). A mention in the school brochure and a notice on the classroom door will help to remind your class and their carers what clothes to bring and when.

Ensure that children are involved in the processes of planning, performing and evaluating their work and extend opportunities to develop other aspects of their learning (language, mathematics, personal and social development) within, through or related to the practical physical activities described later in this chapter.

What should they be able to do?

First some general expectations. *There will be vast differences in experience, interest, physique, temperament, attitude and effort when the children come into your class.* Whatever their previous experience, they may still need some reminders to move safely in a large space with others, on equipment or with apparatus, although they should be much more aware and independent than

in their first years of schooling. They should be able to discuss the reasons for changing into suitable clothing for each activity and should be encouraged to get ready quickly and independently and help others.

Throughout the year, all children should show increasing control and awareness when performing basic actions. Many will be agile and energetic and have a wide range of actions which they can perform successfully. They will enjoy the challenge of learning new skills, some more easily and with greater control than others. They should be developing their ability to clarify or refine their actions (for example make

a shape clearer, use their whole body) when asked to do so, or when working with a partner. Watch for some children who may need particular encouragement or those who need additional challenges. Most children will be able to combine actions (for example, link a number of movements in gym or dance; dodge an opponent and pass a ball to a partner), some more fluently and easily than others.

They will begin to make links between PE and work in the classroom on the heart and 'my body' and understand more about how their body reacts to exercise (for example, heart beating faster because of the need for oxygen). As the year progresses you will notice that they will be able to sustain energetic activity for longer periods, although this will vary tremendously from one individual to another.

Although the sequence of progression through the stages of motor development is similar for most children they do not progress at the same rate or at an even rate and so there will always be a wide range of differences in the ways children in your class achieve various actions/movements. This is natural as every child is unique. Observe and enjoy the actions and progress of each child and continue to create an atmosphere of success, fun, satisfaction and support.

Key area: Dance

Depending on their previous experiences, most children will show a variety of expressive qualities and will begin to show greater sensitivity in their movements. They will be able to explore and demonstrate contrasts in movement, if differences in shape, size, direction, level and speed are exaggerated.

They will be able to isolate and use different body parts and will be able to use them to gesture, travel, support their body weight or to lead movement as they explore different shapes and body positions. Most children will be able to do this in time with different forms of accompaniment (sounds, music), recognizing and responding to changes in rhythm and phrasing. As you would expect, there will be great variations in the ways that they do this, some demonstrating more improvements in timing and rhythm than others. Most children will enjoy dancing and will be able to move confidently, with increasing co-ordination. Some will still need encouragement to create and clarify motifs or phrases of movement and to link them into a sequence, whether individually, with a partner or in a small group. They will develop more awareness of group and partner relationships and be able to observe their partner or others and comment on how a pattern or phrase of movement was performed.

Develop links with other areas of the curriculum and encourage the children to use their imaginations. A clear stimulus or focus will help. They should be able to capture moods or qualities with increasing clarity as they interpret words, music and ideas in their actions or gestures. Watch for their ideas; develop and use some of them to feed in new suggestions to others in the class. By the end of the year, most children will show an increasing ability to observe and repeat short phrases of movement with varying degrees of accuracy and fluency, and contribute ideas of their own. They will demonstrate increasing body awareness when performing a variety of travelling, turning and jumping actions and should be able to include other actions like scurry, linger or whirl as their movement vocabulary increases. They should be encouraged to side-step

and skip, or make up their own step patterns, and most of them will be able to do this rhythmically and continuously in time to music. As a group in a large space, they should be developing their ability to use the space thoughtfully and well, using a variety of pathways (figure of eight, curving, straight, zig-zag), and showing increasing awareness of their own personal space (in front and behind).

They should be better able to describe their actions to others and should begin to explain what they liked or found interesting about the movements of others. They will be able to discuss ideas and make simple comments and judgements which will help them to work on improving the quality and precision of their dancing. Encourage your class to express their own ideas in response to the tasks set and so help them to expand their vocabulary of movement ideas.

Key area: Gymnastics

Most children will be agile and adventurous and keen to participate in gymnastics and use the large apparatus. Although some may still need encouragement, others may need reminders to be more cautious and aware of others. They will need time to try out and practise their gymnastics actions on the floor (jumping, rolling, moving on hands and feet, balancing) selecting and inventing appropriate movements for different themes before trying them on different parts or arrangements of the large apparatus.

They will be able to use and perform accurately a variety of jumping, hopping and stepping patterns and should be encouraged to practise them when warming up (for example from one foot to two feet, two feet to two feet). Encourage the children to work on the quality of these actions, to improve their leaping and to clarify different patterns of jumps and hops. They will be able to land more confidently and safely from their jumps and some will make clear shapes in the air before they land.

Children will be increasingly able to move about the floor and apparatus in a variety of ways using their feet, hands and feet, and other body parts. Throughout the year, help and expect them to show increasing control and awareness of their actions as they explore the various possibilities which are presented to them in their lessons. Encourage them to be inventive and imaginative in response to tasks and suggestions. They should be able to balance with increasing confidence and control in a variety of positions holding still, clear shapes (wide, thin, tucked, twisted) on large and small parts of their bodies (sides, tummy, shoulders, seat, one foot, or head, hand and foot).

Give them opportunities in nearly every lesson to take their weight on their hands (all fours, two hands and one foot, bunny jump or cat spring) so that they will begin to develop strength in their upper bodies. Check that hands are flat on the floor and arms are straight as they hold still shapes or move on their hands and feet (for example while bunny jumping or walking on all fours). They will also use their hands to hold on to, climb, hang and pull themselves along on the apparatus.

Most children will be able to share the space and apparatus with others considerately, but some will still need help and reminders to do so,

particularly where there is some favourite apparatus. Many will use the large apparatus confidently but should be encouraged to clarify their actions while answering the tasks set. Help them to develop a greater awareness of what they are doing and how they can improve their own performance through observation, demonstration, review and practice. They will be able to link several actions (for example: jump, roll and balance) into a short sequence with increasing fluency and understand some ways in which they might do this more smoothly, with clear starting and finishing positions.

Teach, then check, that all children have the opportunity to use all pieces of apparatus over a series of lessons and share the responsibility of setting it out and putting it away. Insist that children lift and carry equipment efficiently and safely.

Key area: Games

Most children will be energetic and keen to participate in games. They should be aware of the space and others as they play, but they will still need reminders to use the space well. Running, chasing and dodging games will provide opportunities for them to practise and improve their ability to stop, start and change direction quickly and nimbly.

They should be able to roll, tap, bounce, throw, or kick a ball with accuracy towards a still (or slowly moving) target (between skittles, into a hoop, to a partner, or between markings on the floor or wall). Most will be able to do this (or can be challenged to try) in more difficult circumstances (a smaller target, from further away, with less preparation time). They should be able to pass a ball accurately to a partner using hands and feet (stationary and on the move) and encouraged to signal and pass ahead into the space. All children should be able to receive a ball (or quoit or beanbag) with their hands in different ways (two hands, one hand, high, low) thrown by themselves or a partner. In small-sided invasion games (3v1, 2v3) many will be able to run into the space to receive the ball and pass to a team-mate avoiding the opposition. The majority will also be able to bounce a ball (large, medium or small) and dribble it with one hand while moving in different directions to avoid the opposition. Many will be able to use a bat in different situations with increasing consistency and success.

They should be given lots of opportunities to co-operate in small groups (pairs, threes or fours) to make up their own games. As they do so, they will show an increasing ability to negotiate, plan and discuss ideas with others. They will be able to invent simple rules for their games (take turns to start the game, scoring). They will be able to work at the consistency and accuracy of their skills and will be able to identify what can be done to improve their performance.

Encourage your class to take responsibility for looking after the equipment, and putting it out and away. (It is helpful if it is colour coded so that each colour group can check the contents of their own baskets.)

Practical ideas

⟡ Making a start

Dance

Starting the lesson

Try different ways to start your dance lessons:

⟩ moving, shaking, bending, stretching different parts of the body; matching a partner's sequence with step patterns and arm actions;

⟩ follow-my-leader phrases to practise and refine travelling actions (skipping, side-stepping, creeping, striding) with various forms of accompaniment (percussion, music or voice);

⟩ using phrases of 16 or 8 beats. Try different directions (8 one way, 8 another) and variations (striding forwards, tip-toeing backwards), encourage them to respond to the rhythm and gradually raise the heart beat. Children will enjoy doing this to popular tunes or disco music.

Phrases of movement

Within the context of the theme or focus for each lesson, work with the children to build individual motifs or phrases of movement, individually, in pairs or in small groups. Encourage them to vary the level, (high, medium, low), shape and direction (sideways, diagonally, up and down) of their actions and to vary their pathways (straight, curving, round-a-bout, zig-zag). They will be able to choose their own starting and finishing positions to help them compose and perform simple dances with clear beginnings, middles and ends.

Ending the lesson

Encourage relaxation and a cool down by using music for slow walking or stretching or simply calm music to sit or lie and listen to at the end of every lesson.

Gymnastics

Focus or theme

Encourage and help children to think carefully about their actions by selecting a focus or theme for their attention. Whatever the theme chosen, they should try out ideas in the floorwork part of the lesson and then try them on the apparatus.

Organization of apparatus

Children will need to be taught to handle and use the apparatus carefully – emphasize the safety factors:

⟩ divide the class into five or six groups (to ensure all children have a range of experiences and to help spacing);

⟩ each group should be responsible for handling the same apparatus each lesson (change over each half term);

⟩ make a plan of the apparatus to be used, which will support the theme;

⟩ establish a fair and logical pattern of rotation of groups (for example, zig-zag, clockwise, or straight swap if there are groups with similar apparatus) so that, over a period of several lessons, the children can explore fully each group of apparatus in turn (have a maximum of two apparatus changes in one lesson);

⟩ teach each group how to get out their apparatus (positioning to carry it, bending knees not back, all looking in direction of carrying apparatus) and where to put it (use chalk marks initially to help indicate the positioning of apparatus);

⚡ check apparatus fixings and placement before it is used;

⚡ establish ground rules (for example, working quietly and considerately, making use of the spaces);

⚡ insist on a quiet working atmosphere, but discuss why with the children;

⚡ encourage children to share space and equipment, particularly when there is limited apparatus;

⚡ establish a consistent routine for stopping, coming down and sitting away from the apparatus.

Children will enjoy the responsibility of lifting and carrying the apparatus and co-operating with their group to make sure it is carefully and safely placed and checked by you and them.

Games

Travelling actions

Use a variety of travelling actions (walk, jog, run, hop, jump, gallop, skip, or stride) to practise stopping, starting, and changing direction (sideways, backwards). Start on the spot or moving slowly and gradually speed up the changes so that children develop the ability to respond quickly and to sustain activity for longer periods.

Class games

Use a variety of class games to start and/or finish the lesson. Start with those with which some children are familiar, for example Tag games, and gradually introduce new ones which involve dodging and marking (for example, 2v1 Pass Ball). This will encourage listening, quick responses to your stop and start commands and will give the children the opportunity to become more aware of the space and others as they dodge and move.

Equipment

● Establish safe and careful use of equipment by teaching the children to take responsibility for putting it out and putting it away. When playing in pairs or groups check that spare equipment has been returned to the baskets.

● Children will be familiar with a variety of equipment, but they still need lots of practice to use it in different ways effectively and skilfully. Allow some time to consolidate skills by including a short practice time specifying the activity or apparatus. (Select from rolling, stopping, retrieving, collecting, aiming, catching, throwing, kicking, passing and hoop, rope, ball, or quoit).

● Introduce individual challenges within a chosen or specified activity. *How many? Can you beat your own record?*

● Develop shared, co-operative challenges (for example, *with a partner, how many?*). Provide opportunities for made-up games in pairs or threes using a specified action (for example, passing, catching or bouncing). This will allow children to be inventive, use their initiative and share ideas as they discuss and negotiate with a partner or small group. Give them time and help as they practise and consolidate their selected actions. They will thus become more aware of some of the fundamentals of games play in a situation in which they are in control, and not feel inadequate as they may do when they are trying ideas which are imposed upon them. These challenges and made-up games meet the National Curriculum suggestions for improving skills and understanding and playing small-sided games.

🏮 Developing key areas

Dance

Themes

● To give children the opportunity to create, plan, modify and present dance ideas in different forms and structures, provide a wide range of experiences to stimulate dance. Use classroom topics or themes or simple movement ideas as starting points for several lessons. (How many will depend on the topic and the experience and interest of the class, but at this stage children should be able to sustain their interest and develop their ideas over a series of lessons.)

● Use language and imagery to help focus on the particular movement qualities of the chosen stimulus. Stress and develop the qualities of each action rather than 'being' a particular animal or object (for example, bird = hovering, swooping, circling and settling).

Machines

Suggest a chocolate-making machine, perhaps after reading *Charlie and the Chocolate Factory*.

● Explore and discuss key words associated with machines (for example, 'pistons', 'cogs' and 'wheels') and key actions involved in chocolate making (for example mixing, pouring, flattening, pressing, cutting). Focus on movement qualities (for example strong, direct, firm, quick or slow) using parts or the whole body (pressing, jerking, punching) to simulate machine actions. Try lots of marching, jumping and bending, first individually and then in pairs (action/reaction: one up, one down, one arm forward, one back), then develop jobs for parts of the machine (slicing and cutting, pressing and squashing, kneading and chopping). Over a series of lessons, develop into a group, and possibly a whole-class dance following the complete process of making chocolates (or sweets).

Fairground

Select aspects to explore. For example:
▶ crowds: walking, pausing, rushing, turning, queuing, watching;
▶ hall of mirrors: the children mirroring your shapes and actions then a partner's, changing shapes, growing and shrinking, jerky and smooth, laughing and pointing;
▶ ghost train: rhythm and pathway, making a tunnel, frightening things appearing and vanishing, skeletons, monsters;

▶ roundabout: rising, falling, motif or action, high and low, circle formation;
▶ coconut shy: aiming/throwing action; a miss, a miss, success!

Weather

Select aspects to explore and develop key action words and qualities. For example:
▶ rain: pitter-patter, drip drop, drizzle, splashing, gushing, pouring, puddles, floods;
▶ wind: blowing, gusting, settling, whooshing;
▶ frost: jagged, sharp, frozen, patterns on the floor and rooftops;
▶ fog: spreading, smothering, settling slowly.
Develop contrasting ideas over a series of lessons or select a few ideas to expand in greater depth. Link with work on weather in Geography (see page 107).

Gymnastics

Use a focus or theme as the main objective of the lesson to help children develop their ability to think about their movements and to become more aware of the different ways they can use their bodies.

Turning, spinning and travelling

Turning or spinning involves the rotation of the whole body, often moving to face a new direction simultaneously. Although the three axes, vertical (head to feet) sagittal (side to side) and horizontal (back to front) can be introduced, it is easier for children to focus on turning on their feet (spin on one foot, turning jump); turning on their hands and feet (front support to back support, cartwheel); turning using the body (side rolls, forward or backward rolls). On apparatus, encourage children to roll around poles or bars, to move off apparatus with a change of direction, to arrive on the apparatus having changed direction.

To develop cartwheels, encourage turning bunny jumps, bringing the feet down to the side together. Then encourage sideways movement using hands one after the other (right, left) followed by feet one after the other (left, right). Later encourage wide shapes and regular rhythm. Encourage attempts at a backward roll by starting from a curled shoulder-stand, twisting the knees to side over the shoulder and rolling over on to the knees (feet).

Balancing — like and unlike parts

To develop the idea of teaching different ways of balancing, focus on like and unlike parts taking the weight of the body and develop the children's control by encouraging the tension necessary to hold a still shape on an increasingly small base. Focus on using like parts (shoulders, two feet, two hands) and then develop different combinations using unlike parts (shoulders and foot, knee and hand). Use travelling actions to help link the balances so that ideas can be linked fluently in a short sequence.

Twisting and travelling

Twisting involves part of the body facing a new direction while another part remains fixed or facing the original direction. Encourage twisting, holding still twisted shapes, or twisting and then turning or twisting and uncoiling. Use travelling actions to link two or more twisted movements (for example twist and hold, untwist and travel, twist and uncoil).

Body shapes in balance and travel

Focus on the shape of each movement or balance by encouraging a variety of twisted, stretched wide, stretched long or thin and curled shapes or actions. It is possible to choose two or three of the shapes and join them with travelling actions to link in an action sequence both on the floor and on apparatus.

Games

Striking/fielding games

Examples of these include French Cricket, Non-stop Cricket or Rota Rounders in groups of four. Ensure each player has a turn to use the bat, to bowl or to field (x2), and that the turns are fair.

Teach and practise under- and overarm throwing with accuracy, and catching from longer distances. Practise striking (use a T-ball base and padder tennis bat to begin with). First encourage strikers to try co-operatively to hit the ball into the hands of the bowler. Later encourage them to aim the ball past the fielders into spaces, while fielders begin to judge where the ball is likely to go and practise retrieving it quickly and returning it accurately.

Invasion games

Examples of these include 2v2 or 3v3 Skittle Ball without a skittle guard. This is a game of Pass Ball aiming to knock down the opposing team's skittle without entering a 2m-diameter chalk circle round the skittle. Teams can use a third or a sixth of a netball court. Encourage the children to practise:
▶ passing to partner on the move – emphasize throwing ahead for partner to move to;

▶ different dodges (sprint and stop, sudden change of direction) – encourage moving into a space to receive the ball;

▶ in different contexts (for example, with a shinty stick, bouncing and passing, using an oval ball or using feet).

Making up games

Introduce making up a game which uses set pieces of equipment (for example, ball and cones; a bat, a ball and a hoop) or which includes specific skills (for example, bouncing and passing). Provide some guidelines, allocate spaces and size of group and help children to make rules, devise a scoring system and shape the game. Once they have been created and possibly modified, games can be described and introduced to others.

Introducing new key areas

Athletics

Ancient Greeks and the Olympics

Four activities can provide the basis for a unit of work which will bring alive the study of the Ancient Greeks:

▶ a short sprint: called a *Stade* run (one length of the stadium). Use about 40m or the length of a netball court. *Diaulos* were two lengths of the

stadium. Introduce the Greek word *apite* for 'go', and the term 'starting from scratch', which originally was a line marked in sand;

▶ a standing jump: without weights and then with weights (*halteres*);

▶ an underarm throw (*linear*): throw a beanbag into a hoop, and gradually increase the distance from the hoop. Encourage step and follow through. **Safety:** Make sure everyone throws and then collects at the same time;

▶ a longer run: called a *dolichos* (long-distance foot race). Use, for example, 4x80m or 4x60m. Run around a cone or 'turning gate'.

Include opportunities for the children to write about running, jumping and throwing in their topic work.

10-step award scheme

This award scheme has been devised to involve all children (including those with special needs) in a variety of athletic activities. Seven of the activities are introduced here as examples. Introduce patterns of hops and jumps (for example step, hop, hop; jump, hop, hop; step, hop, hop) individually or as a follow-my-leader activity before introducing the specific jumping actions which are part of the 10-step award scheme. Children can work in six groups trying two different activities each week (for example, a jump and a turn, a jump and a throw). Allow time for lots of practice and lots of trials, with the children taking responsibility for setting up the equipment and timing, measuring and recording.

▶ a standing long jump: stress the swing of arms and leaning forward into the jump;

▶ three spring jumps: three continuous standing long jumps;

▶ obstacle pick up: five beanbags placed at two-metre intervals are picked up and returned, one at a time, to the start; timing ends when all five have been returned;

▶ 6x10m shuttle run: a timed run back and forth between two lines ten metres apart;

▶ a standing overhead soccer ball throw;

▶ a seated overhead soccer ball throw.

Outdoor and adventurous activities

There is no one way to teach outdoor and adventurous activities (OAA). Some schools may take children for an activity week which may incorporate some OAA with residential experience. Other schools may take children for visits to an environmental or activity centre for this part of the

PE programme. A selection of activities are included here which can all be set up within the school grounds, either as a unit of work, a short series of lessons or as part of geography or mathematics assignments.

Blindfold trail

After discussing what it might feel like to be blind, children can work in pairs with one child blindfolded. Start with them walking in a large clear space in the hall or playground and then gradually introduce obstacles for them to manoeuvre around. Emphasize trust and responsibility. Try with the leader holding the partner, then using verbal instructions only.

Using a compass

Teach map and compass skills in the playground or school grounds:

- finding where you are on the map;
- orientating the map;
- identifying features;
- finding a bearing from the map;
- pacing between landmarks/features.

The tasks need to be devised to suit the particular circumstances of your school's grounds. For example, *20 paces south south-west. What is in front of you?*

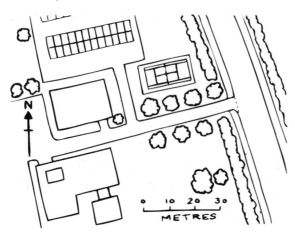

Problem solving

This includes, for example, bridge-building: using planks and old car tyres or crates, each group has to build a bridge and cross the 'river' (which is a little wider than the length of the planks) without anyone or anything touching the river.

Swimming

Swimming is important for safety, survival, confidence, fitness and recreation, but it is very unlikely (unless your school has its own pool) that classes will be taken swimming for more than a short time during their primary schooling. Teaching swimming, therefore, will be unique to each school and very dependent upon facilities available, authority guidelines, staffing and expertise available, previous experience of the children, timetabling, transport, funds and many other factors.

If you are accompanying your class to a pool, the following guidelines may help you:

- prepare the children well before the lessons take place: tell them what to expect (depth of water, location of changing rooms, toilets and fire exit), what to bring (bag for wet clothing, swimming cap) how to take care of dry clothes (use of lockers); discuss safety (pool code of practice: walk don't run; no shouting, jumping or pushing) and consider hygiene requirements (visiting toilets; blowing noses, foot check, foot bath);
- some children will be confident and competent swimmers while others may be quite fearful of the water and find the pool a daunting or frightening experience. You and/or the instructor will need to consider carefully how the children should be grouped;
- alert the instructor to any medical conditions (such as ear infections, asthma) and discuss any special arrangements;
- insist that children listen and watch attentively and establish a routine for waiting (sitting) until they are told to get into the pool;
- check the procedure for stopping the class (for example whistle, voice, hand signal);
- be in a position where you can see *all* the children and observe their efforts and responses;
- encourage and support the children with your interest in their progress.

Ideas bank

BBC dance programmes

Listen to the tapes, select a movement or thematic focus, use the accompaniment and develop the ideas in your own way with your own class rather than using the voice on the tape.

Dance residency

It may be possible to invite an educational dance company or professional artistes to work in school for a workshop/demonstration or alongside teachers. Consult local advisers for information.

Playtime

Consider ways of using some games equipment at playtime.

Athletics and maths

Practise of timing, measuring and recording can form part of a practical mathematics activity.

Assessment

Because of the fleeting nature of physical actions, detailed observation of a class of children constantly on the move is difficult. However, it is a good idea for you to get a general impression or overall feel for the class response before looking more specifically at the movement of individual children. Consider questions such as the following.

- How do the children respond, listen to your instructions/suggestions?
- How well do they:
  - use their initiative;
  - follow others;
  - do a bit of both?
- How well do they use the space? (Then think how could they be encouraged to use it better.)
- Are they able to use different directions? Are they aware of others when they do so?
- What could you say that might help them?
- How well do they sustain energetic activity?
- Are there other observations you need to make?

Then try to watch how individual children respond and move – continual review of the class with a focus on a few children at a time is recommended. There will also be times when you note achievement which is particularly significant for a child or the class, or look for specific actions or responses.

- Do they use the whole of the body when required? Which parts could they make more use of?
- How controlled are their movements ?
- In which ways could they refine their movements? (For example, the fluency of the action – is it easy or awkward?) .
- Can they notice, talk about and discuss their ideas and actions in PE?

Dance

- How well do they respond to my voice, the rhythm, sounds or music?
- How imaginative/creative are they?
- Are they achieving the qualities required? When? If not, why not? What might help?
- How well can they isolate and use individual body parts? Do they use some parts more fully than others?
- Do they use different levels, directions or speeds effectively?
- How well do they remember a phrase or sequence of movements?
- Can they use appropriate and inventive starting and finishing positions?
- Can they follow their partners' pathway or match their actions?

Gymnastics

- How well do they use the apparatus? Are there pieces of apparatus which I need to encourage them to use?
- How inventive are their actions?
- Can they hold still shapes on large and small parts of their bodies for the count of three?
- How confidently can they take their weight on their hands (on all fours, bunny jumps)?
- Can they choose, repeat and refine their favourite movements and select appropriate actions?
- Can they remember two or three actions and perform them one after the other with a starting and finishing position?

Games

- How well do they move about the space in different directions and in different ways?
- Can they stop, start and weave in and out of each other?
- Can they use the equipment imaginatively and confidently in a variety of ways?
- How accurately can they roll or throw towards a stationary target?
- Can they make up and play a variety of simple games?

At all times take care to stress the positive aspects of children's movement and to enjoy and encourage their attempts. There will be as many different responses as there are children. Remember that sometimes excitement, stress or the many demands of a situation, particularly in games, may cause some children to use less advanced movements.

Information Technology

In Year 4 you will be continuing to build upon a range of basic skills and techniques which children will have developed in previous years. They should be encouraged to identify tasks which they think may be undertaken more effectively using IT. Now is also the time to get the children thinking much more about the power of the IT tools to which they have access. In all areas of IT they should be encouraged to experiment with some of the more sophisticated elements of software packages.

What should they be able to do?

Key area: Communicating and handling information

Most children should now be familiar with word-processing packages. They should be combining different types of information, including clip art, pictures, other graphic elements and tables, into their work. They should have a good awareness of their audience, thinking about issues such as text size, language used and the overall look of the finished document. The most able children should now be using more sophisticated editing techniques, such as search and replace, as a matter of course, and should also be introduced to some of the more advanced features associated with desktop publishing, such as moving and shaping blocks of text and pictures to achieve particular effects.

They should be writing their ideas straight down at the computer on a regular basis, using the power of the computer to help them to draft and redraft their work. They should also be considering the finished look of their work, taking into account fonts, size of text, and alignment. In addition they should be aware of the use of similar commands in a wide range of computer packages and be beginning to realize that, once they are familiar with one computer program, new ones are likely to work in very similar ways. They should be given experience of using both Draw and Paint programs so that they are able to evaluate the effectiveness of each.

Children should already be familiar with the idea of a database for storing and retrieving information, and they should be encouraged to use this as a method of collecting and analysing information from many areas of the curriculum. Most children will probably still need the basic format of the database provided for them with field names and some examples included, although they should be encouraged to add or delete fields as they feel appropriate. They should, by now, be considering the need for carefully thinking about the questions they wish to ask. They should also be able to sort lists of data both numerically and alphabetically, and be able to present the information in a range of graphical formats. They should be becoming more confident in their use of databases, and should be beginning to investigate relationships between the items of data – for example, *Are there any links between the mode of transport children use to come to school, and how far away from school they live?*

They should also be familiar with CD-ROM databases, such as *Encarta*, and be learning strategies to enable them to search effectively for information on specific topics.

Key area: Controlling, monitoring and modelling

Children should be aware of the everyday applications of spreadsheets. In particular, the use of the *What if I changed this?* type of question can be very powerful in emphasizing how a spreadsheet can model a real situation. By this stage, they should be able to enter simple formulas into spreadsheets and to use a spreadsheet for useful purposes, for example finding the area of a rectangle by typing in the length of two sides. The most able should also be encouraged to predict what might happen before the data is typed into the spreadsheet, and to look for patterns in data.

Children in Year 4 should already have worked with programs such as LOGO and be familiar with programming structures such as REPEAT. Now they can take their first steps in using a computer to control lights using a similar programming approach.

They should be able to look at the first stages of monitoring the environment by using some form of data logger, and be aware of the advantages of using such an approach.

Practical ideas

Making a start

Alliteration

The children make use of the facilities of a word processor to highlight particular words in alliterative sentences. The first letters of words can either be made bold, italicized, or given distinctive colours. Alternatively, they could make the letters bigger or more distinctive by using a different font. This will give them a lot of practice in highlighting (selecting) parts of words and changing their attributes.

Footwear

Make a database of the footwear that is worn by children in the class. Encourage the class to discuss the different fields that need to be created and then produce an outline database framework. This could be done in groups with the children assisting. Typical fieldnames might be 'owner', 'age', 'sex', 'type of footwear', 'colour', whether or not this is their 'favourite type' of footwear, 'sole pattern', 'type of fastening', 'size'. An activity of this kind could be kept very simple, or it could be extended to include two or three different shoes per person or to extend the data collection to other classes in the school. The analysis of the data should be the important emphasis of this activity. Once the children have looked at simple questions such as *Which is the most popular colour for shoes?* they should be encouraged to look more deeply into the data. They

can consider questions such as *Do boys' shoes generally have different fastenings from those of girls?* or, by collecting further data, *Is there a relationship between shoe size and height?* They should be asked to display results graphically and to explain how they interpret their graphs.

Introducing new key areas

Insulation

Each group of children could do a separate experiment using a temperature sensor in a fixed quantity of ice which is surrounded by a sample of material in an attempt to prevent the ice from melting too quickly. By using a computer sensor, the group has some choice over the length of time for which the readings are taken and the gaps between individual readings. At the end of the experiment, the group can print out a graph of their results and fix a small sample of material to it for display. Subsequently, other groups of children repeat the experiment, but each time they use a different type of material. When all the groups have completed the experiment, have a class discussion about the displayed graphs. Discuss what the experiment has shown about insulation and also the advantages and disadvantages of using a temperature sensor for this activity compared with a thermometer. (See also Science, page 72.)

Recipe card

The children use a desktop publishing package to produce a recipe card for their favourite dish. Give them a basic format of title, photograph or drawing of the finished recipe, ingredients and method, which needs to be printed out on an A5 card. Show them examples of recipe cards and cookery books. Depending on their previous experience, you can either provide them with a basic template into which they input the information or you can leave them free to lay out the material as they wish. Ideally, this will be a part of a design and technology activity where they are actually designing and making a product. If you have a scanner, photographs can be taken, scanned in and incorporated into the recipe card. Encourage the children to think about the way they write the recipe so that the intended audience can easily follow it.

Reinforcing key areas

Research at the burger shop

In this activity, set up a spreadsheet for a fictitious burger shop and ask groups of children to analyse the data by answering a series of questions. If you have a local burger shop, you could ask the manager if he or she would be willing to supply some data in

response to a letter from the children. You can then suggest to the children that they write to the manager, producing the letter on the computer. The basic spreadsheet consists of nine columns, with one for 'item', one for 'cost' and one for the 'sales' for each day of the week. The children can add formulas to the spreadsheet to find out, for example, the value of total sales in a week. The questions can range considerably in complexity. Simple questions such as *On which day were the most cheeseburgers sold?* can lead on to things such as *What was the daily average amount of money taken on hot drinks during the week? How does this compare with that taken on cold drinks?* which again could be extended to consider what time of year these figures are for. The more data you include in the spreadsheet, the more opportunities the children will have of exploring their own particular areas. The data collected for the spreadsheet can also be used for making different types of graphs for mathematics work.

Holidays in Greece

Discuss with the children the sort of information that is required when you book a holiday. This will enable you to come up with the fieldnames for a holiday database. It is probably more manageable to concentrate on one country. Use old holiday brochures to identify the resorts, the apartments, the hotels, the amenities and the costs. In this activity the children should have some freedom to design the structure of the database themselves. You can then ask each group to answer a series of questions such as *Which apartment with swimming pool would be cheapest for a family of four, and what would be its disadvantages?* or *Which hotel would you recommend for a quiet holiday that did not require too much walking?* The activity could be extended to role-play activities with children booking holidays in their 'own' travel agents. There are obviously some good links with mathematics in this activity.

Ideas bank

A noughts and crosses game

Ask the children to make a simple game that could be printed on the back of a cereal packet. As an example you could suggest Noughts and Crosses, where they will need to produce a playing grid and some small cards with 'O' and 'X' (five of each). Encourage them to make the pieces as interesting and individual as possible. A Draw package would probably be the most suitable for this activity, although a primary-focused Computer-Aided Drawing package could be introduced at this stage.

Assessment

By the end of Year 4 you would expect most children to be able to:
- use IT as part of their work in a number of curriculum areas;
- create a short piece of extended writing;
- draft and redraft simple sentences, saving these between sessions;
- insert and delete characters, words and phrases;
- import, move, resize and edit images;
- save on to hard or floppy disk, and print independently;
- add and edit data in a simple database;
- check accuracy of data entry and results;
- interrogate a database to find the answers to simple questions and question these results, and begin to investigate relationships between different sets of data;
- have produced some artwork using an art package, making use of the mouse;
- paint pictures with straight lines and appropriate regular shapes, saving and loading between sessions;
- make a screen robot trace out simple regular shapes;
- use a spreadsheet to answer *What if?* type questions;
- use PENUP, PENDOWN, change line colour and use REPEAT command to build up complex sequences of instructions;
- have used a data logger to sense environmental data and display it in graphical form.

Design and Technology

Designing and making need to be practised in Year 4 in a variety of contexts and with a range of materials. The aim is to develop design and technology capability as a combination of know-how and know-what. The National Curriculum suggests some areas of knowledge and understanding but design and technology draws on others, such as scientific and mathematical concepts. Examples you might use with Year 4 children are described below. You can use them directly, adapt them or use them as models for activities which suit the particular needs of your teaching situation.

Some design and technology activities in Year 4 develop knowledge and understanding. For instance, by studying a solution to some practical problem children can extend their knowledge of control and structures. They can examine the object, mentally disassemble it, name its parts and explain their function. Another activity might be to develop and practise a skill or way of doing something. A focused practical task often serves this purpose. The task can be used to develop either a designing skill, such as considering the practical feasibility of an idea, or a making skill, such as planning a sequence of events.

By themselves, these tasks are unlikely to provide sufficient opportunity for Year 4 children to develop and show their designing and making capabilities. A simple, practical problem which requires some independent designing and making is better suited to this. You can limit the choice of materials to those that are likely to be useful and hence provide clues to ensure a successful start.

It is important that there is the opportunity for progression in design and technology capability. In Year 4, additional 'standard' ways of solving certain practical problems are taught. For example, you can introduce sheet materials slotted together at right angles to make self-supporting

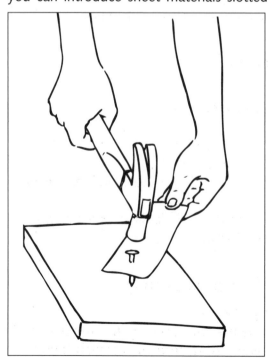

structures. Materials may require more shaping than in earlier years. Continue to introduce alternative ways of joining materials. Children of different capabilities can attempt the same task (essentially differentiation by outcome). You can tune a task to particular children's capabilities by the amount of support you provide and the reserve you show in intervening, but there may be some children who need a slightly different provision because they need to develop particular knowledge and skills.

Year 4 children should continue to develop skill and confidence in using a variety of hand tools. Plan for safe working. Consider the safety of the child using the tool, the safety of others and also of yourself. Check tools regularly and withdraw any from use that could be unsafe and repair or replace them. Store tools securely when not in use. The place where the children use the tools should be in view. Year 4 children should be expected to take some responsibility for safe practices and for organizing their workspace. They should recognize some potential hazards which their activity presents and avoid them.

What should they be able to do?

When they begin Year 4, children should already have practised and consolidated some designing and making skills and have examined variations of one or two simple manufactured products. This is developed in Year 4 by:

- increasing their understanding of some aspects of the manufactured world;
- making explicit what counts as design and technology capability;
- extending the range of contexts experienced;
- developing and extending designing and making skills;
- increasing technological knowledge and understanding.

Key area: Contexts

Fairly abstract ideas in other areas of the curriculum can often be made concrete and meaningful by using them in design and technology activities. You may find, however, that some aspects of design and technology suggested in the National Curriculum are not covered and sometimes you might organize a separate design and technology activity. In Year 4, such contexts and activities will generally relate to practical problems encountered in the home, the school and the immediate locality. Nevertheless, there may be contexts beyond these which have meaning for children (for example, the plight of rainforest animals threatened by forest clearance).

Key area: Designing skills

Children should practise generating and clarifying ideas and choosing what is likely to succeed. To be useful, designing needs to be specific. Help children to recognize any major omissions or potential difficulties in their designs. They should select materials suitable for the task; they should be conscious of the need to make the product safe for the user, and they should show a concern for the product's appearance. Encourage them to communicate their ideas so that they can do so with increasing ease and effectiveness. You will have to teach some technological knowledge and know-how directly (for instance, how to cut slots in sheet material).

Key area: Making skills

The majority of Year 4 children should:

- learn to construct a linear plan of action for realizing their designs;
- be willing to adapt the plan as the occasion demands;
- learn which tools to use for working a range of common materials;
- practise measuring and marking out what they need, avoiding waste;
- learn how to shape, join and combine a range of common materials temporarily and permanently;
- be able to choose, justify and apply some finishes;
- practise simple evaluations of their products which test them and identify their strengths;
- begin to reflect on what they would do differently next time.

Key area: Knowledge and understanding

Materials and components

Remind children of the properties of materials they have used by renewing their experience of them. They should also explore the properties of new materials and forms of materials (plywood,

for example) and take these into account in designing and making activities. Children can compare the properties of various forms of sheet materials (for example, sheet wood, plywood, sheet plastic), examine their structure and relate it to their properties.

Mechanisms and control

Extend children's knowledge of mechanisms to include the pulley, belt-drive, pneumatic shock absorbers, and the transmission of electrical power.

Structures

The children should learn how sheet materials can be made self-supporting and more rigid, explore further uses of frameworks, and build with repeating modules (bricks, for instance).

Products and applications

Whenever possible, you should present real products which illustrate the mechanisms and structures the children will make in simple ways. These are to be at least mentally disassembled. On occasions, children can do a mini case study of the various versions of a product, highlighting in simple terms how and why different materials and shapes have been used. Most children should be able to express views about which materials they think are best suited to the task and justify their views.

Quality

Emphasize that the quality of their work is important. Discuss the appearance of their products and whether they will function effectively. You may sometimes have to ask a child to remake a component rather than accept one that is very badly made. However, discourage undue waste.

Health and safety

Continue to give attention to developing in the children a conscious concern to avoid injury to themselves and others (for example, by making posters showing how to use a tool safely or listing safety products they have seen, such as hard hats, goggles, screens and overalls).

Vocabulary

Knowing the right words helps children to communicate, think and learn. Their vocabulary develops rapidly at this age and their work and case studies provide opportunities for supplementing it with some technological words ('cross-cut', 'belt', 'pulley', 'cogged wheel', and so on).

Working at higher or lower levels with the key areas

Sometimes, working at different levels is achieved by altering the degree of support you provide. It is always possible to provide simpler tasks with different contexts, but this can make a child's inadequacies, real or otherwise, apparent to all. An alternative you might try is to use a context which allows a variety of possible products or materials (for example, fairground, packaging). You can then allocate tasks to ensure that everyone is working at an appropriate level. If there is a child whose special needs make a particular task impossible, this approach can be a sensitive solution.

Children with well-developed design and technology capabilities can be stretched by withholding some support, by expecting more know-how in their products, by providing practical extension tasks and find-out-about tasks. These are activities intended to broaden a child's technological knowledge. They are simple, structured research tasks such as *Find out about bicycles/kitchens/telephones old and new.* Examples of old and recent versions of these are drawn and compared. *Name the various parts. Which ones are the same? Which ones are different? Choose one pair of things that are different and write a sentence to explain why they are different.* You will need to have suitable books and/or software available for such tasks.

Practical ideas

Making a start

Cross-curricular themes or subject-focused topics can generate design and technology activities. At the same time, something which catches the children's interest may arise from a recent event in school, a picture, story or theme which sets the scene for a problem. The children should be taught to clarify their design ideas by responding to *What? Why? How? How else?* questions and by explaining and justifying their intentions. While making, they should be aware of what is and is not working well.

Providing contexts

Children may have some intrinsic interest in solving a problem but they should also see purpose in what they do. The feeling of relevance comes from some obvious need that a task satisfies. Prior knowledge and know-how will also have to be brought out and related to the task in hand. Some strategies to effect this follow.

Stories

The best stories to use are those which lead up to a need or problem which is then resolved. For example, in *The Hobbit* (J R R Tolkien), houses have circular doors and windows. *How can they be made? How can they have hinges fitted which work?*

Visits and visitors

Planned visits which relate to other areas of the curriculum can often have a design and technology element. You can use a television programme or video to provide a 'visit' where it is not otherwise feasible. You might show some technological solution to a practical problem (a waterwheel, for instance, a windmill, a canal lock gate and so on) or how something is made (building a boat, perhaps). You might also use a TV story to set a scene for a problem, as you would use a story in a book.

Often, local people have craft skills which children may not see very often. There may be someone who crochets, does embroidery, carves, makes lace, rugs or pottery, who is willing to show what they do to the children. Structure such events so that the children are prepared for them, take part in them, and follow up what they have seen.

Challenges

In a sense, all design and technology tasks are challenges, but this is when a task is presented explicitly in that form. For example, ask the children if they can design and make a vehicle which could handle rough terrain like that on Mars.

Supporting designing
General

Make what counts clearer to children by beginning with a simple manufactured product (a pencil sharpener, say) and ending up with its design. They run the process of designing and making backwards: mentally disassembling the product, drawing it from different viewpoints, writing an account describing how it works, and producing a plan for its assembly (possibly presented in the form of a sequence of pictures).

Exploring the task

Ensure that the children know what the task means and encompasses. Ask questions to stimulate the recall of relevant prior knowledge. Supplement this so that the task is meaningful. Year 4 children should contribute to the preparation for a task by using simple sources of information in response to structured questions.

Stimulating ideas and focusing

To help children generate ideas, state the problem and ask for responses to it. Review the suggestions in turn and get the children to consider what is feasible in the classroom and what has most chance of success. Encourage them to be explicit about the vague bits of a design. You might progress to group work in which the children explore the questions *Why? What? How?* together and report back to you.

Developing new knowledge

It may be necessary to develop additional knowledge at this point. Related artefacts can be useful for this purpose, particularly if they are everyday objects in which the parts are visible. The children should examine them and explain how they work or were made. Some things might safely be dismantled and reassembled. (Examples include a ballpoint pen, a torch and a bicycle pump.)

Pictures of artefacts may be used in the absence of the real thing.

Supporting making

General

Encourage the children to think more for themselves. There will be times when you will know that the product might have been better if you had given specific instructions but the aim is to encourage some independence of thought and action.

Choosing materials

Materials will have been considered at the designing stage but now the children may be faced with variations. Materials come in a variety of forms and sizes. Expect them to mark out their designs. Discourage waste by, for instance, giving the children a fixed budget to 'buy' materials.

Modelling

Younger children are sometimes so eager to make something that they fix things together and find afterwards that things do not fit or work as intended. Discuss with children the need to try things loosely before fixing them permanently. Have them check they can still fit the final items. Your aim is to develop the habit of mindfulness.

Quality

The purpose of the exercise is not simply to make a product which works or satisfies a need. Remind the children of the looks and performance of a well-made product' perhaps by showing them well-made and badly-made carrier bags.

Introducing key areas

Contexts

In these examples (a) sets the scene, (b) is a focused practical task, (c) is a designing and making task and (d) are other tasks. They may be used as they are, adapted, or may serve as models for other activities.

Land yacht (framework)

(a) Show pictures of boats with sails as a starting point. *What is making them move? What if there was no water? What would we need to make them move on land? Would they need to be boat shaped? What other shapes could we have?* A version for use on land then follows.

(b) The children make a rectangular framework from strip wood and strengthen it at the corners with card triangles. Axle supports are fitted for four wheels. A sail is made from a rectangle of card and glued to the front of the framework. Blowing at the sail should propel it along.

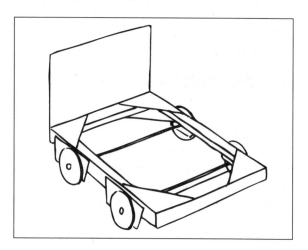

(c) This is an opportunity to show that other ways of solving this problem exist. It also extends the children's repertoire of know-how. *Suppose we had no strip wood, how else might you make a land yacht?*

(d) Look at photographs of land yachts and compare them with the children's models.

The fairground (belt drive)

(a) Use a picture of a fairground to stimulate ideas about what to make for a model fairground.

(b) Introduce simple belt drives which make things rotate. For instance, a model roundabout can be made from a coffee jar lid nailed loosely on a rectangular wooden block. A bobbin is fixed nearby similarly and a rubber band stretched around the bobbin and lid. When the bobbin is turned, the rubber band makes the lid turn. Card figures are glued to the jar lid.

(c) The children work in pairs and choose a fairground item to make. These can be displayed as a collection against an appropriate frieze. Encourage them to make items which move.

(d) A number of construction kits allow various belt-driven devices to be made (LEGO Technic, for example). The chain drive on a bicycle is a variation of the belt drive.

Recycled materials: packaging

(a) Packaging can be a small topic in its own right. You can explore various ways in which objects are protected in the mail.

(b) Introduce the problem of biscuits which break so readily in their packets. Ask the children to design and make a package for a biscuit so that, when dropped one or two metres, the biscuit does not break.

(c) Show the children a toy car and tell them it is to be sent in a rocket to Mars and dropped for some astronauts waiting on the surface. *How can they protect it?* (The 1997 Mars lander was protected by large balloons. Small sandwich bags, inflated and sealed, may be used to simulate the effect.)

Pencil case

(a) Examine different ways of storing pens and pencils.

(b) Describe the problem of preventing woven fabrics from fraying. Demonstrate seams as a solution to this and then get the children to practise seams by making a tea-towel from a piece of plain, light coloured fabric. They can add waterproof designs to the tea towels with fabric pens.

(c) Ask the children to design and make a pencil case from fabrics. A temporary fastener is to be included. Encourage imaginative solutions. For instance, a card tube can give a sock shape some stiffness as a pencil case.

Lifts (pulleys)

(a) Use a picture of a skyscraper to stimulate discussion about the problem of movement up and down the building. *Suppose you wanted to go from the bottom to the top. What would it be like if you used the stairs?*

(b) Demonstrate the action of a pulley. Show how it can be used to lift and lower a small box on the end of a string.

(c) Give children a large cardboard box which is to serve as a skyscraper. They should make several floors in it and design and make a lift to work between the floors using a pulley and string. As an extension, they could incorporate a crank handle to wind the lift up and down (the crank handle may have been introduced in Year 3).

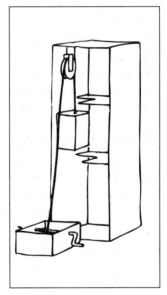

Ideas bank

Visible door stops

There are two main kinds of door stop: a wedge and something heavy. The problem with the wedge is that it may be kicked away and people stub their toes on the other kind. *How can we make a door stop which does not have these problems?* Have some wedges of wood pre-cut. The children can design and make card or wooden animals or figures to stick to a wedge. To extend their experience with sheet materials, they may cut shapes using shaper saws, if available.

Carrier bag

The children see your carrier bag burst, dropping heavy tins of food on the floor. They are asked to make a bag which is strong enough to take the tins without bursting. Give them a limited budget to 'buy' the materials. Test the bags on completion.

Biographical sketch: Margaret Knight

Margaret Knight (1838–1914) was an inventor who lived in Maine in the USA. She invented the satchel-bottomed paper bag, still quite common today. As a child, all she wanted was a knife, a gimlet and pieces of wood. With these, she made toys for her brothers. As well as the paper bag, she also invented clasps for fastening dresses and machines used in shoe-making. Talk about Margaret Knight while involved in packaging activities to introduce a personal dimension to design and technology.

Egg supports as structures

Examine egg boxes as structures. Children can design and make a stable egg cup using reclaimed materials. The same may be done with papier mâché to introduce this as a construction material.

Pneumatic animals

The children can make large animals from cardboard boxes and give them jaws which work. These can be opened by including a balloon in the animal's mouth and inflating it through a tube from the back. The balloon can look like the animal's tongue as it pushes the upper jaw open.

Noah's Ark

Working in groups, the children can design and make pairs of card animals for an ark. The animals are made from card cut into flat outlines. Pairs of legs are cut as a single unit. These have a slot made at the top into which the body is inserted. The ark can be made from card boxes.

The village

Explore the features of a village. As a class task, have the children design and make some aspect of a model village. The houses may be made from boxes. Strip wood frameworks can be used to make model pylons. These can carry wires which operate one or two street lights from a battery. An extension is to study Tudor houses which have an exterior framework.

Bread maker

There are bread makers available which take the ingredients, mix, knead, proof and bake them. If one is available, show the children the ingredients and make them into bread. The sequence is a good example of a programmed cycle. The children should not have access to the bread maker or its electrical connections – deal with it yourself and ensure everyone is safe.

Case study: the Namibian hut

In Namibia, building materials are expensive. The Namibians have overcome the problem by using empty bottles which are free and greatly reduce the amount of brick and mortar needed. Bottles are laid side by side to make a circle. A thin layer of mortar is spread over them and the next layer of bottles is laid. This continues until the walls are built. The bottles, being curved, can take a lot of weight.

Case study: clay

Clay has been a building material for a long time. Until recently, the walls of some buildings were made from clay, straw and animal dung. Given protection above and below, they could withstand the weather quite well. Wattle and daub houses had walls made from interlaced wooden slats covered with a clay and dung mix. When blocks are fired, clay makes bricks which are more weather resistant, although many wattle and daub houses still exist today. Some animals use clay to build with. There is the 'potter wasp' which makes a small globe of clay to lay eggs in and, of course, birds often line their nests with it. Children can make small clay bricks and try them out.

Assessment

In design and technology, both knowledge and skills are assessed. While a product can provide some evidence of skills, it cannot tell you everything. In particular, you need to know about designing and making skills which do not show themselves in a product. For instance, did the children plan ahead and follow the plan? This means that you need to observe them as they work.

What do they know?

This is not closely defined but they should:
- know of some simple mechanisms, like a belt drive, the use of a pulley, and pneumatics to produce a required movement;
- know of instances where structural strength has been obtained from particular shapes;
- know how an increasing number of everyday objects function;
- know about the effect of forces on some materials of different shapes;
- know some working characteristics of materials they have used and the tool used to cut and shape these materials;
- know hazards associated with tools and materials they have used;
- have extended their vocabulary so they can discuss tools, materials, and technological matters relating to the products they have made and disassembled.

What can they do?

They should:
- be able to gather information and use it to generate ideas relevant to the task in hand;
- be able to produce a labelled drawing as a design and, where useful, draw it from another viewpoint;
- be able to supplement their drawings with other ways of communicating their intentions (for example, a clear description, a loose assembly of materials);
- be willing to consider an alternative solution as a possible course of action;
- make realistic suggestions about how to proceed and accept compromise solutions;
- generally avoid difficulties by ordering the way they will work and by drawing on their knowledge of the properties of materials;
- be able to choose and apply a particular finish;
- choose materials, tools and techniques purposefully;
- use tools with some accuracy, cutting and shaping materials with sufficient precision for assembling the product;
- show their knowledge of safe and considerate practices in their making activities;
- produce products which are perceptibly similar to intentions and be able to identify and justify changes during their evaluation of the product.

Religious Education

RE, unlike the subjects of the National Curriculum, has to be planned from a local rather than national document. Agreed Syllabuses differ in the way they present the programme of study but are remarkably similar in what they expect children to do in RE. It is very likely that your Agreed Syllabus expects children to:

● develop a knowledge and understanding of religious traditions;
● explore fundamental questions arising out of people's experience of life;
● develop their own ideas and values arising partly out of what they learn in RE.

In terms of continuity and progression in RE we should be helping children to develop a systematic knowledge and understanding of some religions as well as developing their thinking about religious issues and understanding of common themes across religions which will contribute to their understanding of religion in general.

In these Yearbooks, RE is approached in one of two ways. Some topics are what we call human experience topics. They focus on significant questions or issues in relation to what it means to be human. Such questions as 'Who is my neighbour?' or 'Why do people suffer?' provide a conceptual focus for exploring both human experience and religious beliefs and practices which relate to the question or issue.

In this chapter, another approach is taken: the focus is a concept drawn from religion, namely worship. It is not a concept specific to any one religious tradition but is derived from the study of religion in general. So this chapter explores both common and specific examples of worship in religion. The specific examples are described below under the first key area.

What should they be able to do?

Key area: Knowledge and understanding of religions

Worship is a concept and activity common to all religious traditions (with the possible exception of certain types of Buddhism where meditation may be the more appropriate concept), and this topic gives you the opportunity to do a number of things. First, it is possible to explore different types of worship, such as certain forms of prayer, singing, dancing – even work! This is best done through specific examples drawn from the various religions.

In the Christian tradition, for example, there are different types of prayer, including petitionary, intercessionary and thanksgiving. Types of devotional prayer, such as saying the rosary in the Roman Catholic tradition, can also be compared with the type of Muslim devotional prayer using the subha (prayer beads) through which a Muslim will meditate on the 99 beautiful names of God. Communal worship, such as that which takes place in a place of worship, can be studied, particularly by visiting such places. The ritual of aarti in the Hindu temple, or of the liturgy in a Christian Orthodox church, can be contrasted with the silence of a Quaker meeting or vibrant worship in a Pentecostal church.

A useful way of presenting worship to Year 4 children is to explore the concept under a number of different headings, for example 'What and why do people worship?' This will mean helping the children to develop an understanding of the focus of worship – which for most means God in one form or another – and some of the reasons for worship – which include the need to honour and express key beliefs and values, reinforcing the sense of belonging to a community, and an expression of personal, inner feelings. You can help children explore some of these elements by looking at examples of the two main categories of worship, public and private worship.

The next category worth exploring is best described as 'How people worship'. This chapter provides examples of this, using artefacts from all the major religious traditions. It is essential here to introduce the children to the relevant words which describe different forms of worship; terms like 'liturgy', 'mass' and 'praise' in the Christian tradition, for example, can be compared with 'ibadah' (worship), the different forms of 'salah' (set, formal prayer) and 'du'a' (individual prayer) in the Muslim tradition.

A final possible category to explore is 'Where people worship'. This would, obviously, include looking at places of worship and visits to them. (See Ideas bank, page 157.)

Key area: Exploring human experience

There are several elements in helping the children to explore worship within the context of human experience. First, worship is a way of communicating which involves symbolism and ritual. It will be important for the children to understand something of the way that these play significant roles in people's lives. Aspects that can be explored are the giving of gifts, the wearing of special clothes, dancing, playing music and so on. These can all be explored as ways of 'saying something' without using words.

A second element is the idea of people gathering together in a special place and at a special time. These general concepts can be explored in terms of the children's own experience which you should draw on as much as possible.

In addition to these concepts, the children can be encouraged to think about and respond to a variety of relevant questions, related to their learning about worship under the Knowledge and Understanding of Religions. These might include *What is most important in life? How do people show that something or someone is important to them? Why do people worship?*

Key area: Responding to religion and human experience

Responding to questions plays an essential role in this element. The children should be encouraged to respond personally to the type of questions outlined in the first two key areas. You can help them learn how to answer such questions with statements like *'I think ...'* or *'I believe ...'* This leads them to appreciate that people can respond to questions in their own way, and will help them develop important attitudes such as respect for another's point of view. If you give children this opportunity, some of them may begin to be able to make connections between their own feelings about what matters in their life and how others express feelings and value, through worship, of what they think is most important.

Because this topic makes great use of religious artefacts and, where possible, visits to places of worship, important attitudes can be generated by the way you teach the children to handle artefacts and the way that you encourage them to conduct themselves in the various places of worship. This should also contribute to feelings of respect for the lifestyles and concerns of people who are different from them. Such positive examples are essential if the children are to understand the concepts involved in the first two key areas and are to grow up with tolerance towards other people's customs and beliefs.

Most children should be able to express their responses to what they have learned using various media, including pictorial and written forms. You can also expect them to take part in discussions.

Practical ideas

Making a start

Introducing worship

Divide the class into groups and give each group a picture showing worship (Westhill and Folens produce good photopacks – see the resource list on page 159). Select a different tradition for each group, and pose them two questions: *What are the people in the picture doing?* and *Why are they doing it?*

Ask one member of each group to note down the answers. When you have given them enough time to do this, ask each group to talk about their picture to the rest of the class. Focus on bringing out the common theme of worship, perhaps introducing different words for different forms of worship in the examples and what or who the people or person in the picture are/is worshipping. Examples could be God, or a supreme being, something beyond normal life, or names for God in different traditions, for example 'Allah' (Islam), 'Waheguru' (Sikhism), 'Lord' (Christianity/Judaism). Also talk about the possible answers to the second question, which could include words like 'praise', 'communication', 'thanksgiving', 'adoration', 'love', 'awe'. (Most photopacks include teaching notes which will inform you fully about the pictures.)

Developing key areas

Christian worship

Look at some pictures

Look at a selection of posters showing Christians worshipping in different ways. Examples can include singing (praise), praying, reading the Bible, ritual. Ask the children to pick out the important features of the worship and make a list together of the different ways in which Christians worship. You can use some carefully chosen questions with the posters such as, *What are the people doing? Are they listening, singing, being still? How do you think they feel? Try and think of words which describe their feelings. Can you tell anything about how they feel from their faces and gestures and so on?*

Look at some hymns

Look in school hymnbooks or other collections for words of hymns and prayers. Ask the children each to copy out one that appeals to them. Then ask them to answer questions such as, *What ideas about God, Jesus, or about what it means to be a Christian are contained in hymn or prayer.*

Talk about prayer

If possible arrange for the children to talk to some Christians. (They might be people in the school) about how and why they pray. *What do they think happens when they pray? Do they think prayer works or makes a difference?* Explore with the children, and use examples, of the main kinds of Christian prayer: adoration, confession, thanksgiving, intercession, petitionery. Children could make a display of different examples with suitable illustrations.

Write your own prayers

Compile a class book of prayers composed by the children.

Give them some guidance, such as, *Write a prayer which expresses: being sorry for something, praise for God's greatness, asking God for something on behalf of yourself/on behalf of others.*

Holy communion

Using artefacts

You will need a chalice and paten as well as some altar breads. Sit the children in a circle. Wrap each artefact in a cloth or put it in a feely bag, and pass them around the class asking the children to feel, smell, shake each one and try to guess what it is. When everyone has made a suggestion, ask the child holding an artefact to unwrap it and place the object in the centre of the circle. *Has anyone seen these things before? Where did you see them?* Emphasize that Christians use these artefacts in an act of worship called 'holy communion', 'Eucharist' or 'mass'. (You might ask the children to look these words up and write down their meaning.)

Tell the story

Explain to the children that this communion is an act of remembrance. *What/who do Christians remember during this worship?* Read to them or read together the story of the last supper. Explore questions such as *What were they recalling at the last supper? For what were they hoping? What do you think Jesus wanted the disciples to remember about him?*

Organize a meal

In groups, talk about a person or event worth remembering. It might be the opening of the school or some other important local event, or the birth of a famous local person. Plan a memorial meal. *What will be remembered? How will it be celebrated and with what food?* Keep it simple. Distribute some selected passages of the Eucharistic prayer (see, for example, the Anglican *Alternative Service Book*). Discuss the important words that the priest says and make up your own prayer or form of words for your celebration.

Do this in memory of me

These are very important words in the Eucharistic prayer. If you have contacts, try to visit your local church and talk to the vicar about what things Christians do, apart from the Eucharist, to remember Jesus. Examples would be local church activities, or the work of the Salvation Army or Christian charities like Christian Aid.

Make a display

As part of art work, place a picture of the Eucharistic artefacts in the centre of a display and illustrate examples of Christian activities, 'in memory of Jesus', around them. Discuss in what ways these activities can be described as worship.

Watch a video or visit a service

It would be good for the children to have some experience of an actual Eucharist. Check with a local church and try to arrange a Sunday or even early weekday visit. Alternatively, *Christianity through the Eyes of Christian Children* (CEM, see page 159 for details) is a good available video. From the same source is available the *Believe It or Not* series, really meant for Key Stage 3, but useful if used selectively.

Use your ideas for Assembly

Get the class to prepare a special Assembly on ways of worship. Using pictures, writings and their prayers they can present what they have learned. Explore with other classes, or the headteacher, ways in which different methods of worshipping might be included in the Assembly programme.

Other traditions

The next section includes information and activities related to Muslim prayer and outlines examples of worship in other traditions from which you may wish to select according to your school population or your Agreed Syllabus. It also gives the opportunity to explore different elements in worship, such as preparation for prayer, music, use of the senses, meditation and so on.

Religious education

Muslim prayer

The prayer mat

Show a Muslim prayer mat to the class. Invite the children to feel the texture of the mat and to examine the designs and pictures. If there are pictures of Makkah or the Ka'ba on the mat explain their significance for Muslim prayer. Tell the children that Muslims are taught to pray five times a day. They may not always be able to go to the mosque so a prayer mat can be used wherever they are. Explain how the prayer mat becomes 'mosque' or place of prayer as it provides a clean and suitable place for prayer, even in the midst of a busy street or market place. If you have Muslim children in the class, draw on their experience.

The compass

Show a Muslim compass to the class. Perhaps a large chart or picture of a compass could be used. Explain how the compass is used by Muslims to ensure that they face the Ka'ba in Makkah when they pray. Discuss how we face the 'front' in class or face the teacher when we need to concentrate on some teaching point or look at a picture. Talk about how we face in a particular direction in order to give our full attention to something or someone, for example, the headteacher in assembly; a pop star at a concert.

The adhan (call to prayer)

● Take the children outside. Allow them to wander around the playground as individuals. Ring a bell or call them to stop and face the teacher. Discuss the idea of individuals becoming a group or class with each member attending to the same task. Liken this to the Muslim call to prayer.

● Play them the call to prayer. (Recordings are available from Gohil Emporium, see page 159 for details.)

Make prayer clocks

Use an appropriate information book, for example, *Muslims 2* (Westhill), and ask children to research the names and times of the five daily prayers. Ask them to make coloured versions of the 'salah' clock, naming each time for prayer. Decorate the clock with Islamic designs and patterns.

Preparation for prayer

Ask the children to use reference books to find out about 'wudu'. Explain that wudu is the preparation for prayer. Discuss the use of water for washing, cleaning and purification, which shows the importance of prayer and shows how Muslims separate a holy time, such as prayer, from everyday life. Invite the children to tell or write about how they prepare for important occasions, for example, a party, a meal, a day out.

Jewish worship

There are two essential elements of Jewish worship that you might like to explore: worship in the synagogue and worship in the home. Some ideas about synagogue worship are given in the next section. In terms of the home, it is best to concentrate on 'shabbat'. Teach them about how and why Jews celebrate shabbat. You might ask a Jewish person to come in and talk about shabbat in their house. From the children's own experience it is worth focusing on thankfulness and special time as the human experience aspect of worship. Explore what Jews are thankful for, and consider some of the blessings: 'Blessed are you, Lord our God, King of the universe...' (these can be found in the Jewish prayer book). Discuss with the children what they themselves are thankful for. Talk about the idea of holy time, time set aside from the everyday. *How important is this? Do all the days seem the same to you or are some days different? Which days? Why? Ask the oldest person you know to tell you about what Sundays were like when he/she was little.*

Hindu worship

Again you could concentrate on the temple or the home (see below for the temple). In concentrating on the home, it is worth showing the children a 'puja tray' (a good supplier of Hindu artefacts is Gohil Emporium – see page 159). In order to explore different aspects of Hindu worship, it is a good idea to concentrate on how the senses are used, for example: smell – incense is used for prayer beside the image of the deity; touch – worshippers will touch the image before prostration; sight – the colourful images in the home shrine or at the temple; sound – worshippers ring a bell to 'get the attention' of God before worship; taste – the giving of 'prashad' (blessed food) is an important aspect of Hindu worship. You could burn some incense. Once again, draw on the experience of Hindu children in the class or the school or of a Hindu person who is used to talking to children.

Sikh worship

There are many different forms of Sikh worship (see below) but one form worth concentrating on is music. Music is very important in Sikh worship as it 'lifts' the spirit to God. Sikhs believe that God is present in all beings and can be experienced but is beyond human understanding. Music can lift human attention from self (a spiritual affliction for Sikhs is self-centredness, 'manmukh') to God (god-centredness is 'gurmukh'). 'Shabads' (hymns from the holy book) are sung and the singing is called 'kirtan'. Many Sikh children have lessons in the

PUJA TRAY

A	Water container	E	Deva Lamp
B	Haldi container	F	Spoon
C	Container for Kum Kum	G	Bell
D	Incense holder		

gurdwara, learning instruments such as the tabla, harmonium or sitar. You might be able to arrange for someone who plays one of the instruments to come and play to the class. You can get good audio tapes of Sikh worship, both prayers and singing, from Gohil Emporium (see page 159).

Buddhist worship

See 'Visiting a Buddhist centre' (page 159).

Ideas bank

This section contains ideas and advice on visiting places of worship. For all visits you should obviously make contact beforehand to find out if/when it would be convenient to come and explain the purpose of the visit to whoever is in charge. Politely discourage offers of a formal talk to the children unless you can be sure that its length and level would be suitable. Prepare the children beforehand, explaining what they will see and do, and telling them about appropriate behaviour.

Visiting a Christian church

Of course, there are many different types of Christian places of worship; you could choose a very visual building like an Orthodox church or a sparse Quaker meeting house. It is good to vary visits in order to explore different forms of Christian worship. If you visit a fairly conventional church, make sure you concentrate on the aspects that relate to worship rather than treating it like a church study which you might be doing as part of history. Things to point out are the altar, lectern, pulpit, kneelers, prayer-books and so on. Some of the symbolism in Christian churches may well help with exploring the variety of Christian worship.

If possible, try to go to a church during a service. You might be able to combine with other classes and arrange for a special service. For variety, consider visits to an Orthodox church for liturgy or a Black Pentecostal church for praise.

Etiquette

There are no special requirements in most Christian churches except respectful behaviour (and no head covering for boys).

Visiting a Sikh gurdwara

Sikh worship has a number of interesting elements that could be explored. A visit to the gurdwara could include experiencing the 'Akhand path' (the continuous reading of the Guru Granth Sahib, the Sikh holy book) and the receiving of 'Kara Prashad'

(a sweetmeat offered in the prayer hall). There would also be the opportunity to experience 'langar' (a shared meal given to all as an example of Sikh 'sewa', or service to others) and the Sikh stress on equality of all humans.

Etiquette

You must cover your heads and remove your shoes. When you enter the prayer hall, a small bow in front of the Guru Granth Sahib may be expected. It is a way of expressing respect and showing politeness to the community. Always avoid turning your back on the holy book or pointing your feet towards it. When in the prayer hall you will be offered Kara Prashad – it may not be to everyone's taste. Tell the children that, if they want some, they should take it in both hands, but they should not take it if they don't want it, as this is seen as wasteful.

Visiting a Hindu temple

The best time to visit is when 'aarti' is being performed. In most Hindu temples in this country this will mean between 10.00 and 11.00 in the morning. Prepare the children thoroughly for this visit. The inside of a temple is bright with many images – 'murtis' – of the gods. Explain to the children that Hindus don't actually worship lots of gods but that, for them, 'Brahman', ultimate reality, is the world's soul and all the images are really expressions or aspects of the one reality. Clarify this by discussing how one person can be many things: a mother, a teacher, a wife, a daughter and so on.

Etiquette

You will need to remove your shoes before entering the temple. If you are offered a gift of fruit or sweets, it is polite to accept. Hindu temples are good places to take photographs, but always ask permission.

Visiting a Muslim mosque

A good time to go is on a Friday lunchtime for juma (congregational) prayer. Get there early enough to hear the 'adhan' (call to prayer). On a Friday there will also be a sermon ('khutbah'), which is very often in English as well as Urdu. You will see Muslims offering their own prayers, 'du'a' , as well as the formal, set 'salah' prayer. Mosques tend to be very symmetrical which illustrates the central Muslim belief in 'tawhid' (the oneness and unity of God). You can point out the 'mihrab' (the recess in the wall that faces Makkah), and the 'minbar' (a small 'pulpit'.) from where the 'imam' delivers the khutbah. If you can't go on a Friday check the local prayer timetable for other 'jamaat' (the daily prayers in the mosque).

Etiquette

You must all remove your shoes and all girls should dress modestly (trousers are best) and cover their heads. Boys are not required to cover their heads but it is often polite to do so as many Muslim men wear caps during prayer. Do not point the feet towards the 'qibla' wall (that facing Makkah). Males and females may be asked to sit separately, but often you would sit together as a group at the back of the prayer hall.

Visiting a Jewish synagogue

Avoid Fridays as Jews will be getting ready to celebrate shabbat. Also avoid festival times (check with the SHAP Calendar available from The National Society RE Centre – see Resources). As there will be no worship going on, a good guide will be able to show you the 'ark' (cupboard) where the 'torah' scrolls are kept, as well as the 'bimah' (platform from where the torah scrolls are read). Look out also for the 'ner tamid' (the eternal light burning above the ark). You should also be able to see the 'tallit' (prayer shawl) worn by men.

Etiquette

All males are required to cover their heads.

Visiting a Buddhist centre

Many Buddhist 'places of worship' are small – often houses, although there are some larger buildings. Ask your guide to concentrate on describing the shrine with its Buddha image, flowers, candle, incense and seven bowls to welcome the guest. This will help explain something of Buddha's teachings in an accessible way. Remember that Buddhists don't worship Buddha but use the image to be reminded of the qualities of Buddha. The main practice in Buddhist centres is meditation and it would be good to ask about this and, maybe, practise some. Be sensitive about this and make sure parents and everyone at school know what you are doing. If you do get the chance to do some basic meditation it will concentrate on the breath; to explore this further, *Buddhism for Key Stage 2*, a video published by Clearvision Trust (see below) is useful. You could also use such a video and this advice in the classroom if you can't, or don't want to, make a visit.

Etiquette

You will be expected to remove your shoes. Some Buddhist monks are not allowed to touch women, so if you are female, don't expect to shake hands. There are no dress requirements but there may be quite a long time spent sitting on the floor.

Resources

Artefacts, pictures and other resources are available from: Articles of Faith, Resource House, Kay Street, Bury, Lancashire BL9 6BU, Tel 0161 763 6232 (mail order); CEM, Royal Buildings, Victoria St, Derby DE1 1GW. Tel 01332 296655; Clearvision Trust, 16–20 Turner St, Manchester, M4 1DZ. Tel 0161 839 9579; Folens Publishers, Albert House, Apex Business Centre, Dunstable LU5 4RL, Tel 01582 472788; Gohil Emporium, 381 Stratford Road, Birmingham B11 4JZ, Tel 0121 771 3048 (mail order); The Jewish Education Bureau, 8 Westcombe Avenue, Leeds LS8 2BS, Tel 0870 7300532; The National Society RE Centre, 0171 932 1190; Westhill RE Centre, Westhill College, Selly Oak, Birmingham B29 6LL, Tel 0121 415 2258 (mail order).

Assessment

When you have finished this topic you will have a pretty good idea whether the children have enjoyed it. You should also be able to judge by the outcomes how much they have learned. Evaluation can take the following form.

What do they know?

There is a great deal of information which the children could have picked up. Being selective it is possible to suggest that most children should know:

- the names of different places of worship;
- some of the different ways in which religious people worship;
- some of the correct terminology for different types of worship;
- some details about artefacts used in worship.

What can they do?

You can expect children in a typical Year 4 class to respond at different levels. In this topic, for example, you can expect all or most to be able to:

- talk about different types of worship using correct vocabulary;
- show respect when visiting places of worship or talking to people;
- handle artefacts appropriately and with sensitivity;
- express their ideas in written or visual form.

You can also expect some children to:

- understand and explain the reasons why people worship;
- understand and explain the reasons for different forms of worship;
- explain with reasons, in personal terms, what they think and feel about worship.

What have they experienced?

The children should have:

- handled religious artefacts used in worship;
- researched aspects of worship in different religions;
- visited at least one place of worship;
- experienced more than one form of worship;
- talked to a religious believer about worship.

How have they made their knowledge public?

The children should have made a public display of their knowledge through discussion, writing and illustrations. They should also have behaved appropriately when visiting places of worship, handled artefacts with due sensitivity and spoken to and listened to others, both classmates and visitors or people on visits, in a respectful way.